The Two Lives and One Passion
of Louise Marshall

The Two Lives and One Passion of Louise Marshall

◇◇◇◇◇◇◇◇◇◇

Founder of the Cabbage Patch Settlement

LINDA RAYMOND AND BILL ELLISON

Front cover passport photograph of Louise Marshall
courtesy of Filson Historial Society, Louisville, KY

Printed in the United States of America

ISBN 978-1-941953-51-8
Library of Congress Control Number: 2017949895

Book design by Carly Schnur

Butler Books
P.O. Box 7311
Louisville, KY 40257
Phone (502) 897-9393
Fax (502) 897-9797

Miss Louise Marshall
Founder of the Cabbage Patch Settlement
April 9, 1888–February 5, 1981

DEDICATION

Tracy Holladay became executive director of the Cabbage Patch
Settlement three years after Louise Marshall's death.
Cabbage Patch Settlement House

To the devoted men and women who, over the years, have
served the Cabbage Patch Settlement's families with love,
dedication, and Miss Marshall's philosophy. We recognize—
especially—Tracy Holladay. As the settlement's executive
director since 1984, Holladay has worked to give Miss
Marshall's Cabbage Patch and its children both a vibrant
present and a secure future.

CONTENTS

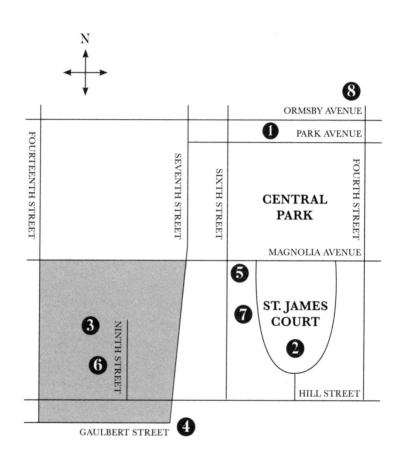

N

MISS MARSHALL'S
NEIGHBORHOOD

Louise Marshall grew up, lived, and worked her entire life in an area that encompassed little more than one square mile of prosperity and poverty. This map shows both of her worlds and locates key landmarks that were important at various points in her life. (Some streets and buildings have since disappeared.)

1. 422 Ormsby Avenue, one mile south of Broadway and downtown Louisville. It was the Marshall family home where Louise grew up and lived much of her adult life.

2. St. James Court, an elegant collection of homes for prominent and prosperous Louisvillians, including author Alice Hegan Rice, who wrote *Mrs. Wiggs of the Cabbage Patch*

3. The Cabbage Patch neighborhood (shaded area) around the turn of the 20th century, when it was home to about 600 African Americans and Irish and German immigrants. The area stretched from roughly today's Seventh Street to 14th Street and from Magnolia Avenue to Gaulbert Avenue.

4. People's Hall, a tavern building used by Stuart Robinson Presbyterian Church for the mission Sunday school that piqued Louise Marshall's interest in the Cabbage Patch

5. Stuart Robinson Memorial Presbyterian Church (1888–1977) at Sixth and Magnolia Streets

6. The first Cabbage Patch Settlement House, 1461 South Ninth Street, built in 1911

7. Today's Cabbage Patch Settlement House, 1400 block South Sixth Street

8. Puritan Apartment Hotel, Fourth Street and Ormsby Avenue, Louise Marshall's nominal home in her later years

PREFACE

During the Great Depression, Louise Marshall undressed at night under a single, bare light bulb and wrapped herself in a blanket to sleep on a cot in a desperately poor neighborhood—although she had a comfortable bedroom in a fine house less than a mile away. In the morning, when she put on her black dress and got down on her knees to teach grown men to earn a living by scrubbing floors, her day revealed nothing about her taste for ocean cruises in first-class accommodations or her stays in elegant European hotels. At the Cabbage Patch Settlement she founded in 1910, some people knew that Louise Marshall was wealthy and suspected that she used her wealth to send poor boys to college. But Louise Marshall never talked about herself, never revealed her wealth, the suffering in her childhood, her fun as a flighty debutante, or her flirtations with young men who adored her. She talked, instead, about her need to live her faith by serving the struggling people around her. She had plenty to say about that.

The prosperous friends who invited Louise Marshall to their homes for coffee served in fine china cups did not understand why she drove a Chevrolet instead of a Cadillac or why she spent her days with people who smelled bad. Settlement work had become an acceptable temporary occupation for single women who had just finished college, but what Louise did was different. She didn't talk like the Progressive reformers. In fact, she didn't work for political reform. She believed in changing people one by one. She advocated individual virtues: respect, character, discipline, excellence, and pride. That sounds plain enough, but her friends and family didn't really understand. Maybe she was a saint, they said. Maybe she was crazy. Everyone in both her worlds agreed on only one thing: Louise Marshall was absolutely devoted to the Cabbage Patch Settlement and its people. It was her only passion.

We came across Louise Marshall and the lifesaving work she did during the Depression when we were researching church history for another book. We were struck by how little has been written about a woman who has had a profound effect on thousands of lives—more than 100,000 by the University of Louisville's account 10 years before her death in 1981.[1] That neglect by history seemed wrong to us, but we didn't know if we could find enough material on Louise Marshall to justify a biography or if we would like her enough to do the work. We still don't know if we like her. But we found a remarkable story of faith, love, courage, dedication, and mystery. It's a story Louise Marshall didn't want known. She wanted people to focus on the Cabbage Patch Settlement, not on her.

We teased Louise Marshall's story from Cabbage Patch Settlement records, oral histories, and memorabilia—40 cubic feet of documents—transferred to the Filson Historical Society just as we began our work; from more than 30 interviews we did ourselves with people who knew Miss

---

1. Woodrow Strickler, remarks for University of Louisville graduation ceremony, May 16, 1971, CPSHR, FHS.

Marshall or her work; from public records, contemporary newspapers, and diaries. More recent scholarship provided additional context.

Historians tend to ask how Miss Marshall fit into the settlement house movement that began with England's Toynbee Hall in 1886, and Jane Addams's famous Chicago Hull House in 1889. By 1910, when 22-year-old Louise Marshall incorporated her Cabbage Patch Settlement, the American settlement house movement was well established with perhaps 400 settlement houses in the United States; even Louisville already had three other settlement houses.[2] That year, Jane Addams published her autobiography, *Twenty Years at Hull House*, in the hope that others engaged in similar work would find it useful. Addams's work provided Louise Marshall a template for what a settlement house could be and what programs it could offer. It did not provide a pattern for what the Cabbage Patch Settlement would become. Louise Marshall was not Jane Addams—however much they may have been alike.

Certainly, they had similarities. Addams and Marshall were both Presbyterians and daughters of prosperous Victorian families. (Louise Marshall was the great-great-granddaughter of US Chief Justice John Marshall.) Both identified areas of crushing poverty where they established programs to improve the plight of the people. However,

---

2. Allen F. Davis, *Spearheads for Reform: The Social Settlements and the Progressive Movement 1890–1914* (New York: Oxford University Press, 1967), 14. The number depends on the definition of "settlement house." Davis says that most settlement houses were in the Northeast and Midwest and asserts that the few settlement houses in the South were of little importance.

Addams was an erudite college graduate, a student of philosophy and the classics. Louise Marshall was a voracious reader of theology, news, and nonfiction who never finished high school. Addams's faith faltered. Marshall's faith drove and sustained her. Addams brought educated young women and men into her settlement house to teach and set examples of better living. Marshall recruited and paid to educate settlement workers from the Cabbage Patch neighborhood because those from the neighborhood understood the people and their problems. Addams embraced the key tenets of the Progressive Era and worked to elevate the masses by advocating legislation to attack the root causes of poverty and suffering. Louise Marshall rejected those campaigns and believed that the key to improvement was changing individuals. For her, saving individuals was an end, not, as with some Progressives, a beginning. Her tool of choice was love, not legislation. On one rare occasion when she entered a public debate, she argued against the child labor legislation advocated by Progressives because she believed children needed to work. While Addams traveled broadly in support of her cause, Louise Marshall visited filthy homes in her hometown. She loved, inspired, and scolded naughty, stinky children and worked to strengthen their families. The children stood in awe of Miss Marshall. They loved her, hated her, and later credited her with changing their lives.[3]

---

3. Jane Addams, *Twenty Years at Hull House* (New York: Macmillan, 1920); Allen F. Davis, *American Heroine: The Life and Legend of Jane Addams* (New York: Oxford University Press, 1973); Jean Bethke Elshtain, *Jane Addams and the Dream of American Democracy, A Life* (New York: Basic Books, 2002); Louise W. Knight, *Citizen: Jane Addams and the Struggle for Democracy* (Chicago: University of Chicago Press, 2005).

Given her lack of impact on the course of the settlement house movement and the issues it espoused, it may be tempting to write off Miss Marshall as irrelevant to scholarship and uninteresting to today's readers. We believe that would be wrong for several reasons.

Over almost 70 years, Louise Marshall pulled thousands of people from certain ruin and created a ripple effect of success for subsequent generations. She showed rare courage defending her settlement children from society's evil and was badly beaten more than once for her trouble. She enjoyed attractive men and the advantages of wealth, but she loved her Cabbage Patch children more. She gave them her life and much of her fortune. Her story remains compelling.

Louise Marshall also established an institution—the Cabbage Patch Settlement—that is still changing lives using the philosophy and techniques she established. The Cabbage Patch Settlement is remarkable for both its longevity and its continuing success. The broader settlement house movement faded as social legislation, much of it passed in the wake of the Great Depression, provided safety nets. However, the Cabbage Patch Settlement had some of its most memorable successes in the years following World War II. Today the Cabbage Patch remains strong, if more finely focused, and continues to change the lives of vulnerable young people. It still refuses the government funding and Metro United Way campaign money that would restrict its policies or make it dependent on another organization. The settlement's approach deserves further study by educators and by social scientists, including those interested in the settlement house movement's varied forms.

The Two Lives and One Passion of Louise Marshall

The Cabbage Patch story is well known, at least in Louisville. This book focuses on Louise Marshall's story, the tale that most of those who thought they knew her never heard. The story will certainly interest the many thousands of people who were touched by the Cabbage Patch or those who still support its programs. Elderly alumni of Miss Marshall's days at the Cabbage Patch—they call themselves "Patchers"—still meet periodically to celebrate their friendships and recall old times at the settlement. Other people, who never knew Louise Marshall, heard us tell the story as we worked and found the tale engaging and sometimes inspiring. I recall especially an elderly employee at a government office where I searched for old Marshall wills. As we worked, I told him about Miss Marshall. At the end of the morning, I pulled out my wallet to pay my bill. The man shook his head firmly. "No charge," he said. "That story needs to be told."

We agree. Louise Marshall's story needs to be told.

—*Linda Raymond and Bill Ellison*

CHAPTER 1

HONORIS CAUSA

For graduation 1971, the University of Louisville mustered all its usual pomp to award four honorary degrees, three of them to men with towering international reputations in medicine, music, and diplomacy. The fourth, a Doctor of Humane Letters (*Honoris Causa*), the university awarded to Miss Mary Louise Marshall, a tiny, graying woman little known outside her hometown.[4]

University President Dr. Woodrow Strickler presented the degree (the only one Louise Marshall ever got). In brief remarks, he credited her with more than 60 years of devoted, unpaid work among the "poor and destitute" at the Cabbage Patch Settlement House, which she founded in 1910 in the Cabbage Patch neighborhood near downtown Louisville, Kentucky. Louise Marshall, he said, had provided thousands

---

4. "University to Distinguish Four with Honorary Degrees," *Louisville Cardinal*, May 16, 1971 commencement issue. The University of Louisville honored three others with degrees that day: Charles Yost, career diplomat who promoted peace as a representative of the United States in the United Nations and around the world; former U of L School of Medicine dean Dr. Murray Kinsman, who published extensive research on cardiac output; and John Jacob Niles, internationally known for collecting, composing, and performing Appalachian mountain music.

of young people with the way to a "better life." He put the number of those she influenced at more than 100,000.[5] That understated what she had done by a good deal. Louise Marshall did not just influence people; she changed lives.

The restrained smile with which Miss Marshall accepted her hood and diploma did not reveal much either. It did not even hint at the steel will that both defied the expectations of her privileged Victorian upbringing and rejected great issues of the Progressive Era that followed. Nothing in her demeanor that great day suggested the absolute commitment she demanded of herself and others or her icy rejection of those who disappointed her most. Nothing credited the conservative Christian faith that powered her. No one mentioned the quirky personality that, even years later, caused friends to shake their heads and smile.

Ten years later at her funeral, the Rev. Dr. Henry Mobley would do a better job of summing up Louise Marshall. "Anyone who knew Louise Marshall," he said, "would agree that she was a character."[6]

But that was later. On the spring graduation day in 1971, when the university focused its attention on her, the best clue to understanding Louise Marshall was the list of people she invited to share the occasion. She had spent her life straddling two worlds; her guest list embraced both.

Her family was on the list, of course, her sisters, nieces, and nephews. She had even invited her brother Burwell, although they had hardly spoken in years. (Her brother Richard, the

---

5. Dr. Woodrow Strickler (commencement script, University of Louisville, May 1971), CPSHR, FHS.

6. Thomas R. Chambers, PI, July 13, 2011.

family black sheep, had been dead for two decades. Most people did not even know she had an older brother.) Board members who had supported the Cabbage Patch through the years had been invited. So had the Cabbage Patch boys—now men—she had groomed to carry forward her good work: Roosevelt Chin, Charles Dietsch, James Cooksey, and Joseph Burks. The Escue Tomerlin family was there, also—two generations of Patchers who had pulled themselves out of the Great Depression's desperation to solid ground because Louise Marshall stood beside them.[7]

Indeed, some people would later argue that nobody knew Louise Marshall as well as those she served at the Cabbage Patch. While the Progressive Era powered social change for the masses, Louise Marshall focused on individuals, especially the women and children who had little status in turn-of-the-century America. She loved children, especially the bad boys. She treated each of them with respect, even when she spoke sharply—as she often did. Louise Marshall may have been a child of privilege, but when people from the Patch sat down with her to talk about family strife, alcoholism, struggles in school, violence, and despair, a bond formed.

"She really didn't talk about herself," said Ruth Tomerlin Chaffins, one of the longtime Patchers. "The ways she presented things, you knew that she had gone through similar things. She was an amazing woman."[8]

She *was* an amazing woman. Everyone agreed on that. What they didn't agree on—what no one really understood—

---

7. "List of Miss Louise Marshall" (invitees to graduation ceremony), CPSHR, FHS.

8. Ruth Tomerlin Chaffins, PI, July 6, 2011.

was what shaped the woman who merged her identity with the Cabbage Patch to change so many lives.

No one knew because Louise Marshall did not want them to know.

CHAPTER 2

BORN TO WEALTH, PRIVILEGE, AND PRESBYTERIANISM

Although she lived her whole life in Louisville, Kentucky, Louise Marshall spoke with the cultured accent of old Virginia gentry. She used that tone in June 1974 when she sat down with Lynn Gant, a Cabbage Patch board member, for a taped oral history interview. Lynn Gant started by asking about Miss Marshall's family and background.

"My dear," Miss Marshall responded crisply, "I can't conceive of anyone being interested in that."

"Everybody is," said Gant.

"My dear," said Miss Marshall, "we're going to stop this right now."[9]

Fortunately, Lynn Gant did not stop.

––––––

9. Lynn Gant and Louise Marshall, taped interview, June 25, 1974, CPSHR, FHS.

US Chief Justice John Marshall was Louise Marshall's great-great-grandfather. His picture still hangs in the settlement, and he is mentioned on the historical marker in front of the building.

Mary Louise Marshall lived most of her life with her feet planted in two very different worlds. That stretch was partly the unavoidable result of Burwell Keith Marshall's marriage to Elizabeth "Lizzie" Veech, a union that joined the venerable, if slightly tatty, Marshalls of old Virginia to the upright and very prosperous Veeches of Louisville, Kentucky. Rapidly changing times also played a role in shaping Louise Marshall, as the Victorian Age's corseted expectations gave way to the Progressive Era's determined optimism and catapulted women into the 20th century. Most important of all, however, was the decision Louise Marshall made herself, while still very young, to step back and forth across the stark boundary between her well-heeled Louisville neighborhood and the barefoot poverty of the Cabbage Patch half a mile away.

If that dualism bothered some people—and it did— Louise Marshall doesn't seem to have concerned herself with the contradictions. She knew who she was: a humble—if highly opinionated—servant answering God's call to serve others. In time, after she had decided who she was and who she could not be, she gave herself single-heartedly to the Cabbage Patch Settlement she founded and to the people the settlement served. In the end, many people would conclude that Louise Marshall *was* the Cabbage Patch and the Cabbage Patch was Louise Marshall. That suited Louise Marshall just fine. She didn't want attention for herself.

As a portrait still hanging in the Cabbage Patch Settlement's boardroom suggests, however, understanding Louise Marshall's story requires understanding both the distinguished John Marshall family of old Virginia and the strong-willed, pioneering Veeches of Kentucky. Indeed, Louise got many of the qualities that made her a character— the qualities that made people love, hate, and admire her, often at the same time—from her forebears. Those qualities were as much a product of her genetic makeup as her hazel eyes and brown, wavy hair. Thus, this story begins with US Chief Justice John Marshall, whose portrait looks down on all modern-day boardroom meetings at the Cabbage Patch Settlement. Marshall was Louise Marshall's great-great grandfather, a point of considerable, well-justified pride to the Marshall side of her family. John Marshall fought in the American Revolution, serving beside George Washington, and went on to become the Chief Justice who defined the US Supreme Court's role in the ensuing democracy. John Marshall was also a rich man, a slave owner, a large landholder, and a man who could keep a family feud smoldering for years.

John Marshall once said he was "destined for the bar from infancy," and so, it seems, were succeeding generations of Marshalls, including Louise's father, brother, and (unexpectedly) her older sister. Louise and her family also embraced John Marshall's willingness to resolve differences through litigation rather than negotiation and his penchant for bitter family dispute. Even the more modern Marshalls "would go to court over some of the most nitpicking things," said a later Marshall family son-in-law. "The thing was no one would yield."[10] Indeed, the Chief Justice's running political and legal disputes with his cousin Thomas Jefferson were legendary. Called upon to administer the oath of office to the newly elected President Jefferson, Justice Marshall reportedly turned his back on the ceremony. Nonetheless, John Marshall sired a family with a passion for land acquisition and launched future generations toward the new frontier, Kentucky, where the disputes would continue.[11]

---

10. Thomas R. Chambers, PI, July 13, 2011.

11. R. Kent Newmyer, *John Marshall and the Heroic Age of the Supreme Court* (Baton Rouge: Louisiana State University Press, 2001), 37–39, 77.

Louise's grandfather, Nathaniel Burwell Marshall, owned property, too, but departed from the family's legal tradition to become a distinguished Louisville doctor and medical educator—but only briefly. He died when Louise's father Burwell Keith Marshall was only eight years old.[12] Nathaniel left his beautiful wife, Sallie Ewing, with both property enough to support the family, if properly managed, and the unpleasant duty of collecting the rents, a ritual that may have shaped young Burwell's penny-pinching attitude toward money. Burwell Sr. told his own son (also named Burwell Keith Marshall) that he "watched helplessly while his mother borrowed money on her bankers' advice to finance real estate investment" that went bad. The bad investments and a series of economic disruptions "basically wiped the widow and her family out" financially, Burwell's grandson, Burwell Keith Marshall III, wrote many years later. Louise's father became "a taciturn, humorless man with a temper."[13] Those qualities had a lasting, painful impact on his children. In time, Burwell Sr. reverted to the family's traditional profession and began studying law at the University of Virginia, where he took highest honors in Latin.[14] By then, old Chief Justice Marshall had become the stuff of history and family legend, but the character that defined him continued on to his

---

12. Ancestry.com. *Virginia, Prominent Families,* Vol. 1–4 (database online), Provo, UT: Ancestry.com Operations Inc., 2001; Louise Marshall, taped interview by Lynn Gant, June 25, 1974, CPSHR, FHS.

13. Burwell Marshall III, email to Bill and Linda Raymond Ellison, June 3, 2013.

14. "B. K. Marshall Funeral Today," *Louisville (KY) Courier-Journal,* July 2, 1932.

progeny, including Louise, with sometimes-heartrending results. Louise Marshall reveled in the Marshall legacy; she was stubborn, contentious, litigious, and smart.

Burwell Marshall Sr. left Virginia to finish his legal education at the University of Louisville. There he graduated with distinction and set a standard for perfection he later expected his own children to meet, whether they could or not. His diploma in 1878 was accompanied by a certificate showing that he had obtained "the highest honor available and answered without error every question in the examination." Within a year, he had established a law practice in downtown Louisville.[15] His next project was to court Lizzie Veech—who was not dazzled by the Marshall pedigree.

The Veech family's roots also stretched back to the nation's beginnings when John Veech, lately of Ulster, Ireland, came by flatboat to the Falls of the Ohio where the city of Louisville was starting to emerge. There he built a log cabin and a reputation as an Indian fighter. Over the years, the Veeches became owners of land and slaves at a plantation east of Louisville that they called Indian Hill, where they developed a reputation for breeding fine trotting horses. The Veeches also raised beautiful, hardworking, strong-willed women, iron-spined daughters who would forge pioneering careers in medicine and law. Those women's stiff-necked determination caused a future generation to coin a phrase, "Veechie," which described someone who could be hard to deal with but who was *never* rude.[16] Louise Marshall would

---

15. Ibid.

16. Meme Sweets Runyon, PI, October 17, 2011.

mix those tough Veech genes with the pugnacious tendencies she got from the Marshalls, a formidable combination. As many people would learn to their sorrow, Louise Marshall knew how to be Veechie.

Before he retired to Indian Hill to raise his six children (including Louise's mother), Richard B. Veech, big, tall, and handsome, had been a banker, financier, and railroad president.[17] Veech shared the Marshall passion for land and owned more than 1,000 acres of prime real estate, more than enough to make Louise's mother Lizzie, and the other Veech children, wealthy. Veech wealth also financed religious causes. It was said that Grandfather Veech "made the money and the missionaries spent it."[18]

Besides wealth and social standing, Lizzie Veech brought to the marriage a family history of adamant Presbyterianism. John Veech had been Scotch Presbyterian, and the affiliation stuck through the generations. (Legend has it that one later Veech kinsman, killed in a steamboat disaster, washed ashore still gripping the Bible he'd been reading.) Lizzie's own mother was the product of Puritan stock, making flexibility in religion doubly unlikely.[19] (Old Mrs. Veech, "a tiny soul," reportedly wouldn't allow her "great big" husband the sin of racing the horses he raised.)[20]

---

17. Louise Marshall, taped interview by Lynn Gant, June 25, 1974, CPSHR, FHS.

18. Ibid.

19. Kathleen Jennings, *Louisville's First Families: A Series of Genealogical Sketches* (Louisville, KY: Standard Printing, 1920), 100–105.

20. Louise Marshall, taped interview by Lynn Gant, June 25, 1974, CPSHR, FHS.

When Lizzie Veech married Burwell Marshall Sr., there was only one question about who would switch churches. His Episcopal father may have been a pillar of Christ's Church in Louisville, where he was secretary of the vestry, but when Burwell Marshall married a Veech, he was bound to become a Presbyterian—if Presbyterians were Christian. Marshall said, "Lizzie, I'll study this just like I do my law cases and see if it's Christian."[21] He concluded that Louisville's Second Presbyterian Church did qualify as Christian, and Marshall seemed to make the transition smoothly. Burwell Marshall became a deacon and Sunday school teacher at the Second Presbyterian Church, and the couple's household would be deeply Presbyterian in a day when Presbyterians had a reputation for being austere churchgoers who feared God, hell, and most human pleasures. (Their church reinforced the stereotype by frowning on card playing, dancing, drinking, and reading the newspaper on Sundays.) That was fine with the newly married Marshalls. The Marshalls were "Presbyterian to the core—and the core was Presbyterian," their granddaughter Elizabeth Johnson Haynes said years later.[22]

Louise Marshall's parents, Elizabeth "Lizzie" Veech and Burwell Keith Marshall, married June 21, 1883, and set up housekeeping conveniently near Burwell's office on West Jefferson Street in downtown Louisville. Then, at some point, they took a trip to recall the Marshalls' Virginia roots and to meet Burwell's Virginia relatives. Lizzie was "absolutely disgusted by the fact that they simply sat on their disheveled

---

21. Mrs. Nicholas Dosker, interview by Mrs. William Harvin, February 23, 1987, CPSOHP, FHS.

22. Elizabeth Johnson Haynes, PI, July 11, 2011.

mansion porches and didn't do anything but fan themselves and speak of the old days," Elizabeth Haynes said.[23]

Sloth and mourning the past were not ethics Lizzie was about to embrace for herself or her children. Her upbringing, her station in life, her times, and her religion all required something very different of women: energy, cheerfulness and motherhood, among other things. Marrying Burwell Marshall was a good start; late 19th century women, especially Presbyterian women, were, after all, born to be supportive wives and mothers.

"Sweetness is to woman what sugar is to fruit," the Rev. E. J. Hardy wrote in 1887. "It is her first business to be happy, a sunbeam in the house, making others happy . . . her raison d'etre is to give out pleasure to all as a fire gives out heat."[24]

A Presbyterian Church report put it more starkly: "The woman was created out of and for the man . . . The first law of human government is, 'Thy desire shall be unto thy husband, and he shall rule over thee.'"[25]

Lizzie met all the tests. She and Burwell loved each other dearly. She was able to calm and comfort him through difficult times. She called him, always, "Mr. Marshall." And when they went to bed on cold nights, she let him thaw his cold feet on her warm back.[26] She ran a conservative,

---

23. Ibid.

24. E. J. Hardy, *Manners Makyth Man* (New York: Charles Scribner's Sons, 1887), 42–43.

25. Ernest Trice Thompson, *Presbyterians in the South*, vol. 3 (Richmond, VA: John Knox Press, 1973), 387–388, quoting from a report by the Synod of Virginia in 1899.

26. Thomas Chambers, PI, July 13, 2011.

straight-laced household where even Mr. Marshall had to observe her rules: When he wanted to smoke, he had to go outside on the porch.[27]

She also promptly got down to the business of producing children. Richard Veech Marshall was born in 1884, without a hint of the disappointment and shame he would bring to the family. A daughter, Elizabeth Veech Marshall, who would comfort, surprise, and delight, arrived two years later.

With each addition, the family moved to new lodgings. By the time Mary Louise Marshall was born in 1888, the family needed a real home. Lizzie's father, Richard Veech, was ready to build a suitable house for them on land he owned on Ormsby Avenue. Louise Marshall would grow up in that stylish suburban neighborhood south of downtown Louisville, where the future revealed itself to anyone who wanted to take a trolley ride.

Just a few blocks down the trolley line, beyond the Veech property, Louisville's business leaders had for five years organized the annual Southern Exposition, a collection of modern wonders including, most spectacularly, an electric railway and the world's largest installation of the new incandescent lights. However, in their zeal to improve Louisville's economy, those civic leaders failed to point out that a few blocks west of the exposition's brilliance the cost of industrial progress was also visible for anyone who wanted to see it. Among Louisville's factories and railroad tracks nestled a neighborhood with sordid shelter for a new class of working poor. The Southern Exposition would eventually yield its

---

27. Katherine M. Davis, telephone interview by authors, September 27, 2014.

land to fashionable homes for Louisville's most prosperous citizens. The industrial slum, known as the Cabbage Patch, would continue to fester.

Both neighborhoods would shape Burwell and Lizzie's new daughter, Louise.

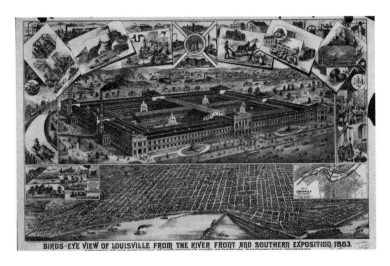

BIRDS-EYE VIEW OF LOUISVILLE FROM THE RIVER FRONT AND SOUTHERN EXPOSITION, 1883.

Louisville's Southern Exposition, just south of downtown Louisville from 1883 to 1887, promoted development of the stylish neighborhood where Louise Marshall grew up. The exposition buildings were demolished in 1889 to make room for residential development, including today's St. James and Belgravia Courts and Central Park. In the background are the railroads, factories, and shabby houses of the Cabbage Patch.

CHAPTER 3

MISERY'S LESSONS

Despite wealth, privilege, and family connections, Louise Marshall's childhood included a full measure of trouble. She almost never talked about the pressures, disappointments, conflict, violence, or depression of those early years, but the trials would pain, shape, and, eventually, serve her well. When she reached out to help others who struggled, she knew something about their miseries. Those she helped didn't know how she could understand, and she never told them. Victorians did not discuss such family secrets.

Some of those who knew what happened in the new house on Ormsby Avenue blamed Louise's father. Certainly, Burwell Marshall's expectations were high, his Presbyterianism rigid, his respect for rules unbending, and his honesty unassailable, but there was a duality about him, too. While Burwell Marshall ran a humorless, regimented household with expectations that were sometimes unrealistic, he could also be a devoted "Papa" who could deny his children little. Louise's younger sister, Sallie Ewing, would later say that Louise "just wrapped him around her finger.

He thought she was wonderful."[28] Certainly, Louise adored and desperately wanted to please her father, no easy task.

It's also worth noting that by the time the Marshalls moved into their new house on Ormsby Avenue, society was changing fast, driven by technological innovation that put pressure on their old Victorian norms and ideas and made some conflict inevitable, especially for those who clung to the old ways and values. Indeed, as one century turned to the next, technological innovation was everywhere. Louisville was becoming the nation's 20th largest city, well on its way to a population of 161,129 in the 1900 census. The Marshalls' new neighborhood was a showplace for the changes.

Burwell Marshall, Presbyterian that he was, was perfectly ready to walk a mile and a half downtown to his law office and back again for lunch every day. But for others less open to exercise, a modern electric trolley opened the area south of downtown to new residential development. With their purpose of boosting Louisville's economy accomplished, the Southern Exposition buildings a few blocks south of the Marshalls' home were demolished. That made way for an upscale neighborhood known as St. James Court, home to a prosperous new class of men who managed booming Louisville industries such as tobacco, liquor, and transportation. Other men who shared the prosperity built large, stylish houses along the streets that crossed Ormsby, and their families became part of the Marshall children's social set.

The Marshalls' new house, built in the trendy Richardson Romanesque style, was neither the largest nor the grandest

---

28. Mrs. Nicholas (Sallie Ewing Marshall) Dosker, interview by Mrs. William Harvin, February 23, 1987, CPSOHP, CPSHR, FHS.

in their Ormsby Avenue neighborhood; industrialist James B. Speed's mansion up the street clearly outshone it. But the Marshall house had ornate touches: stone arches over windows echoed the stone arch over the front door. Fancy brickwork climbed the tall chimney. A stylish, patterned tile floor greeted visitors under the recessed front entrance. Inside, wide doorways led to big rooms with 16-foot ceilings and fine, highly polished hardwood floors.[29] Most important, the house was big enough to house a growing crowd.

Louise Marshall was one or two years old when her family moved to their new home at 422 Ormsby Avenue. Built for them in Richardson Romanesque style, the house wasn't the grandest in that neighborhood, but it was large enough for a family of seven and four live-in servants.

Linda Raymond photo

---

29. Elizabeth Dosker Chambers, interview by Mrs. William Harvin, March 19, 1987, CPSOHP, CPSHR, FHS.

By the 1900 census, 11 people were listed as living at the Marshall house on Ormsby.[30] The census taker listed Burwell K. Marshall as head of the household, his wife Elizabeth and their five children—Richard, then 15; Elizabeth, 13; Louise, 12; Sallie Ewing, 8; and Burwell Keith Jr., 3. The household's residents also included four servants: Cecilia Reerdon, who was listed as white, and Rebecca Howard, Eliza Barnett, and Elijah Barnett, who were recorded as black.[31]

Prosperous and privileged though the Marshalls were, they were too Puritan to admit it. They liked to think they lived simply, a contention that was subject to challenge. An irreverent young man who later married into the family once pointed out that the family had a coachman to help with the buggy and horses, a cook, a laundress, a seamstress, and a maid upstairs. It was true. The live-in staff was bolstered by servants who came in during the day as help was needed.[32]

Louise's favorite was Miss Maggie Dearing, the seamstress who came to Lizzie's sewing room in the spring and fall to make clothing and other things the family needed. "That sweet lady" endeared herself to Louise for life by giving her a hairpin box full of mints, a memory that Louise savored into old age.[33]

Burwell Marshall was the unquestioned head of the household—unquestioned at least until Richard reached the

---

30. The house was originally numbered 414 Ormsby but was later renumbered 422 Ormsby, the address the Marshalls used for most of their lives there.

31. Twelfth Census of the United States, June 1900.

32. Elizabeth Johnson Haynes, PI, July 11, 2011.

33. Louise Marshall, taped interview by Lynn Gant, June 25, 1974, CPSHR, FHS.

age of rebellion. Sallie Ewing later said their father was "the meanest man in the world."[34] When it came to business, the assessment stuck. As an attorney, he had a reputation as a lone wolf with a willingness to go for the kill, a virtue for lawyers of his day. He was the lawyer other lawyers turned to when they needed representation.[35]

At home, Burwell Marshall ran a regimented household committed to Presbyterian virtue, frugality, and academic excellence. In Burwell Marshall's household, mornings started with family prayers that everyone was expected to attend. Prayer would provide a foundation for the day to follow; the family would pray again at the table before each meal together. Despite the family's wealth, Louise's father always told the children "he couldn't buy anything more for us," Louise recalled later, and their mother always assured him that she didn't buy the children anything they didn't need.[36]

When Louise was old enough to start school, her father reached into his Episcopal past and sent her to Kentucky Home School. Founded in the vestry of Christ Church Cathedral, the school had a reputation for high "standards of scholarship."[37] There, to please her father, Louise memorized the Episcopal catechism (as she would later learn the Presbyterian catechism) and began a long, agonizing effort to

---

34. Tom Chambers, telephone interview by authors, May 24, 2012.

35. Burwell Keith Marshall III, PI, March 16, 2012.

36. Louise Marshall, taped interview by Lynn Gant, June 25, 1974, CPSHR, FHS.

37. Patty B. Semple, "Schools of Louisville in the Past and Present," *Louisville (KY) Post*, October 25, 1921.

learn to read.[38]

What no one knew—and what a little girl couldn't tell them—was that her eyes couldn't focus.[39] Apparently, her eyes had different refractive powers, possibly a condition called anisometropia, now correctable with glasses. An anxious Burwell Marshall brought in tutors and doctors for Louise, but the problem continued undiagnosed. A renowned eye doctor prescribed fresh air and exercise. Louise took the required long walks, but she simply could not read—or master the subjects that required reading.

"I just couldn't," she said later. "It wasn't a question of wanting to."

Burwell Marshall, who had excelled in academics, expected his children to excel, too. "It was a terrible blow to him," she said later.[40]

The children walked to school, of course. Kentucky Home School, with classes for little children, was by then conveniently located nearby. But Louise aspired to be like Elizabeth, who was nearly two years older, so each day after school, she and a friend would hide until Elizabeth walked by. Then they would walk home with her, feeling much more grown up.

At home, nonsense doesn't seem to have been much tolerated. One day, Louise arrived home from school and gleefully announced to her mother, "Did you know that my great-grandfather was John Marshall?"

38. Louise Marshall, taped interview by Lynn Gant, June 25, 1974, CPSHR, FHS.

39. Lewis Johnson, telephone interview with authors, July 18, 2011.

40. Louise Marshall, taped interview by Lynn Gant, June 25, 1974, CPSHR, FHS.

"It doesn't matter who your ancestors were," Lizzie Veech Marshall replied. "It matters how you behave in school!"[41] That rigidity may help explain why Lizzie Marshall, who was close to Elizabeth, never seems to have established much empathy with her middle daughter.

After-school hours were regimented. Burwell Marshall was determined that his children would have every advantage, so for four afternoons each week, Lizzie Marshall scheduled wholesome cultural activities for her daughters. One afternoon a French teacher came to the house for what became a French club for girls from the neighborhood. Another day a woman from the neighborhood taught embroidery, an activity Louise loved, despite her eye problems.

For piano lessons, the girls had Miss Mildred Hill, who later became internationally famous for a song she wrote with her sister, "Happy Birthday to You." With Louise, however, she had no success. "She was lovely," Louise Marshall recalled, but not stimulating. "Papa was determined we were going to play, but I didn't care a thing in the world about it."[42]

On Wednesday afternoons, Louise and her sisters left their neighborhood friends and walked the mile to Second Presbyterian Church for a program called "Ministering Children." There Lizzie Marshall's close childhood friend, Lizzie Robinson Cecil (Mrs. John Cecil), taught the Bible and helped the children memorize Bible verses, activities that proved important for Louise later.

---

41. Dr. James J. Cooksey, PI, July 14, 2011.

42. Louise Marshall, taped interview by Lynn Gant, June 25, 1974, CPSHR, FHS.

On Sundays, of course, the Marshall family went to church, to Second Presbyterian, a tall-steeple, silk-stocking church across from what would become the Louisville Presbyterian Theological Seminary in downtown Louisville. After the morning service, the minister often came to the Marshalls' home for dinner. In the afternoon, Burwell Marshall would tell the children Bible stories. The children also went to Sunday school, which led Louise to mischief. When she moved out of the infant class into "the big room," she had a teacher (she recalled his name as Mr. Victor Lloyd Jenson Brooks) whom she took pleasure in tormenting in ways only a child could conceive or appreciate.

The Marshall family attended Second Presbyterian Church, a striking Gothic structure at Second Street and Broadway within walking distance of their home. The church was destroyed by fire in 1956, and the congregation moved to a chapel it had built in Rolling Fields east of Louisville.

"I did all sorts of bad things to him," she told an interviewer later with some relish. "I just bedeviled the life out of him." She never could explain how or why she did it.[43]

The Marshalls also believed in travel as a part of a child's education. They regularly went by train to Florida and toured around North America to Yellowstone National Park, to the Thousand Islands area of Canada, and to places that Burwell Marshall felt had historic importance, such as Grant's Tomb in New York. Then, while Louise was still quite young, they went to Europe, where the great landmarks looked amazingly like the "Perry Pictures," sets of educational cards with pictures, that her mother had been showing her since she was tiny. The trip ignited a lifelong love of Europe's wonders. Coming home was a letdown. Home looked drab by comparison, and Louise said so. The solution, her father responded, without a trace of humor, was that she should never leave home again.[44]

As she grew older, Louise moved to Semple Collegiate School, which had been founded by very well-educated, progressive women with a "solid professional reputation as skilled teachers." There, teachers worked with small classes on activities designed to provide a strong academic education through thinking rather than memorization.[45] The school was apparently a good fit for

43. Louise Marshall, taped interview, undated tape fragment, CPSHR, FHS; Louise Marshall, taped interview by Lynn Gant, June 25, 1974, CPSHR, FHS.

44. Kim McConnell Schiewetz, email to Bill and Linda Raymond Ellison, September 24, 2014; Louise Marshall, taped interview by Lynn Gant, June 25, 1974, CPSHR, FHS.

45. "Semple Collegiate School," in *Encyclopedia of Louisville*, John G. Kleber, ed. (Lexington: University Press of Kentucky, 2001), 802.

Louise, and she thrived there for a time. But her time at Semple ended abruptly in a quintessentially Marshall moment.

Progressive institution that it was, Semple introduced its young women to the new sport of "basket ball." The women's game was considerably different from the men's version with rules that limited movement and encouraged teamwork among teams of nine women. Men might shed clothing for freedom of movement, but women's bodies were, of course, well covered by long stockings and commodious bloomers and blouses. Louise loved basketball.

Elizabeth enjoyed basketball, too, so at first the sisters played each other. Then the school principal made a rule that siblings were not to compete. The girls observed the rule until the school organized a game that pitted Elizabeth's class against Louise's class. Louise pointed out—probably with Veech-like emphasis—that the contest would violate the rule against sibling rivalry. The principal ruled that an exception was in order.

"I was aggravated," Louise said later. "I defied the principal and wouldn't play because she had made the rule . . . and she just broke the rules and decided we would play whenever she said . . . I refused to do it."[46]

Louise's parents were called in and her teacher was invited "to tell Papa and Mother what a bad little girl I was." Burwell Marshall, well steeped in reverence for the rule of law, was not amused. "He picked us up and took us out of school." Louise Marshall would wonder later if her father erred by not supporting the principal. His decision opened a dark and

---

46. Louise Marshall, taped interview by Lynn Gant, June 25, 1974, CPSHR, FHS.

mysterious chapter in Louise's childhood, one that would cloud and shape her life. Suddenly Louise moved from the small, protected, encouraging atmosphere of private schools to the wide, roiling halls of the public Louisville Female High School in a big, new building with hundreds of students. "I was just terrified," Louise said later. "I just couldn't study at all."[47]

Certainly the school, which would shortly be renamed "Louisville Girls High School," met Burwell Marshall's desire for academic rigor. Its faculty of more than 30 women had degrees from well-respected institutions—Vassar, the University of Chicago, Wellesley, and the University of Michigan, among them. English classes required students to read—and write about—more than a dozen substantial works of literature each year. College-bound students took four years of Latin. Everyone studied science in gleaming new laboratories. Graduates went on to the best colleges where, the school's publications proclaimed, "in every instance they forged to the front" of their classes.[48]

Louise liked English, and she adored her history teacher, who helped link history to Louise's love of travel. "She was to me a very interesting person, interesting mind," Louise said later. That positive relationship, however, was more than overshadowed by the large classes of 40 students and more, reflecting the democratic give and take of a public school, rather than the nurturing five- or six-girl classes Louise had

---

47. Louise Marshall, taped interview by Lynn Gant, June 25, 1974, CPSHR, FHS.

48. "Fiftieth Annual Report of the Girls' High School, Louisville, Ky. 1905–06," Jefferson County Public Schools archives, Louisville, Kentucky.

always known.[49] The tongue-in-cheek "Commandments for Freshmen" printed in the school yearbook suggested the change in atmosphere. The list began, "Remember thy opinion is not wanted, neither is it of value on any subject whatsoever." It ended, "Never forget that in case of doubt thou art always wrong."[50] Louise, unfortunately, was a freshman.

"There were just so many girls," Louise Marshall said. "So many. The place was so big . . . I was just terrified the whole time I was there. I'd never been in crowds, and when you went through the halls, you were just like a bunch of cattle. It was awful to me."[51] If there was any comfort in the discovery that Louise's eye problem could be improved with glasses, it's not recorded. For an anxious teenage girl, the thick lenses that allowed academic progress probably didn't do much for social life or confidence. It probably didn't help either that Elizabeth was pretty and popular or that the Marshall boys seemed to keep things stirred up at home.

Louise Marshall didn't like talking about her teenage years and admonished later interviewers not to mention them, so details about those years are sparse and sequences confused. Some patterns seem clear, however. Richard, separated from his sisters by age, gender, and expectations, seems to have confounded his father's hopes and, probably, stirred up considerable conflict at home. Elizabeth responded by acting

---

49. Louise Marshall, taped interview by Lynn Gant, June 25, 1974, CPSHR, FHS.

50. "Louisville Girls High School Record 1853–1908," Jefferson County Public Schools archives, Louisville, Kentucky.

51. Louise Marshall, taped interview by Lynn Gant, June 25, 1974, CPSHR, FHS.

as her parents' comforter and Louise's role model. Sallie Ewing viewed Louise as her protector. (Louise saw Sallie Ewing as a little kid.) And Burwell Jr. struggled with a problem that even the age's advanced technology had not solved: polio.

Around the turn of the century, poliomyelitis—long one of the world's most dreaded diseases—became a force in the United States. Periodic epidemics swept Louisville in the early 1900s, and one of those waves caught young Burwell Keith Marshall Jr. Then, as now, doctors had no cure for polio, and in the early 1900s, there was little they could do to help. Those with polio struggled to breathe and suffered as their joints throbbed and their muscles weakened and stiffened. The disease was excruciating and more often crippling than fatal.

The Marshalls all shared Burwell's suffering. "You were a sick little boy who suffered so terribly yet so courageously," Louise wrote to Burwell years later, after their relationship had turned contentious. "We all loved you so and longed so to relieve your pain."[52]

The Marshalls worried, pampered Burwell, and, no doubt, prayed. In time, with long rest, the disease relented. Burwell had to wear a brace on his left leg. The doctors eventually decided to cut a tendon in the leg to remedy a lingering problem. Burwell walked again, but with a limp for life.[53]

The limp didn't keep Burwell from enjoying his years as a handsome, active public school student at Louisville Boys High School. Burwell crowned his senior year with

52. Louise Marshall to Burwell Marshall Jr., February 1935, CPSHR, FHS.

53. Burwell Keith Marshall III, PI, March 16, 2012; Elizabeth Johnson Haynes, PI, July 11, 2011.

his appearance "to the delight of everyone" in blackface as a steward in the class play, *The Dictator* by Richard Harding Davis. The glowing review noted that "the only trouble lay in the fact that his part did not enable him to demonstrate his ability to better advantage."[54] Burwell would graduate, go on to become the lawyer his father wanted, and raise a son of his own, Burwell Keith Marshall III. But for reasons that Burwell wouldn't discuss and no one else seemed to understand, Burwell Jr. would never get along with his sister Louise.

Richard's path was very different and very painful; he would end up estranged from the whole family until the end of his life. Thirteen years Burwell's senior, Richard was a tall, handsome young man in the mold of his grandfather Richard Veech, for whom he was named—but Richard wasn't satisfied with himself. Louise recalled her older brother as "beautiful-looking with dark brown curly hair." As she remembered him, Richard didn't like the curl and tried his best to straighten his hair. "But he couldn't because it was there," Louise said.[55]

If Louise felt the weight of her father's high expectations, Richard, as the firstborn son, must have found his father's hopes crushing. Convinced that private schools were superior, Burwell sent Richard to private prep schools. In 1902, as Richard approached college age, the *Courier-Journal* published a story about the University of Virginia, the university Burwell had attended as a young man. The *Courier-Journal* story emphasized the academic and moral values that

---

54. *Mustered Out*, yearbook published by the Louisville Boys High School Class of 1917, Louisville Free Public Library, Louisville, Kentucky.

55. Louise Marshall, taped interview by Lynn Gant, June 25, 1974, CPSHR, FHS.

Burwell held dear: The university's professional courses were known widely for their "scientific precision, thoroughness and breadth." Moreover, the article said, the university's "moral and religious atmosphere" was "markedly beneficial. . . . Altogether there is not a college in the country . . . where there is more orderliness and sobriety."[56]

With that ringing endorsement, and his father's checkbook, Richard was launched in his father's footsteps toward the University of Virginia and a career in the law. Unfortunately, Burwell Marshall also made young Richard cosigner on Burwell's bank account, giving the young man unfettered access to family funds. More unfortunate still—despite the university's high moral standing—Richard quickly discovered a number of distinctly un-Presbyterian pleasures, drinking alcohol, gambling, and enjoying women among them.

"He was somebody women just fell for easily," Richard's nephew Lewis Johnson said later. "Three times in a row, he gambled away the money" his father had given him.[57]

Burwell learned of the problem when his bank account emptied. Richard was yanked back to Louisville without ceremony.[58]

For roughly the next six years, Richard would live at home—where the city directory listed him as a boarder—and continued to confound his father's hopes and best efforts to set him up in business. Richard first went to work as a salesman

---

56. "The University of Virginia," *Louisville (KY) Courier-Journal*, June 23, 1902.

57. Lewis Johnson, telephone interview with authors, January 1, 2013.

58. Tom Chambers, PI, July 13, 2011; Burwell Keith Marshall III, PI, March 16, 2012.

(perhaps a traveling salesman) for Peaslee-Gaulbert Co., which dealt in paints, oils, mirrors, and glass lamps. The company was founded by three highly respected Louisville men. By the time Richard joined the company, it was a major manufacturer and employer with 4,000 employees and branches throughout the South. Richard had been given a fresh chance to succeed in a first-rate enterprise.[59] He would disappoint his family again.

"The behavior of Richard put a strong stamp on all of them," his niece Elizabeth Johnson Haynes said years later. "He was the typical scapegrace. He drank too much. He ran up debts at the University of Virginia . . . Upright, honest to the bone was absolutely the stamp of their [the Marshalls'] character. You can imagine how hard this was for them to take and how much of an impression it made on the younger ones about their own behavior."[60]

Louise's big sister, Elizabeth, did her best to comfort her parents. Indeed, she would become the family's next lawyer. However, her parents, always upright, became absolutely rigid, especially on the issue of alcohol. Years later when Louise was asked to describe her father, she said, "Let me tell you what kind of man he was. If they were on the 10th floor of some building downtown and if you invited him for a jigger of whiskey and set that jigger of whiskey on your desk and said, 'Mr. Marshall, you can either drink that jigger or jump out that window,' you wouldn't be able to catch him to keep him from jumping out."[61]

---

59. *Caron's Louisville City Directory*, (Louisville: Caron's Directory Co., 1904–1910); "Louisville Fifty Years Ago," Louisville Board of Trade, March 9, 1923.

60. Elizabeth Johnson Haynes, PI, July 11, 2011.

61. Dr. James J. Cooksey, PI, July 14, 2011.

However Louise may have viewed Richard's failings, she seems to have enjoyed the occasional evening when he'd sit and talk with her. On one such occasion, she convinced him to ask her friend Sallie Guthrie for a theater date.[62] Louise was growing up. And like Richard, she was struggling with their father's expectations, at least when it came to education.

When Louise Marshall later told an interviewer not to mention her high school experience because it went "very badly," her painfully disappointing academic record was only the surface problem.[63] In the shadows of those high school years, Louise endured a traumatic attack that injured her both physically and emotionally. Family and friends differ on the nature of the event and exactly when it happened; some of them won't discuss it at all. It may have involved someone close to her. As an adult, Louise told her good friend and associate, Dr. James Cooksey, that she was assaulted and had "a terrific reaction to that." The resulting depression (Cooksey, a psychologist, thinks it may have been post-traumatic stress disorder) was so profound that Louise's family sent her away to an institution, perhaps in Massachusetts, to recover. "She just said it was something she had to work to overcome," Cooksey said.[64]

Like others who knew something about the trauma, Elizabeth Johnson Haynes believed that it "laid a heavy hand on" Louise. Some, like Cooksey, add that the trauma, her

---

62. Louise Marshall, "Private Note Book for the fall of 1906 and the year of 1907" (her handwritten diary), CPSHR, FHS.

63. Louise Marshall, taped interview by Lynn Gant, June 25, 1974, CPSHR, FHS.

64. Dr. James J. Cooksey, PI, July 14, 2011.

struggle with depression, and the therapy that eased it also sharpened Louise Marshall's empathy and provided tools she was able to use later.[65]

"As a result of what she had found, she could help lots of folks through some really difficult times that had sort of unhinged them," Cooksey said.[66]

The episode may also have caused her father to relent on some of his expectations, at least concerning his vulnerable middle child. For girls of Louise's social class, high school was a decision, not a given; many girls (and boys) ended their formal education with eighth grade graduation. Some well-to-do girls like Elizabeth Marshall graduated from high school and went on to college. But they were exceptions. Other girls moved from eighth grade to the next phase of their social education; they began active social lives that provided both schooling on being charming hostesses in society and an intense ritual designed to introduce them to the men they would marry. Whatever Burwell Marshall may have expected, turn-of-the-century society did not consider a classical education necessary for women. Louise apparently did not stay in high school to graduate—although she continued to read, study, and value education all her life.[67]

---

65. Elizabeth Johnson Haynes, PI, July 11, 2011.

66. Dr. James J. Cooksey, PI, July 14, 2011.

67. The decision not to continue her education sets Louise Marshall apart from most of the other women in the Progressive, settlement house, and social gospel movements. Women in those movements generally had college degrees, focused on the great issues of the industrial age, and used language that reflected social theory. Studies of those women suggest that they were often concerned with fulfilling their own needs to break out of Victorian society's stringent expectations for women.

The archives of the Louisville public school system have records showing that Elizabeth, Sallie, and Burwell Marshall Jr. all graduated from public schools. The records say nothing at all about Louise. Burwell Marshall Sr. later offered Louise an opportunity to go to school in Washington. She considered the idea seriously but didn't take him up on it. She had other things on her mind.[68]

Victorian society demanded that socially prominent girls develop their social graces and make a debut into polite society. Elizabeth, Louise, and Sallie all did—although Louise would later say she didn't think much of all the fuss.

In 1915, the *Courier-Journal* women's section ran a long article on butterfly-like debutantes who "made good," a story that included Elizabeth and Louise Marshall as examples of debs who had become accomplished women. The story conjured the vision of a debutante, "a lovely girl all a-sparkle, tripping along with her bright eyes peering at you from a great fluff of fox fur . . . almost lost in a whirl of billowy skirt." The deb's life, the story said, was a mad, breathless dash from one party to another, "often accomplishing an unheard of number in one day; never losing her bright graciousness and vivacity and . . . never having a thought above clothes, beaux, teas, parties."[69]

It's hard to imagine the upright Marshalls a part of that picture, but the scene at the Marshall house was changing as the three girls grew up. Elizabeth, small, blonde, and very pretty was the "butterfly that drew the admirers" first, filling

---

68 Louise Marshall, "Private Note Book for the fall of 1906 and the year of 1907" (her handwritten diary), CPSHR, FHS.

69. "Louisville Women who have 'Made Good' in the Business World," *Louisville (KY) Courier-Journal*, September 19, 1915.

the parlor with young men. As the beaux began to come, the Marshalls found themselves with crowds for dinner. Between beaux and family, they often had 18 people for a meal.[70]

Whatever the cause, the end of her formal schooling seems to have begun an extraordinarily happy period of Louise's youth. Young men discovered the lovely girl with dark wavy hair and started calling to see Burwell and Lizzie's second daughter. That development was so utterly delightful that Louise began keeping a diary to record her burgeoning social life. Whatever she would become later, in 1906 and 1907, Louise Marshall was very much the giggling, boy-crazy, fashionably dressed society girl that the *Courier-Journal* had described. For that brief period at least, when she was 18 and 19 years old, it was clearly a life she enjoyed.[71]

During a summer trip to Danville, Kentucky, Louise melted when Tom Lanier gave her "quite a rush" and she had "quite a time" according to her diary. Next, she met Max Barker, a Louisville lawyer's son, who sent a gift and started calling. "I [was] immediately girl crazy about him," Louise wrote. "I was wild about him."

When she wasn't wild about a guy who liked her, Louise looked for guidance to Elizabeth whose approach to men sometimes lacked finesse. Elizabeth believed in being rude to young men she didn't like in the hope that they would get the message. Louise tried the technique with limited success. In one

---

70. Elizabeth Johnson Haynes, PI, July 11, 2011.

71. Louise Marshall, diary. Unless other credits are noted, the following description of Louise Marshall's life in 1906 and 1907 and the quotations from her are drawn from her diary, "Private Note Book for the fall of 1906 and the year of 1907," CPSHR, FHS.

instance, her mother introduced Louise to a promising medical student who pursued Louise up and down the aisles of Second Presbyterian Church—despite more than enough rudeness to convey Louise's feelings about her mother's taste in men.

Louise's most important failure to discourage a beau was E. Boyd Martin, who saw Louise taking the family horse and buggy downtown to leave for her father, offered help tying it up, and walked her to the trolley to get a car home. In no time at all, E. Boyd (as Louise referred to him) was a regular in the Marshall parlor—to Louise's dismay. "I didn't like him a bit, and he knew it," Louise wrote.

A schoolgirl's notebook became Louise Marshall's diary during her teenage years when her house was a mecca for young men wanting to socialize with the three Marshall daughters. Louise enjoyed the attention so much that she recorded her flirtations in this diary.

Courtesy of Cabbage Patch Settlement House Archives

E. Boyd, however, was not daunted. He managed to sit at Louise's table at a Presbyterian Orphanage fund-raising dinner and played a trump card: He invited her to see a stage show. "Of course you know I liked him then," Louise told the diary. "He was so sweet." For the remainder of the dinner, E. Boyd didn't need to ask for anything. Louise kept his plate well supplied.

Thus began an up-and-down relationship that would be important when Louise started her work. Those who knew Louise late in life as an austere presence eternally dressed in navy blue or black, would have wondered at the young woman in pink silk. Her interest flitted among fawning young men—Max, the "regular lady killer" about whom she was crazy, Tom Lanier in Danville, E. Boyd, who alternately soared and sank in her estimation—and enough others to supply escorts for horse shows, dinners, dances, and all the other events a society girl attended.

Lizzie Marshall's interest in Louise's suitors seems only to have embarrassed her daughter. To Louise's horror, Lizzie told some of her own women friends about the upcoming theater date with E. Boyd. "I felt very, very silly," Louise complained to her diary. Then E. Boyd was late picking her up for the outing—raising Louise's fears that he'd forgotten. He hadn't. Louise enjoyed the play. But she remained conflicted about the young man. "I like E. Boyd terribly well," she wrote, "but wasn't crazy about him." As 1906 ended, Louise's social life throbbed with activity. However, something E. Boyd said on their first trip to the theater began to sink in. "He told me, of course jokingly, that he was going to Pittsburgh to work and then coming back to get me. I looked sort of disgusted, and Boyd said he didn't mean to mention such a disagreeable subject." Clearly, Louise had made a conquest.

E. Boyd was only one of a crowd of young callers who gathered in the Marshall parlor on evenings when they didn't have a competing dinner, dance, theater engagement, roller-skating date, or party to attend. It was an exceptional night when Louise's diary reported, "Nothing doing." Usually there was plenty doing. On one occasion, the merriment in the Marshall parlor became so loud that Louise's father went onto the landing of the stairs to bellow for the young men to quiet down. Lizzie Marshall stopped him. "Mr. Marshall," she said, "would you rather that they *not* come?" Those were sobering words for a man who hoped to see three daughters wed.

In the end, only two of Burwell and Lizzie's daughters would marry. Louise would finally decide that, while E. Boyd was "a dear," she simply was not in love with him—or anyone else. E. Boyd married someone else and became a highly respected theater critic. Friends would say that Louise had married her work. However, the network of relationships Louise formed during those giddy evenings in the parlor would be critically important to sustaining the settlement house she later founded. Over the years, Louise would find herself calling on many of those same men for help. She never forgot how to flirt with them, even when she was very old, and they never stopped responding to her. Flirting was an essential skill for a woman trying to raise money for a cause.

Revealing though it is, Louise's diary may be most remarkable for what it does not say. Although Sunday entries routinely chronicle her attendance at Second Presbyterian

Church in the morning and Sunday school in the afternoon, it's clear that during the winter of 1906–07, Sundays didn't really begin for Louise until the Sunday night callers began arriving in the Marshall parlor. Louise Marshall's diary says very little about the activity that would become her life's passion: working with children in the Cabbage Patch, just half a mile from her world of high society.

CHAPTER 4

FINDING THE CABBAGE PATCH AND A CALLING

Debutantes that they were, Elizabeth, Louise, and Sallie Ewing Marshall honored the Victorian ethic that society women should support good causes. They all helped with a Presbyterian Mission Sunday school located near the line where St. James Court's prosperity melted into the Cabbage Patch's poverty. But over the years, only Louise stuck with the mission project and its people. The reason, she'd say later, was that she went visiting. When she did, she discovered her second world—and her life's work.

The initial portal to that world was the Sunday afternoon Bible school at Stuart Robinson Church, which the Marshalls' Second Presbyterian Church began at Sixth Street and Magnolia to serve the trendy new St. James Court neighborhood. At first, the Stuart Robinson Sunday school, just a few blocks from the Marshall home, provided a welcome alternative to the downtown Sunday school Louise had sometimes disliked.

Turn-of-the century Presbyterians were always looking for new mission opportunities, and just west of Stuart Robinson, in the Cabbage Patch neighborhood, an opportunity was ripe, or so the fashionable churchgoers thought. Railroad lines and new industries were breaking up the small farms where poor people had grown and sold cabbages. Small white wooden houses, backed by sheds and privies, nestled up to railroad tracks and factory fences without benefit of civic planning or utilities. Dirt roads and cow paths wandered where they would. The 600 or so blue-collar residents of that seven-square-block area were a motley mix of Irish and German immigrants and African Americans. All were poor, and many were unchurched, although many of the Irish and Germans had Catholic roots. In the winter of 1904–05, Presbyterians led by Col. Bennett H. Young rented a former saloon and dance hall at 2033 South Seventh Street in the old Cabbage Patch neighborhood to house a mission Sunday school. Colonel Young (the title reflected his past as a Confederate war veteran) tapped Burwell Marshall Sr. for money to rent the building and drafted him to teach. When Marshall went to teach at the mission, his children went with him.

What the Marshalls saw on their Sunday afternoon walks to the Cabbage Patch mission was arguably the world's most famous slum. In 1901, Alice Hegan Rice, who lived elegantly on St. James Court, had written a sentimental story called *Mrs. Wiggs of the Cabbage Patch* that caught the world's imagination. The novel sold more than 650,000 copies, enough to keep it on the best-seller list for two years. Translated into French, Spanish, Norwegian, Danish, German, Japanese, and Braille, the novel made the Cabbage Patch an international tourist destination. People came to Louisville, alone and on tours, to see the famous Patch, buy postcards of Mrs. Wiggs's house, and glimpse the real woman who inspired Mrs. Wiggs. It didn't dim interest when the book became a stage play and then the basis for four movies. The first two were silent films; the third, in 1934, starred W. C. Fields and ZaSu Pitts.[72]

Mary Bass, shown here in later life, was the prototype for the fictional Mrs. Wiggs, a central character in Alice Hegan Rice's 1901 novel, *Mrs. Wiggs of the Cabbage Patch. Courtesy of Cabbage Patch Settlement House Archives*

---

72. 70 Jacqueline M. Hersh, "Cabbage Patch," and Gail Richie Henson and James Duane Bolin, "Alice Caldwell (Hegan) Rice," in *Encyclopedia of Louisville,* John G. Kleber, ed. (Lexington: University Press of Kentucky, 2001), 153, 761-62.

Rice's book painted a world where Mrs. Wiggs bore poverty philosophically in the absence of Mr. Wiggs, who "traveled to eternity by the alcohol route." She lived in a "strange neighborhood, where ramshackle cottages played hopscotch over the railroad tracks." Mrs. Wiggs's 15-year-old son, Jim, supported the family, including three little girls, Asia, Australia and Europena, named for continents, and a small brother, Billy. The people in Rice's world were proudly independent "deserving poor" who needed only a hand up from a benevolent hero from Rice's own elevated social class.[73] The book appealed to an audience reeling from the rapid pace of social change. Even the nation's president, Theodore Roosevelt, would find wisdom in Mrs. Wiggs. "I am old-fashioned or sentimental," he wrote to Mrs. Rice. When he read a book, he said, he wanted "to feel that I am a little better and not a little worse for having read it."[74]

The Cabbage Patch Settlement House wasn't even an idea when Mrs. Rice wrote the novel in 1901, but the book prepared the way by establishing the Cabbage Patch in the public mind. Later, when Louise Marshall asked for money for the Cabbage Patch, many people remembered proud, brave Mrs. Wiggs, who had asked for help only when her son died.

Mrs. Wiggs wasn't on the Marshall family's mind when they marched to Seventh Street to teach Sunday school. A Sunday school needed teachers, who were not easy to find for

---

73. Alice Hegan Rice, *Mrs. Wiggs of the Cabbage Patch* (New York: Century, 1901).

74. Mary Boewe, *Beyond the Cabbage Patch: The Literary World of Alice Hegan Rice* (Louisville, KY: Butler Books, 2010), 52.

such a neighborhood, and the mission was short a teacher for a small class of eight- and nine-year-old boys. Louise, then 16, was asked to teach them. "I loved the Bible so," Louise Marshall said later. "I think you get more out of it when you teach, so I began at a very early age."[75]

To recruit boys for her class, Louise went visiting. What she found was a haunting world unlike the one in *Mrs. Wiggs* or the one Louise had known on Ormsby Avenue. In the real Cabbage Patch, men's drinking threatened their families' lives; water from public pumps provided no surplus to regularly wash dishes, bodies, or clothing; people who lacked beds—with or without bedbugs—slept on hay; babies who died were buried in the yard by grieving parents who couldn't pay for a cemetery plot; and privies provided what passed for sanitation. When the people of the Patch had money to buy food, a filthy local grocery sent them home with provisions well mixed with bugs.

Victorian women had a duty to perform acts of charity, but most visited the poor only briefly, did their duty and left quickly—much in the style of Mrs. Wiggs's heroine. Louise went deeper, stayed longer, did more, and took friends and relatives who were quickly revolted by what they saw and smelled. Louise's little sister, Sallie Ewing, gamely agreed to help Louise carry food and clean up for a woman with a new baby. They found the mother in a room "filled with wet clothes drying, hanging all around," Louise Marshall said. "The smells, and the filth, and the baby in the bed right there by the side of the mother, just a newborn baby, and

---

75. Louise Marshall, taped interview by Lynn Gant, June 25, 1974, CPSHR, FHS.

[the mother] sitting up munching bread. It just did something terrible to Sallie Ewing."[76]

Such scenes did something very different to Louise, but that something wouldn't become clear for years. In the short term, she was dedicated to the little group of boys in her class. In an age before antibiotics, illness was always life threatening, especially to those without good nutrition, so in November 1907, when one of her boys, Charlie Jamerson, had been very ill, Louise took Charlie soup with help from a friend who had a "machine" (as she called the automobile).[77] Louise's devotion to her boys didn't waver even when the Marshalls made their annual trek to Florida for a few weeks. Louise wrote to each of the boys every day she was gone, even when the group had grown to 40 boys.[78]

The Cabbage Patch work made Louise's suitors, even rejected suitors, suddenly very useful. When one of Louise's little boys, Ben Hynes, stopped going to school and missed Sunday school, Louise drafted a brawny friend, Clem Spalding, who'd been the very popular captain of the Centre College football team, to help her search for young Ben in the Cabbage Patch. Ben hid in a stable on 11th Street, a distinctly inelegant neighborhood. "I went out and got him," Miss Marshall said later. "I got him and sent him back to school." Both Ben (whose relationship with Louise Marshall

---

76. Louise Marshall, taped interview by Lynn Gant, June 25, 1974, CPSHR, FHS.

77. Louise Marshall, "Private Note Book for the fall of 1906 and the year of 1907" (her handwritten diary), CPSHR, FHS.

78. Gail Ransdell, "Cabbage Patch Project Realization of Dream for Louise Marshall," *Louisville (KY) Courier-Journal,* July 20, 1952.

would last for years) and Clem Spalding were just beginning to understand what a determined Louise Marshall could do. Clem was appalled. "If I'd known what you were doing here, I'd have dragged you out of here by the hair of your head," he told Louise.

Louise, however, had discovered a truth. "You couldn't ram the Bible down boys' throats. You had to live it," she said. "You had to know people and care about them if you ever expected to get close to them."[79] That philosophy would undergird her work for the rest of her life.

The five-year period from Louise Marshall's teenage decision to give her heart to the little boys in her class until the formal founding of the Cabbage Patch Settlement is shrouded in undocumented memory, myth, and often-repeated legend. However, those years somehow transformed a depressed, terrified high school girl into a lively, passionate woman. For Louise, they were years marked by conflict both at the Patch and at home.

Conflict at the Patch was probably inevitable because the Presbyterians had artlessly dropped their mission into the middle of a community struggling with religious, racial, and ethnic prejudice, as well as poverty. The African American majority lived in a society where segregation was state policy and their inferior status was mandated by custom and enforced with violence.

According to a booklet published in 1974, "Negroes lived in the alleys in the back of most of the streets" in the Cabbage Patch and worked as railroad laborers. They reportedly lived

---

79. Louise Marshall, interview on undated tape fragment, CPSHR, FHS.

at peace with their Irish neighbors.[80] Louise Marshall would wait until much later to struggle with tough racial issues.

The Irish, who also worked as cheap labor for the Louisville & Nashville Railroad, had been driven from Ireland by the twin horrors of famine and British (Protestant) domination. They lived in shotgun houses (so called because they were built with all the rooms in a line so a gunshot fired at the front door passed through all the rooms of the house). German immigration peaked in 1881 in the wake of civil war at home, and most Germans assimilated quickly into Louisville's active German business community. But the Cabbage Patch's Catholics, Irish and German alike, knew well the "anti-Catholic prejudices of narrow-minded Protestants."[81] They responded with matching distrust that spelled trouble for young Louise Marshall.

The Presbyterians set up their mission on Seventh Street even as Catholics, who also saw mission potential in the Cabbage Patch, were already at work building a substantial new church and school one block to the south. The competition meant conflict was certain, and it came quickly.

The trouble grew with the Presbyterian mission's success. During the week, the little wooden mission, which came to be known as People's Hall, housed a kindergarten program and, probably, sewing classes with a paid staff member, Miss Grace Pollock. Louise considered Pollock "a lovely creature, a beautiful spirit," who apparently had a working-class background. She and Louise worked well together. Louise

---

80. Stanley Ousley, *Limerick, An Irish Neighborhood*, booklet published to commemorate Kentucky's bicentennial, 1974.

81. Ibid.

added an after-school boys' club called the Covenanters, a boys' organization being tried by churches nationally. Whatever her society may have thought about women and sports, Louise's basketball training served her well. Her boys played basketball and baseball.

Down the street, leaders of the new St. Ann's Catholic Church and school watched children trooping into the Presbyterian mission and worried. When it came to Presbyterians, the Catholic clergy of the day were deeply familiar with sectarian violence and were distinctly non-ecumenical.

"They never did want us there," Louise Marshall said. "The Catholics fought us like everything." A priest—probably the priest for St. Ann's—told the Catholic boys and mothers not to go to the Presbyterian mission. Louise, who was raised to respect church authority, told the Catholic boys to listen to the priest. She told them not to come to her boys' club. "That wasn't very smart of me," she concluded later.[82]

Irish boys probably had plenty of experience dealing with unwelcome advice from priests, and disobeying a priest most likely posed no problem for them. Hearing Louise, young and pretty, say they couldn't come back to her club was something different. They turned their anger on Louise—a response the priest may have encouraged, if myth is to be believed. The neighborhood's Irish men were known for their pugnacious toughness and brawling, and Louise Marshall's boys were their fathers' sons.[83] The

---

82. Louise Marshall, taped interview by Lynn Gant, June 25, 1974; Louise Marshall, interview on undated tape fragment, CPSHR, FHS.

83. Stanley Ousley, *Limerick, An Irish Neighborhood.*

angry boys began throwing things, first at Louise and then at People's Hall.

Burwell Marshall reacted like the protective father and hard-nosed lawyer that he was. He decreed that Louise could not go back to People's Hall, lest she be hit in the head. Quitting wasn't acceptable to Louise. No one wanted the boys to have criminal records either, so a solution was apparently devised using the Marshalls' influential connections. The boys were promptly arrested and taken to court. There, Judge Arthur Peter, an Episcopal neighbor of the Marshalls, heard the case with little to-do and no effort to hear all sides. When a boy's mother spoke up in defense of her son, the judge hushed her. He didn't want to hear anything out of her. We don't know what else was said, but the Marshalls left able to say that they had won the case. However, the boys who didn't want to give up their club would win the day.

The next afternoon, the same tough pre-teens who had thrown things at Louise and then faced her in court arrived at People's Hall in a group. Louise, all five feet, four inches of her, stood alone on the wooden steps to the front door as she always did. Her mother usually gave Louise a basket of apples when she went to the Cabbage Patch, and that afternoon was no different. One by one, Louise offered each boy an apple as he came up the steps to People's Hall.[84] That was the end of the problem.

The episode seems to have provided a lasting lesson for Louise. The Stuart Robinson mission was unquestionably Presbyterian. Later, when Louise founded her settlement

---

84. Louise Marshall, taped interview by Lynn Gant, June 25, 1974, CPSHR, FHS.

house, it would be undeniably religious, but it would also be nondenominational. Keeping it that way would mean struggles later, but Louise Marshall would never allow children's religious affiliations to keep them from the Patch—even if it meant that some of her girls did grow up to become Catholic nuns.

The other conflict to plague Louise, the one in the Marshall home, had no such graceful solution or useful life lesson. Nobody won the very painful clash between Richard Marshall and his father. That much is clear, although neither the Marshall family nor public records shed much light on what happened after Richard's ignoble return from the University of Virginia. According to the city directory, Richard stayed in his first job as a salesman for only two years. His second job as a clerk lasted even less time. By 1908, Richard was listed as manager of H. W. Werst Plumbing Co., a company that recorded his father as an incorporator, investor, and president. A year later, Richard was unemployed again.[85]

"He was a blight on the household," Louise's niece, Elizabeth Johnson Haynes, said later.[86]

Richard may have had one more try working as a salesman before the tension with his father came to a final head.

Everyone agrees that Burwell Marshall and his son faced off for a cataclysmic explosion. In the Louisville branch of the Marshall family, the spark that caused the blowup remains a closely held secret by those who say they know the facts—and the subject of speculation by those who can only guess. Whatever its cause, the clash rent the family with a

---

85. *Caron's Louisville City Directory* (Louisville, KY: Caron's Directory Co., 1903–1910).

86. Elizabeth Johnson Haynes, PI, July 11, 2011.

bitterness that lasted for decades and would seep down to later generations. Richard left home for good. From then on, his Louisville family apparently spoke of Richard to outsiders only rarely. Burwell Marshall never stopped caring about his oldest son—but he wouldn't trust him again either.

His Louisville life over, Richard moved on. By the 1910 census, Richard, 26, was working as a salesman and living in Richland, Illinois, newly married to Helen Chauncey, 21. Helen's family tree, rooted in tiny Olney, Illinois, was considerably less celebrated than the Marshalls'. Helen was an orphan raised by her sister and her stepfather, a hardware salesman.

"As far as I can tell, he married the girl he fell in love with," a clerk in a 10-cent store, said Tom Chambers, who married into Sallie Ewing Marshall's branch of the family.[87] That wasn't the end of Richard's scandalous behavior, but it was enough for the moment.

We don't know how involved sisters Louise and Elizabeth were in the blowup, but by 1909 or 1910, it was time for them to leave town, too, at least for a while. Louise Marshall began a pattern she would repeat again and again. After a difficult period of her life, she would leave her troubles behind for the glories of Europe. She and Elizabeth must have left home for the trip abroad with an enormous sense of relief.

When they returned, Louise would be fully an adult and ready to seek her life's work in earnest.

---

87. Thomas R. Chambers, PI, July 13, 2011.

CHAPTER 5

THREE BEHIND-THE-SCENES MENTORS

In the decade or so after she returned from Europe, something almost mystical happened that changed both Louise Marshall and her Cabbage Patch project. Louise Marshall, once a terrified schoolgirl and silly debutante, became a courageous, effective visionary—although the skills needed to support that vision emerged very slowly. The tenuous Presbyterian mission project in the Cabbage Patch became a vigorous, independent institution that changed lives from the very start.

Later in life, Louise Marshall was never very reflective about the changes in herself, although some of what happened to the mission is a part of the Cabbage Patch's celebrated history. Part of what's missing—or understated—are the roles three strong and very different women played in both transformations: Louise's aunt, Dr. Annie S. Veech, one of Louisville's first female physicians; Louise's neighbor Alice Hegan Rice, whose books made the Cabbage Patch neighborhood famous; and Jane Addams of Chicago, who launched the settlement house movement in the United States. The three moved behind the scenes, but their impact on Louise and the settlement is clear from Cabbage Patch records, family lore, and the context of the times.

To show Annie Veech's relationship to Louise Marshall, her modern relatives often cite a family picture, probably taken at the Richard Veeches' 50th wedding anniversary in 1903 in front of the old Veech plantation house on Indian Hill. Richard and Mary Veech are seated in the middle of the photograph with their children and grandchildren ranged around them. On the front row at one end, young Elizabeth, Sallie Ewing, and Burwell Marshall Jr. nestle between their parents. (Richard is not in the picture) On the other end, on the back row, a teenage Louise stands next to Annie Veech, looking very much like her aunt, who was 17 years older. Louise's relatives say the picture is telling. Auntie Annie, as Louise knew her, was Louise's favorite aunt and a force in her life.[88] Certainly when Annie Veech was in town, Louise's life seemed to change, sometimes toward innovation and adventure.

Like Louise, Annie Veech started life as a privileged daughter in an upper-class, Presbyterian household, a status that offered more boredom than opportunity for a woman who had finished school but not yet married. At first, Annie Veech responded in a way the Victorian age considered appropriate. She traveled. She traveled for 15 years, without ever marrying, and then returned to Louisville so deeply depressed that she took to her bed.[89] Then the 34-year-old spinster had an epiphany.

---

88. Elizabeth Haynes Johnson, PI, July 11, 2011.

89. Elizabeth Dosker Chambers, interview by Mrs. William Harvin, March 19, 1987, CPSOHP, CPSHR, FHS.

The Veech family gathered at Indian Hill to celebrate the 50th wedding anniversary of Richard B. and Mary Veech (at center) Louise Marshall's grandparents. At left, Louise's father, Burrell Marshall (with the dark mustache) and her mother, Lizzie Veech Marshall (standing beside him), pose with Louise's older sister Elizabeth, younger sister Sallie Ewing, and little brother Burrell Jr. In the back row at right, Louise Marshall, then about 15, stood with her aunt and mentor, Annie Veech. The enlargement shows Louise and her favorite "Aunt Annie," who have a family resemblance.

Courtesy of Elizabeth Johnson Haynes

"Until then I had done nothing but have a good time," she told a newspaper interviewer later. "I decided that happiness lay in thinking of others rather than one's self." Annie Veech decided to go to medical school and become a doctor, one of the first female doctors in Kentucky.[90] She made her decision around 1905, a period when Louise was 17 and just beginning to feel the pull of the Cabbage Patch. In 1913, Dr. Veech returned to Louisville with a medical degree and experience treating mothers and young children in hospitals. She wouldn't stay home for long, but it would be long enough to have an impact on both Louise and the Cabbage Patch Settlement.

Alice Hegan Rice was also a world traveler, but when she was home, she wrote books, dealt with a self-absorbed husband who fancied himself a great poet, and mentored young women. Girls growing up around her St. James Court home idolized the internationally known writer who rubbed shoulders with the rich and famous. Sometimes the girls would sit breathless on the Rices' front porch where Mrs. Rice would encourage them to write and to produce elaborate dramas to raise money for good causes. When one of the girls was sick or had a significant birthday, sometimes Mrs. Rice would send an autographed copy of her latest book for the girl to treasure. Mrs. Rice's mentoring also reached a few blocks north of St. James Court to include Louise Marshall. Although Louise Marshall would contend much later that Alice Hegan Rice had gotten rather too much credit for the Cabbage Patch's founding, Mrs. Rice seems to have provided Louise with an important model of how to lead and organize people.

90. "Drs. Annie Veech and Alice Pickett Due Medical-Achievement Awards," *Louisville (KY) Courier-Journal*, May 15, 1956.

Certainly, Mrs. Rice charmed Louise as she did the other girls. Mrs. Rice was a lovable person, Louise said later. "I was very, very fond of her."[91]

The third woman, Jane Addams of Chicago's Hull House, also had an impact on Louise Marshall, although there's no evidence that the two ever met and considerable evidence that they were poles apart on some significant issues. Jane Addams was a thoroughly political Progressive, a Presbyterian whose faith faltered, and a social worker who looked at big issues more than at individual people. But she defined the settlement house movement much as Alice Hegan Rice had defined the Cabbage Patch neighborhood in the public mind. By the time Louise began to think about a settlement house in the Cabbage Patch, the movement Addams spawned had already resulted in three settlement houses in Louisville: Neighborhood House, John Little's Presbyterian Colored Mission, and Wesley Community House. In 1910, Jane Addams published her autobiography *Twenty Years at Hull House* in the hope that it would be of value to others engaged in similar work. That was the very year when a group of Louisville women, led by 22-year-old Louise Marshall, met to incorporate a settlement house in the Cabbage Patch neighborhood. It is inconceivable that those literate women didn't read Addams's book.

Louise seems to have returned from her own European trip with a vision for a real settlement house to replace the increasingly inadequate People's Hall. The work she

---

91. Melville Otter, memory book for 1914, Melville Otter Briney Papers, 1855–1986, FHS; Louise Marshall, interview on tape fragment, CPSHR, FHS.

and others had done filled People's Hall with mothers and children who came for kindergarten classes, women's clubs, a sewing school, boys' clubs, and story hour. People's Hall had never been commodious or comfortable. By 1910, the program needed something bigger, a building that had been constructed for its needs.

Louise went to see her father. "Now, Papa," she said, "it's perfectly ridiculous to spend as much money as you're spending on this little room." Louise proposed that Burwell Marshall give her the money he was spending to rent People's Hall so she could get an adequate place for the program she envisioned. Papa, never a hard sell when it came to his daughter, said yes—but with lawyer-like provisions. The Cabbage Patch Settlement House needed to be properly incorporated and to have a board that would provide a broader leadership base.[92]

For the board, Louise assembled a group of six women in the Marshall parlor, most of them upper-class neighbors and Presbyterians with an interest in the Cabbage Patch mission. Given the era's restrictions on women, they brought wide experience, valuable contacts, and considerable wisdom to the undertaking. Lizzie Robinson Cecil, a minister's daughter, was the dear family friend who had taught Louise to love the Bible at Second Presbyterian Church. Eliza S. Young's husband, Col. Bennett Young, had laid the foundation for the Cabbage Patch by establishing the Presbyterian mission that became known as People's Hall. Fannie Caldwell Macaulay was Alice Hegan Rice's aunt and a gifted teacher. Mary

---

92. Louise Marshall, interview on tape fragment, CPSHR, FHS.

Holloway Tarry, whose husband was a Louisville & Nashville Railroad accountant, would be the organization's secretary-treasurer. Alice Hegan Rice brought her star power and leadership skills. The last member of the founding group was different in every way: Grace Pollock, the uneducated servant who'd come to the People's Hall as a part-time employee and who had become Louise Marshall's close friend and ally. Grace Pollock knew the Cabbage Patch and its people. Louise considered her a saint and laughed into old age at Grace's odd way of putting things. The new corporate board selected its youngest member, 22-year-old Louise Marshall, as its president. The well-seasoned Mrs. Cecil stood behind her as vice president.

Burwell Marshall drew up incorporation papers intended to serve the new organization for 100 years. They established the Cabbage Patch Settlement as a social settlement founded to conduct "what is known as social settlement work" by raising money and building a settlement house for "religious services, the training of the mind and body, care for destitute children and assisting mothers in the care of their children and whatever pertains to the uplifting of people who may be brought in contact with its work."[93]

The incorporation papers—and the group itself—set the Cabbage Patch apart from other settlement houses like Chicago's Hull House and Louisville's Neighborhood House where the resident social workers' jobs often involved both work with individual clients and politicking for the great causes of the Progressive Era: better working conditions for

93. Articles of Incorporation of the Cabbage Patch Settlement House, October 18, 1910, CPSHR, FHS.

women, child labor laws, and women's suffrage. Politics were important to Progressives, who believed the cruel inequities of the Industrial Age should and could be remedied by legislation. However, most of the women in the Marshall parlor were emphatically not political or Progressive. At the beginning of the 20th century, the Southern Presbyterian Church limited its women to activities consistent with female modesty and scriptural authority. In church affairs, women were to remain silent in gatherings that included men and to fulfill their proper functions—such as teaching children— under men's supervision.[94] Forming a corporation and operating with an all-female corporate board must have seemed a bold move, even without politics. If, as some argue, settlement houses were a force for feminism, the Cabbage Patch was an exception. While the women on its board believed they could do a job normally reserved for men, they seem to have respected the Presbyterian Church's position on women and did not press for social change.[95]

The new board members faced two immediate tasks, one more daunting than the other. They needed to find a site for the new settlement house, and they needed to raise the money to build and operate it.

Louise did not wait for the dollars to start coming in before she, Burwell Marshall Sr., and Grace Pollock set out to find a suitable site for the new building. They found a lot at

94. Thompson, *Presbyterians in the South*, 399–401.

95. Ruth Crocker reviews the debate over the role of settlements in promoting feminism in her book, *Social Work and Social Order: The Settlement Movement in Two Industrial Cities*, 1889–1930 (Urbana: University of Illinois Press, 1992).

1461 South Ninth Street, not far from People's Hall and just a mile from the Marshall home. Louise's father, as good as his word, provided $567.40 for the property, fees, and survey. Then Louise took a ride with E. T. Hutchings, one of the boys who had called at the Marshall parlor in the old days. By 1910, E. T. Hutchings was an architect in business with his father. He agreed to design a proper settlement house at no charge. Both Louise and Grace Pollock were delighted. "We've got *architecture* for to put up our building," Grace exclaimed in the way that made Louise smile.[96]

All that remained was to raise $4,000 to make the plan real. Raising money for the Cabbage Patch wasn't going to be easy, not in 1910 and not for the next 100 years.

At first, the results were promising. Contributions from the prosperous board members disappointed Louise, but two friends of board members each gave $500. When Louise contributed her entire $1,000 savings to the project, her father decided to match her contribution by adding another $500 to what he'd already given. "The rest of it was raised just a piddling dollar or two dollars" at a time, Louise Marshall said later, and the toll of those piddling contributions on the board's new president was substantial. As she faced the necessity of calling on friends' fathers to ask for money, all her old anxieties resurfaced. "I had terrible attacks of diarrhea when I was terrified," she said. And that's what happened when she set out to ask for money.

As Louise started out to make the first call, her insides writhing, Sallie Ewing stopped her. "You're sick," Sallie told

---

96. Louise Marshall, interview on tape fragment, CPSHR, FHS.

her sister. "You can't do that." Deep inside, that's what Louise wanted to hear. Louise gave in and let someone else make that day's call. Then she made a resolution: "I make myself do something. I go through with it." In time, the terrible attacks receded, and $3,500 was raised for the new building. "It took an awful lot of work to get that $3,500," she said, "An awful lot of work."[97] The new building was built with a $500 debt and dedicated at a grand celebration on May 27, 1911.

The proper Presbyterian women who made the building possible could not, of course, speak at the dedication. (Church convention frowned on such behavior.) Col. Bennett H. Young, who organized the original People's Hall mission, did the honors in what Louise regarded as his usual overstated style.

"Mr. Young was always doing things he got the credit for without ever really paying the price," she said later.

Colonel Young delivered the day's dedicatory address with extravagant prose, and the next morning's *Courier-Journal* declared the new settlement house "the outgrowth of a philanthropy started" seven years earlier by Colonel Young, who "bore all the expenses in connection" with renting and equipping People's Hall. (That, of course, failed to credit Burwell Marshall Sr.'s very substantial contribution.) The newspaper listed the settlement's directors as a group of women who had become interested in the plan. Louise was near the end of the list. Miss Pollock was credited with supervising the settlement house's work, "having been intimately connected with its growth." Mrs. Rice got credit for heading the women's clubs that totaled 75 members.

---

97. Louise Marshall, interview on tape fragment, CPSHR, FHS.

"Miss Louise Marshall will again look after the interests of the boys," the newspaper added.[98] If the proceedings and coverage produced tooth-grinding frustration for Louise, it was not recorded. Self-promotion was not her goal.

The wonderful new building had a large first-floor room where groups could meet and children could play. The second floor, reached by an outside staircase, had rooms for a resident worker to live and room for sewing and cooking classes and, in time, a branch of the Louisville Free Public Library—all activities consistent with other settlement houses. The side yard provided a playground. The program geared up in the fall of 1911 with room to grow—and it would grow. For all that to happen, however, the organization needed to be better organized and have a systematic approach to fund-raising. Alice Hegan Rice helped with both issues until Louise took over.

In those early days, Louise seems to have focused on what she knew: working with Cabbage Patch boys, using her circle of friends to support the good work, and spreading her vision. In December of that first year, she invited a group of her society girlfriends for a meeting that would shape the future of the Cabbage Patch. They decided to form a circle to raise money for the Cabbage Patch and provide it with volunteer workers. "We had made our debuts a few years before, and our hope was to contribute what we could to our community," the circle's first president, Lida Kelly Muir, wrote later. Louise Marshall focused that idealistic energy on the Cabbage Patch and provided "a fount of ideas to enhance our usefulness to the Patch's dire need," Muir recalled. Alice Hegan Rice,

---

98. "Open Doors, Cabbage Patch Settlement House is Dedicated," *Louisville (KY) Courier-Journal*, May 28, 1911.

who was older and more experienced, served as "a wise and willing adviser."[99]

If there was anything Presbyterian women were really good at, it was holding fund-raising bazaars, and that's what the first circle set out to do. The young women met in each other's homes to sew and embroider the fancy towels, aprons, baby clothes, table linens, and special-order "Wiggs dolls" that would sell at their bazaars. That was work Louise loved, and her passion for the Cabbage Patch's work drove the effort. Mrs. Rice stirred up the St. James Court girls to join the sewing effort. The enterprise thrived. When the early bazaars were held, first in the Cecil home, then at the Rices', young men flocked in to eat the luncheon the young women prepared and to support their lady friends with purchases. The bazaars outgrew the parlors and moved to church basements and storefronts, getting ever larger and more popular. Over 90 years, they would pull hundreds of women into the circle and raise more than $750,000 for the Cabbage Patch.[100]

Still, the few hundred dollars all that work raised in the beginning wasn't enough to operate proper programs that cost close to $1,300 a year. Alice Hegan Rice established another fund-raising staple: an annual letter and report seeking contributions. The first letter's request was modest—too modest. She asked each of 500 recipients to pledge $2 a year to the Cabbage Patch. That did not produce enough

---

99. Lida Kelly Muir, "First President's Message," Cabbage Patch Circle history, CPSHR, FHS.

100. "History of the Cabbage Patch Circle," one undated page, CPSHR, FHS; Martha Elson, "Wesley House Complex for Sale," *Louisville (KY) Courier-Journal*, April 7, 2006.

money either. Louise staged a coup of sorts. She took over writing the fund-raising letters from Alice Hegan Rice.

That ignited Alice's husband, Cale Young Rice, whose ego far exceeded his talent. "Mr. Rice was mighty mad at me," Louise Marshall said later. "He said why did I think I was the class of Mrs. Rice?" Louise Marshall made no claims for the quality of her writing. "I said we had to have more money." There was a certain irony in the exchange; Cale Rice had always belittled his wife's writing. "But he thought less of me," Miss Marshall added. "Of course he was just such an egoist. So pitiful . . . It was such a disappointment [to him] to think that all the attention they got wasn't his—it was all her."[101] Despite Rice's protests, Louise Marshall's letters did, indeed, raise more money—but never enough.

The first Cabbage Patch Settlement House, on Ninth Street just north of Hill Street, was completed in 1911 to house the growing settlement's programs. One of Louise Marshall's former boyfriends, E. T. Hutchings, designed the building. *Courtesy of Cabbage Patch Settlement House Archives*

101. Louise Marshall, interview on tape fragment, CPSHR, FHS.

Alice Hegan Rice was a Cabbage Patch board member, author, neighbor, and mentor for young Louise Marshall. Miss Marshall always made it clear, however, that Alice Rice may have gotten too much credit for the settlement's founding.

Once again, Louise reached out to her old friends for help. By 1911, E. Boyd Martin had given up his courtship of Louise, married the leading lady of a production he directed for the Louisville Dramatic Club, and launched what would be a celebrated career as a local theater critic. When Louise needed help, however, E. Boyd responded by agreeing to a benefit performance of his play, *The Cradle Snatcher*. Louise insisted on doing the casting—basing her choices not on acting ability but on the actors' ability to draw an audience that would pack the Shubert Masonic Theater. The result was both a full house and a performance the *Louisville Evening Post* called "one of the most pleasing amateur plays given in this city." Louise went to the event escorted by her old friend Clem Spalding, who brought her flowers that she remembered fondly for many years.[102]

Now galvanized, Louise Marshall's men friends organized a benefit dance at a venue called White City (possibly with help from the young women of the Cabbage Patch Circle). One enterprising young man put boxes outside a bachelor hotel so its residents could donate cast-off clothing for the Cabbage Patch's regular rummage sales. All sorts of people were drawn into the effort. "That's the kind of thing I liked," Miss Marshall said years later. "I never did like the public eye."[103]

All the fund-raising and the Cabbage Patch's organizational needs were creating conflicting demands for Louise Marshall's time. Alice Hegan Rice helped. In February 1912, she presided over the premier meeting of the Committee of Workers of the Cabbage Patch Settlement House, established to provide necessary coordination for the booming programs. All the women who led programs attended, including Louise Marshall, who reported on the Monday afternoon Boys Club. All the programs, with the exception of Thursday night prayer meetings, seemed to be thriving, and the prayer meetings' failure to prosper was attributed to "unpropitious" weather. The long list of Cabbage Patch activities included a notice of a shower for

---

102. "Fine Performance of 'The Cradle Snatcher,'" *Louisville (KY) Evening Post*, May 3, 1911; Louise Marshall, interview on tape fragment, CPSR, FHS; "Sale of Seats for 'The Cradle Snatcher,'" *Louisville (KY) Evening Post*, April 27, 1911.

103. Louise Marshall, interview on tape fragment, CPSHR, FHS.

Miss Pollock, Louise's dear friend and soul mate, who was getting married.[104]

Miss Marshall told the workers that she had decided to limit attendance at the Boys Club to 12, but the club seems to have provided a crucible for the philosophy and approaches that would underlay Cabbage Patch programs long into the future. Miss Marshall's boys played sports, went on field trips, had a wonderful time, and ended every program with a short devotional period that usually included a Bible story and prayer.

To improve her foundation for teaching those Bible classes, Louise Marshall took time off in the springs of 1916 and 1917 to attend Bible study classes at the Biblical Seminary (later New York Theological Seminary) in New York City where she listened to Bible scholars and filled notebooks with tiny, careful notes.

"She was a great student of the Bible," said Lloyd Redman, a later friend and colleague. "She was a smart person."[105]

The nondenominational religious emphasis set the Cabbage Patch apart from both secular settlement houses like the Hull House and settlements started by churches to win souls for their denominations. To Miss Marshall, personal faith was the whole point. Churches weren't doing the job. "You had to live" the Bible to draw people into religion, she believed. She said it again and again.

---

104. Board of Directors Minutes, first meeting of the Committee of Workers of the Cabbage Patch Settlement House, February 20, 1912, CPSHR, FHS.

105. Lloyd Redman, interview by Keith Cardwell, February 12, 1987, CPSOHP, CPSHR, FHS.

The new settlement house throbbed with activities for both boys and girls. Here Campfire Girls attend a meeting in an upstairs room in 1911.

Courtesy of Cabbage Patch Settlement House Archives

The settlement house yard provided just a little space for games. In 1915, boys practiced high-jumping there. *Courtesy of Cabbage Patch Settlement House Archives*

To Louise Marshall, living the Bible meant knowing and caring about every one of her boys. Her approach to young Ben Hynes, the boy she and Clem Spalding pulled from the stable and sent back to school, illustrated the philosophy she would follow through many years. After she identified Ben as a boy with potential, she hired him to work in the Cabbage Patch office, a job that provided him with a little money, a lot of pride, and an opportunity for Miss Marshall to keep an eye on him. Even Miss Marshall's favorites like Ben had to adhere to the strict rules. Rule breakers were suspended from the program until they'd had time to repent and reform. In Ben Hynes's case, Miss Marshall also drew attention to his misdeeds by chasing him with a broom.

Ben Hynes did well in school, and when he graduated, he went to college, even though he was a poor kid from the Cabbage Patch. In July 1922, Louise Marshall got a letter from Ezra T. Franklin, the president of Union College in Barbourville, Kentucky. The letter asked for $5 to cover the "genuine parchment large size diploma" Ben had earned, and it acknowledged receipt of Miss Marshall's final payment for Ben's tuition. Miss Marshall had been very generous in helping Ben through school, Franklin added. "I believe we have not seen any superior faithfulness on the part of any friend to a student's interest than you have been to Ben Hynes. It has been an inspiration to us to see such unselfish devotion to a boy's needs. We shall remember it many days."[106]

Ben Hynes went on to become an accountant for the huge Standard Sanitary factory that spread across his old

---

106. E. T. Franklin to Louise Marshall, July 17, 1922, CPSHR, FHS.

Cabbage Patch neighborhood and covered the People's Hall site. In time, Hynes developed a hearing problem that he feared would cost him his job. Miss Marshall wrote a letter on his behalf and got a response assuring her that Hynes's office mates were helping him. His job was safe.[107] When Ben Hynes died at 88, he was a Presbyterian with three surviving children, 11 grandchildren, and 10 great-grandchildren.[108] All 25 of those people could trace their family's wellbeing to a teenage girl who went out one night to search a slum for a ragged boy who didn't want to go to school.

Ben was the first of many such boys. The day's theologians and activists would argue about whether God wanted his people to counter injustice by changing laws and institutions, as Jane Addams had done. Louise Marshall stuck with the conservative Southern Presbyterian tenet that faith required changing people one soul at a time. For Louise Marshall, that meant knowing the names, the needs, and the gifts of her boys and their families and following them through their lives. That approach—plus a faith that never wavered—separated Louise Marshall from Jane Addams, who was less certain about religion. Addams arguably gave Louise Marshall a workable pattern for settlement house programs, an appreciation for social work as a profession, and a demonstration that women could, indeed, found and run a settlement house. From that point, they parted company. Louise would build a program that offered its own innovations. One of the first was the work of her aunt, Dr. Annie Veech.

---

107. Louise Marshall to Theodore Ahrens, undated, CPSHR, FHS.

108. Ben Roy Hynes Sr., obituary, *Louisville (KY) Courier-Journal*, August 1, 1991.

Jane Addams founded Chicago's Hull House, a model for America's settlement house movement. Her book on her settlement house was published just as Louise Marshall and her friends started the Cabbage Patch Settlement.

In a day when maternal and infant mortality rates were high—and parents in places like the Cabbage Patch had to bury too many babies in their yards—Annie Veech started one of Kentucky's first well baby clinics at the Cabbage Patch Settlement. Dr. Veech recruited other doctors to work with her at the Patch—and eventually other sites—screening babies, counseling mothers on their care, and making sure children got their immunizations until they were school age. The clinic started on Wednesdays and Fridays during the winter of 1911–12 with five or six babies a session and a determined effort to publicize the service to attract more clients.[109] The Patch kept note cards

---

109. Minutes, CPSH Board of Directors, February 20, 1912, CPSHR, FHS.

tracking each child over the years, from that first baby clinic visit through the kindergarten program, the Bible schools, the sports teams, camps, and other programs. Some men and women who became Cabbage Patch leaders can trace their beginnings all the way back to the baby clinic Dr. Veech began.

For Annie Veech, the Cabbage Patch's well baby clinic was the beginning of a distinguished pioneering career to improve maternal and child care in Kentucky, but the effort would have to operate for a time without her. The nation was preparing for war in Europe. Alarming headlines topped the daily newspapers followed by articles about the suffering in Europe and political machinations as the United States attempted to avoid involvement.

Despite the world's trouble, the Marshall family had a happier matter to celebrate. Sallie Ewing was marrying Nicholas Dosker, a Michigan minister's son who had come south when his father joined the faculty of the Louisville Presbyterian Seminary. Young Dosker graduated cum laude from Centre College, the Presbyterian school in Danville, Kentucky, and went on to graduate from law school where he earned the sorts of honors that would have gratified Burwell Marshall Sr. The wedding took place October 3, 1917, in the Marshall home, well decorated for the occasion with palms and fall flowers. Sisters Elizabeth and Louise were bridesmaids in fashionably short full silk dresses wrapped in "billows" of netting. Both the dresses and the roses the women carried were Louise's best color, pink. Men seated at the bridal table afterward included Louise's old friend, Clem Spalding, by then a doctor.[110]

---

110. "Home Wedding of Miss Sallie Ewing Marshall to Mr. Nicholas H. Dosker," *Louisville (KY) Evening Post*, October 3, 1917.

Even the wedding couldn't hold gloom at bay forever.
World War I was going to touch the Marshalls, and it did
almost immediately. Not long after the United States entered
the war in April 1917, Annie Veech left the Cabbage Patch to
ease pain in France.

In 1918, Louise and Elizabeth Marshall decided to leave
Louisville and the Cabbage Patch to go to war-torn France,
too. On her passport application under "profession," Louise
listed "social work." That wasn't what Louisville's turn-of-
the-century high society expected of a society girl. But then,
going to France as a Red Cross volunteer in the middle of a
war wasn't expected either.

Sallie Ewing Marshall was the first of the Marshall girls to wed. Although
the family did not think much of picture taking, she posed in her wedding
dress in the Marshalls' yard. *Courtesy of David Dosker*

CHAPTER 6

A LAST DANCE IN POST-WAR FRANCE

In November 1918, the members of the Cabbage Patch's Worth While Club simply could not bring themselves to meet, and the Just Right Club was disbanded because of the boys' "ungentlemanly behavior" at a party. What was the point of meeting after all? "They could not bear to come back now that Miss Marshall was gone," reported Jeannie Read Sampson, the settlement's resident worker. Home visits were made to each of the boys encouraging them to return to the Patch, but it was no use.[111] Over the next 10 months, many of the Cabbage Patch's activities would continue to thrive and even grow, but there was no denying the obvious: Things weren't the same when Miss Marshall was going to France to help with the war.

Things wouldn't be quite the same when she got back either. The First World War was a time of profound change for the western world, including Louise Marshall and her settlement house. Volunteering for Red Cross duty in France while fighting still raged took considerable courage and required

111. Jeannie Read Sampson, Report to the Board, November 1918, CPSHR, FHS.

a stretch for a nervous young woman from Louisville—even after the November 11 Armistice. If Louise retained any of her teenage anxiety about crowds, she would be tested in Paris. But for Louise, it was an important trip, one she memorialized in a scrapbook she kept for the rest of her life. Those 10 months in France represented a last serious flirtation with life beyond the Cabbage Patch. Louise Marshall's response to post-war France revealed a woman whose life was neither without alternatives nor crippled by neuroses. It was a precious time for her: heady, demanding, fun, and ephemeral.

Sisters Louise and Elizabeth Marshall volunteered as Red Cross workers together and left the United States November 30, 1918, at midnight—low tide—on the steamship *Kursk*. Smoke from the ship's two stacks disappeared into a clear, cold night. Even for the Marshalls, who relished travel, the trip promised more than enough risk to worry a mother and excite envious friends—as the submarine netting still stretched across New York Harbor reminded them.[112] The risks from Germany were receding quickly. Only 10 days before the *Kursk* left harbor, the German high seas fleet and 19 U-boats had surrendered. What remained of dangers included the normal hazards of the North Atlantic in winter (emphasized by still-fresh memories of the doomed ship *Titanic*) and the quiet, deadly progress of the Spanish influenza, which sometimes swept through passengers in the close confines of a ship, leaving a trail of burials at sea.

---

112. On November 30, 1918 (the day the Marshalls left New York), the *New York Times* "Shipping News" listed the *Kursk* as sailing for Liverpool at midnight. The low water mark at Governors Island that night was 12:10 a.m.

For Marshalls used to traveling in style and comfort, the *Kursk* represented a step down from the great passenger ships with four smoke stacks. Launched in 1910 to transport passengers and cargo, the *Kursk* spent its early years transporting Russian immigrants to Ellis Island. By the time Louise and Elizabeth boarded, the Cunard line had taken over the ship and offered 120 cabins for first-class passengers and space for many hundreds of poorer folk. Louise referred to it years later as a converted "Russian cattle boat."[113]

Nothing suggests that the sisters were daunted by either the dangers or the accommodations. Louise and Elizabeth had committed to the trip, applying for passports and getting the requisite shots and vaccinations in early fall while heavy fighting still raged. An apparently oblivious Sallie Ewing had sent Louise to "far off France" with a sisterly note in verse and a "little pink negligee" to remind her of home. As Louise prepared to leave New York, she received a telegram from a friend, identified only as Janet, who gushed with envy. "I cannot tell you how thrilled I am that you are really setting off," Janet wrote. "It is simply splendid."[114]

The idea for the grand adventure grew in 1917 as Louise's aunt Dr. Annie Veech—and the rest of Louisville—geared up to support the war effort. Louisville had been reading about the flagging Allied efforts and of terrible civilian suffering in Europe, but all the news took on fresh urgency in April 1917 when the United States entered the war. Louisville civic leaders organized a Louisville chapter of the American Red

---

113. Gail M. Ransdell, "Cabbage Patch Project Realization of Dream for Louise Marshall," *Louisville (KY) Courier-Journal*, July 20, 1952.

114. Louise Marshall's World War I scrapbook, CPSHR, FHS.

Cross, a group richly laced with members of the Cabbage
Patch board and Marshall friends and relatives, including
Louise's favorite aunt, Dr. Veech. The Louisville chapter
decided to focus its efforts on relief work for Belgian and
French children, who were dying of disease and starvation at
an appalling rate. In November 1917, Dr. Veech became chair
of Louisville's Committee on Instruction for Women—but
not for long.[115] Dr. Veech and her longtime friend, Dr. Alice
Newcome Pickett, volunteered early for service in France.
They arrived in France in August 1918, and, by November,
Louisville learned that they had been assigned to the Red
Cross Children's Bureau. Dr. Veech went to Blois, south of
Paris and well away from the front.[116] Women doctors were
not allowed to treat men.

Women were, however, considered capable of providing
coffee, food, and endless smiles to soldiers in transit. The
American Red Cross conducted a vigorous recruiting campaign
for 55,000 volunteers to help with canteen duty for "soldier
boys" in both the United States and France.[117] Red Cross
recruitment posters for male drivers and mechanics offered

---

115. "Authority to Form a Chapter" and minutes of meetings, October
and November 1917, Louisville Chapter of the American Red Cross
archives.

116. "Physicians Reach France," *Louisville (KY.) Herald*, November 4, 1918;
"Woman Doctor with Red Cross in France," *Louisville (KY) Courier-
Journal*, August 23, 1918; "Dr. Pickett Recalls World War in France,"
Louisville (KY) Courier-Journal, October 30, 1939; and "Dr. Annie Veech
Led Programs of City, State" (obituary), *Louisville (KY) Courier-Journal*,
July 11, 1957.

117. "Many Sign with Canteen Service," *Louisville (KY) Herald*, September
27, 1918.

to pay salaries and expenses.[118] Women who volunteered to work in French canteens, however, had to pay many expenses themselves. Still a "most remarkable" number of Louisvillians volunteered.[119] Some were rejected for overseas service during a screening process, but, with Annie Veech's support, Louise and Elizabeth became part of the army of Red Cross canteen workers and left for war-torn France.[120]

The *Kursk* dropped the sisters in Glasgow, Scotland, where a customs official stamped Louise's passport December 11, 1918. Louise later told a newspaper interviewer that she worked in a Glasgow canteen—but that was probably only briefly as a part of her Red Cross training.[121] Before she headed south to London, Louise also found an opportunity to visit her Presbyterian roots, the Edinburgh home of Presbyterians' greatest Scottish hero, John Knox, who brought the Reformation to Scotland in the 16th century. Louise preserved the three-pence, half-price ticket from the tour in her scrapbook.

As the pace of preparations picked up, Louise received a permit to wear the Red Cross Foreign Service Uniform, considered more fashionable than uniforms for some other women's services. The grey wool tunic and jacket came with shiny buttons and Red Cross insignia for shoulders and collar. The matching skirt was fashionably short enough to

---

118. Mark Davis, *Solicitor General Bullitt: The Life of William Marshall Bullitt* (Louisville, KY: Crescent Hill Books, 2011), 100.

119. "Many Sign with Canteen Service," *Louisville (KY) Herald*, September 27, 1918.

120. Elizabeth Johnson Haynes, PI, July 11, 2011.

121. Gail M. Ransdell, "Cabbage Patch Project Realization of Dream for Louise Marshall," *Louisville (KY) Courier-Journal*, July 20, 1952.

reveal laced-up boots with heels and pointed toes. A straw hat, intended to be plain and sober, often topped the outfit. In cold weather, even fashionable Parisians loved the Red Cross cape with its red lining. (Elizabeth Marshall had one so elegant that she brought it home and kept it for her daughter.)

Louise also got a US War Edition of *What You Want to Say and How to Say It,* a useful book of French phrases little girls would have been unlikely to learn during their French Club days on Ormsby Avenue. Now Louise's French vocabulary included "Where is the enemy's cavalry?" and "Put the irons on my moustache." The book also helpfully included codes for telegraph and flag messaging and hints on reconnaissance. There's no evidence that Louise found it useful, but she did save the book.

This photo was taken for Louis Marshall's passport that she obtained in November 1918 to travel to Paris as a Red Cross canteen worker.

Courtesy of Cabbage Patch Settlement House Archives

The next stop on the way to France was London. The Marshalls checked into the Thackeray Hotel across from the British Museum. A temperance hotel, the Thackeray offered accommodations with amenities the Marshalls expected, including electric lighting, "perfect sanitation," bathrooms on every floor, and evening fires in bedrooms (for an extra one shilling and three pence). The sisters didn't have much time to enjoy London during that holiday season. On New Year's Day, Louise came ashore in Le Havre, France, where the first of thousands of American soldiers impatiently awaited transport home.

The Marshalls arrived in Paris in a cold rain during one of history's critical moments. At the Paris Peace Conference, great men were negotiating issues of war and peace. Some people considered Paris the center of the world that winter, but what Louise Marshall saw was a city of contrasts. Most of the grand buildings and monuments had survived German bombing, but the Place de la Concorde had been ringed by captured German cannon, still spattered from the battlefield. Some Parisians were beginning to restore the city's fashion and gaiety, even as the French army began releasing its troops, the oldest men first. Those soldiers returned home to a Paris with few jobs and a seething discontent that launched almost daily demonstrations and protests. Veterans with missing limbs shared the streets with vast numbers of young widows in black with long crepe veils relieved only by white ruffled ruching over their foreheads. Those women, another Louisville visitor concluded, were "the saddest sight of all."[122]

---

122 William Marshall Bullitt, "I am too busy to write much . . ." letter, November 1918, William Bullitt Marshall Papers, FHS.

Uniforms for Red Cross canteen workers were functional, if not fetching. Louise Marshall's sister, Elizabeth, is second from right in this line of American Red Cross canteen workers. *Courtesy of Elizabeth Johnson Haynes*

The Red Cross canteens, like this one in France after World War I, provided American soldiers with food, a break from war's hardships, and the smiles of American women. For the volunteers, like the Marshall sisters, providing those comforts was often demanding, exhausting work.

Courtesy of Elizabeth Johnson Haynes)

Superimposed over the French hope and suffering were complicated emotions of thousands of American soldiers, freed from the fear that they would again face horrors like those at the second Battle of the Marne. The Americans yearned to go home, but, in the meantime, they were ready for distractions from the memory of what they'd been through. Those men would be Louise and Elizabeth's primary focus.

It's not clear whether Louise and Elizabeth lived together during their time in France or if they were assigned to the same work sites.

"Their entire life . . . was dancing with the officers at the officers' club," Elizabeth's daughter, Elizabeth Johnson Haynes, would say almost a century later.[123] While both Marshall women clearly enjoyed their Paris experiences, Louise's experience may have been a little more nuanced than Elizabeth's. She did considerably more than just dancing.

Louise checked into a YWCA Hostess House, a French hotel adapted to provide wartime accommodations for women. According to a bulletin in Louise's scrapbook, the Hostess Houses provided "a friendly place for friendly people" with social and dining rooms open to both men and women.[124] The friendliness was qualified, however. "Red Cross girls" were expected to observe a high standard of propriety. "This is not a place for a silly or indiscreet girl," wrote one Red Cross volunteer. Girls—actually fully mature women—who were

---

123. Elizabeth Johnson Haynes, PI, July 11, 2011.

124. Bulletin, The American Church, 21 Rue De Berri, Paris, June 1919; and Louise Marshall's World War I scrapbook, CPSHR, FHS.

silly or indiscreet were promptly sent home.[125]

The Red Cross operated a network of canteens at train stations throughout France to provide food and a place to rest for soldiers in transit. Louise was assigned to the Parrot canteen, one of 13 that operated in the Paris area. For work, canteen workers wore uniforms that were considerably less fetching than the dress service uniform. In deference to French wartime laundry problems, the dresses were grey or blue—baggy with white collars, sleeves, aprons, and nun-like wimples that covered their hair. To the troops coming through the canteens, the uniforms didn't matter. What they saw were smiles on the faces of girls from home.

"All you have to do is to smile at a boy and he lays his heart at your feet," reported Irene Farrell, an Oakland, California, debutante who served as a canteen worker in 1919 and lived in the same Hostess House as Louise, the 18th-century Hotel du Palais Royal.[126]

In the canteens, the Red Cross women served fare that ranged from simple coffee, chocolate, or soup—all served in bowls—to a full dinner: soup, corn beef hash, beans, tangy "frog" bread (French bread), and a dessert for 15 cents. For a soldier who hadn't been paid—the plight of many—the meal was free.

For the volunteers, the job required hard work and long hours. "The girls are so busy they have not a moment," wrote William Marshall Bullitt of Louisville, the Red Cross deputy

---

125. Irene Farrell, letter to Dearest Mother, June 2, 1919, World War I Research Institute Research Institute website, http://ww1institute. org/bios/ifarrell.php.

126. Irene Farrell, letter to Dearest Mother, June 2, 1919.

commander for France and a distant cousin of Louise's. "It is a terribly hard physical strain to be behind a counter, waiting on say 100 or 200 men each standing in line but at least 8 at the head of the line crowded tightly together. . . . There is always such a crowd that it is hard to get to the counter. I should think they would be dead."[127]

Even dead tired, however, the women had to smile. That's what the men needed most.

The soldiers' responses ranged from adoration to a new respect for women. Volunteer Irene Farrell wrote of encountering an American unit of "doughboys," headed by a captain, marching down a French street. "The Captain and boys all saluted me as they passed," she wrote. "I felt as important as General Pershing."[128]

For Louise, doughboys' thanks included endless, often over-the-top poems, pictures, postcards, and a group of good friends, drawn close by their distance from home and their goofy sense of humor. While other Red Cross women slept late in the morning, Louise got up early to have "adventures" with a group she referred to as her "playmates of the Bonhomme Detachment: The Poet, the Twins, Frenchie and Imp" and "Smyser." They called her Ma, Miss Welfare Worker, Mary, or whatever else the occasion suggested. "The Montparnasse crowd" apparently included other women and shared some running jokes, including one about Louise Marshall and Russians. Most of the jokes seem to have had a "you had to be there" quality. When two of the men signed

127. William Marshall Bullitt, pocket diary entry, February 28, 1919, William Marshall Bullitt Papers, FHS.

128. Irene Farrell, letter to Dearest Family, April 19, 1919.

a pact to stop smoking, they trusted the contract to Louise Marshall. "Liquidated damages for breach" were to include 100 francs and "dinner to the other party" in "Kaintucky." If neither party broke the contract, they were to have dinner in Kaintucky anyway.[129]

There is no suggestion that the friendships were anything but platonic, although at least one of the men seems to have been smitten by Louise's charms. Frenchie suggested in a poem of thanks that the soldiers were drawn by Louise's constant cheerfulness and "zest of living." "When she smiles Ah! Boy! The sun comes out and the birdies sing, and I cheer up," wrote another soldier, who referred to Louise as "my 'Manager.'"

The men would come to Louise's hotel when they had a free few minutes or to cheer her up, if—as seemed to happen from time to time—she was ailing or feeling blue.

On one such occasion when Louise had apparently been under the weather, Smyser and another member of the "Cheerful Idiots' Corporation," came by her hotel to cheer her up by extravagantly spending their recently issued pay to seat her in a 20-centime chair at the Luxembourg. Unable to see her, they sent a note, "Be a good girl, Ma, and if you feel rotten, smile; it'll do you worlds of good."[130]

Most extravagant was Bjorn Winger, the grandson of a

<hr>

129. "Agreement: No smoking—all forms proscribed," Louise Marshall's World War I scrapbook, March 26, 1919, CPSHR, FHS; and Eleanor Leuenberger, PI, January 9, 2015.

130. "My dear Miss Welfare Worker," undated letter, Louise Marshall's World War I scrapbook, CPSHR, FHS. Accounts of Louise Marshall's Paris experience are drawn from memorabilia in her World War I scrapbook unless they are otherwise attributed, CPSHR, FHS.

pioneer missionary preacher to the Sioux Indians, who sent Louise page after page of his poetry and a picture of himself with his little sister in the United States. On the back of the picture, he wrote "to our revered friend Louise that she may remember Paris Days and know that we are not ungrateful." One of his poems, he dedicated to "Miss Louise Marshall, human treasure trove." Louise said she was honored to receive the verses he sent and kept his work safe in her scrapbook— and, perhaps, her heart—for the rest of her life.

In the evenings, Louise sometimes went to entertainments presented by and for the troops. She kept the programs, with names of soldiers she knew marked. The program for a musical review by the 88th Division included a song, "There Is Room in My Heart for You," with an unattributed, handwritten notation: "There's a little corner in my heart that needs attention."

Even in heady Paris, Louise practiced her faith and remembered her settlement work. She attended the American Church on Rue De Berri and visited Mission Populaire Evangelique de France, which did social work with Paris's needy, especially children. She kept booklets from both in her scrapbook, one of the very few places she recorded her life beyond the Cabbage Patch.

With spring and improving conditions, Louise found opportunities for travel, including a short trip to Blois, where her aunt Dr. Veech served. Summer brought the allied Victory Parade, July 14, 1919. The Red Cross issued Louise a ticket to watch amid the largest crowds she'd ever seen. Paris vibrated with emotion, reported *Vogue* magazine. Garlands and baskets of flowers hung from everything that would support them, in preparations for a celebration "arranged and desired by millions of hearts."[131]

The victory parade put a period on Louise's French adventure. Leaving Europe had never been easy for Louise, and leaving France with the freedom and closeness of its wartime friendships was harder than usual. Whether she realized it or not, going home would mean making a decision on whether to settle down to managing the Cabbage Patch and its vexing problems, a decision that would last a lifetime. On July 17, she boarded the *Britannia* in Marseilles for the trip home. She took a trunk with French purchases: dolls, prints, a pipe, French gloves, scarves, beaded bags, two fans, and one centerpiece. On August 2, the *Britannia* landed safely in New York Harbor to the immense relief of Lizzie Marshall, who sent a telegram: "My precious child. I have no words to express my joy. Love, Mother."

It was as if the clock at Cinderella's ball had struck midnight. The Montparnasse crowd went home and turned back into pumpkins. "It broke up Miss Marshall's Boys' Club, the most distinctive organization of the AEF" (American Expeditionary Force in France), Craig Smyser moaned in a letter a year later. Smyser's letter was the first installment of a round-robin letter the group had agreed to circulate a year after they left France. Smyser was joyously teaching French and Spanish to freshmen who didn't want to learn at Northwestern University and hoped to spend his life "with chalk dust" in his hair.[132] One of the twins had lost addresses for some of the Paris friends and said he hadn't written to

---

131. "Paris Reviews the Victorious Troops," *Vogue*, September 15, 1919.

132. Craig Smyser, "Dear Fellow-Parnassians," Louise Marshall's World War I scrapbook, May 17, 1920, CPSHR, FHS.

"Ma" Marshall because he'd heard "that she didn't think it proper for us married brothers to correspond with the sister. (I can just hear you saying, 'Oh bosh, I never heard such rot.')"[133]

Most other club members appeared to reenter civilian life happily united with wives, families, and jobs. Only Bjorn Winger and Louise Marshall seem to have struggled with putting the Paris experience behind them. Winger wrote his round robin letter only after "Ma" had laid down the law that he had to do it. His year had been "fraught with listlessness and apathy," dominated by a "sluggish muse" that refused him new poetry. Winger sounded rather like a man struggling with lost love. Shortly after Thanksgiving, Winger had gone to Louisville to see Louise, who had been hospitable as always. Louise, he wrote, had "a rare distinctiveness. There are people on this earth who somehow seem to personify a fellow's ideal and she is one."[134]

Louise's contribution to the round robin began wistfully, "To my Playmates of the Bonhomme Detachment . . . Would that I could look in upon each of you now," and it ended with an uncharacteristic postscript written months later. The letter said that Louise had planned to go to Japan for the World's Sunday School Convention that summer, but she had given up the idea. Instead, she had returned to the Cabbage Patch to "the most fascinating little boys, now almost grown. They grow more interesting every day." The boys had their hearts set on going to camp during the summer, she said, and she

---

133. Fletcher R. Andrews, "Dear Parisians," May 5, 1920, Louise Marshall's World War I scrapbook, CPSHR, FHS.

134. Bjorn Winger, "Bone Sure, Monster," (undated letter), Louise Marshall's World War I scrapbook, CPSHR, FHS.

hoped that would happen.

Louise Marshall had not shaken off Paris, however. In October, she had begun volunteering three days a week with the Red Cross, helping ex-service men with their affairs, filling out claims for compensation and the like. She reported working with a Kentucky mountain man who could neither read nor write.

Louise Marshall struggled with the end of her letter, swinging between her desire to keep the Paris magic going and the realities of home. She hoped to see her old friends "before many moons" at the Marshall home where the latch would always be out for them, she wrote to end the letter dated April 9, 1920. On August 3, 1920, she added a plaintive postscript.

"I think of you all often and wonder what you are doing," she wrote. "I have to continually remind myself that we are now in America, where things are different, and that perfectly harmless things are misunderstood over here. I would that it were not so because frankly I feel just the same about you every one as I did in France." Louise conceded that her dream of a Louisville house party for the Paris group and their spouses simply wouldn't work. The best she could do was to carefully store away the round robin letters her "playmates" had written and to speak of them always with a "gleam" in her eye.[135]

More than 50 years later, standing on the deck of a ship bound for France, Louise Marshall would remember that Paris trip and those men. She would recite their poetry from

---

135. Louise Marshall, letter to "My Playmates of the Bonhomme Detachment," April 9, 1920, including addition dated August 3, 1920; Louise Marshall's World War I scrapbook, CPSHR, FHS; and David Dosker, telephone conversation with the authors, September 4, 2016.

memory and smile. But in 1920, she was coming to grips with a hard reality. She could keep the letters forever, but she was going to have to let go of Paris.[136]

---

136. Kimberly McConnell Schiewetz, telephone interviews with authors, September 3, 6, and 30, 2014.

CHAPTER 7

MARRYING HER MISSION

If leaving the happy camaraderie of Paris was hard for Louise Marshall, resettling in the familiar confines of Louisville was harder. In place of Paris shows and adoring young men, Louisville's demands were difficult and unyielding. Everything that had supported and defined her through her early life was changing or about to change: her family, her circle of friends, the Cabbage Patch neighborhood, and the settlement house she founded, perhaps even the role faith would play in her life.

Turbulent change was everywhere around her, too, redefining what it meant to be a woman, what faith demanded, what technology allowed. American women would get the vote in 1920, and growing numbers of women, buoyed by the respect and experience they had gained during the war, went to work in offices, wore clothing that was less restrictive (and less modest), drove automobiles, and took larger roles outside their homes. Many men and women entered the 1920s in the giddy, misguided belief that the world had endured its last war. They were ready for a good time and oblivious to the suffering in places like the Cabbage Patch. Many women who had been pioneers in the settlement house and

Progressive movements had thrown themselves into the peace movement before the war. When they returned afterward, they found their great movements beginning to fade. Those who remained as settlement house workers became more professional and wanted pay for their work, forcing settlement houses to shut down or to become more business-like as they paid workers and accepted money from new sources. Miss Marshall was not about to trade control of her settlement house for money from the community fund or government.[137] Change would come to the Cabbage Patch, too, but Miss Marshall's settlement house would only get stronger.

The time between the two great wars would profoundly change Miss Marshall, too. The fun-loving young woman who wore pink silk would become the quirky woman everyone recalled wearing stiff navy blue or black. As her public identity merged with the Cabbage Patch Settlement, the distinction between her two lives grew sharper. She had a life most people at the Cabbage Patch didn't see. And the people in that other, upper-middle-class life were increasingly baffled (and sometimes put off) by the way she lived and the things she did.

What didn't change were the unyielding needs of the people who lived in the Cabbage Patch and the grinding

---

137. Michael B. Fabricant and Robert Fisher, *Settlement Houses under Siege: The Struggle to Sustain Community Organizations in New York City* (New York: Columbia University Press, 2002). Fabricant and Fisher argue that settlement house programs and funding contracted during conservative periods, such as the 1920s, because their goals for social reform were "increasingly seen as problematic." Louise Carroll Wade, "Settlement Houses," Encyclopedia of Chicago, http://www.encyclopedia.chicagohistory.org/pages/1135.html.

difficulty of raising enough money for the settlement house to address them. Those needs remained constant despite efforts city fathers made to gentrify the area and to change the Cabbage Patch Settlement. Their efforts were, in part, driven by a work of fiction.

Alice Hegan Rice, her book, *Mrs. Wiggs and the Cabbage Patch*, its sequels, and the movies and dramas based on it were a source of civic pride for Louisvillians. However, the shabby Cabbage Patch neighborhood itself was a bit of an embarrassment, especially as it began to bump against the glittering St. James Court development. In the early 1900s, tourists flocked to Louisville to see the slum described in the book and to glimpse the real Mrs. Wiggs, Mary Bass, who had been known to insult them. Plagued by people who broke off pieces of her fence and front door while raiding her yard for souvenirs, Mrs. Bass finally dumped a pot of "foul-smelling slop" on an unwanted visitor to her back door. The story made it all the way to the front page of the mighty *New York Times*, much to the dismay of Louisville's boosters.[138] Why didn't someone tell Mary Bass "what an honor it is to be Mrs. Wiggs?" railed a Louisville newspaper society writer. "Why aren't you proud of your distinction?"[139]

The "distinction" was also wearing thin for some of the Marshall family's social peers, Louisville civic leaders, and residents of St. James Court, who wanted to keep their

---

138. Mary Boewe, "Back to the Cabbage Patch: The Character of Mrs. Wiggs," *Filson Club History Quarterly 59, no. 2* (April 1985): 196–197.

139. Homer Dye, "Cultivating the Cabbage Patch: Not Kultur, but Cultrah, the Menace to Picturesque Section of Louisville," *Louisville (KY) Courier-Journal,* January 12, 1919.

property values up. They responded by forming the Central Civic League to gentrify the area around St. James Court, including the Cabbage Patch. The group's first meeting was held, appropriately, at the Cabbage Patch Settlement House on Ninth Street where, according to a news article, 50 men committed to improving the area by increasing "its resources and advancing its civic affairs." If anyone at the meeting advocated addressing the residents' actual poverty, that concern was not recorded. Afterward, "women interested in the new organization" served the men dinner.[140]

The leaders also asked the Cabbage Patch Settlement to change its iconic name. The request, made at the June 10, 1918, Cabbage Patch board meeting, fell flat. The board delayed action, and that's where the matter stood when Miss Marshall left for France that winter.[141] It was still on the table, waiting for action, when she returned the following fall, an unwelcome decision that needed to be made.

Although she had plenty of opinions, making decisions seemed hard for Miss Marshall—and no wonder. Nineteenth-century society was heavily vested in the principle that women weren't meant for the rigors of the real world. Homes were sanctuaries, "separate spheres" where men could rest and women were protected.[142] Learning to manage important

---

140. "Civic League Formed to Improve 'Cabbage Patch,'" *Louisville (KY) Courier-Journal*, February 15, 1918; and "Citizens Organize Central Civic League," *Louisville (KY) Herald*, February 16, 1918.

141. Minutes, Cabbage Patch Board of Directors, June 13, 1918, CPSHR, FHS.

142. Nancy F. Cott, *No Small Courage: A History of Women in the United States* (New York: Oxford University Press, 2000), 365.

enterprises and make decisions were not part of a girl's education. Especially in the society where Louise moved, both custom and the law dictated that hard decisions—and the power that went with them—were the purview of men.

The women on the Cabbage Patch board struggled to retain control of their creation, even as they relied on men to provide much of the money they needed. Louise's father, Burwell Marshall Sr., remained supportive, stepping in to help pay an insurance bill or to have painting done when the settlement's treasury went dry. He also searched for a better long-term solution. In July 1917, Burwell Marshall offered $500 to start an endowment fund for the benefit of the settlement house—if the board could raise an additional $2,250 or $5,000.[143] It was a generous offer that could have provided a measure of financial stability for the organization. The board decided their financial situation wouldn't allow them to accept it. During the decades ahead, other men and organizations would offer financial security, but the price was always yielding a measure of control. The women on the board struggled with that cost. The Cabbage Patch Settlement, with Miss Marshall as its president, was their baby.

Still, the lack of managerial know-how was fast becoming a problem for the Cabbage Patch Settlement. Miss Marshall's youthful project had become an important institution that provided life-sustaining services for people who had no social safety net. In 1920, parents and children from the Patch made 8,000 visits to the settlement to take part in clubs and classes,

---

143. Keith Cardwell, "In the Beginning: A History of the Cabbage Patch Settlement House in the Early Years," unpublished manuscript, July 24, 1987, CPSHR, FHS.

use the medical clinics, visit its library, and find help with problems that included providing clothing to children so they could go to school. Annual expenses had passed $2,000 a year, a sum that fund-raising barely covered.

"Each year the Settlement courageously opens its doors with no money in the treasury, and each year it closes them with the treasury again empty but all debts paid," said the annual fund-raising letter in 1919.[144]

Although Louise Marshall was the board president, Alice Hegan Rice remained the face of the settlement for much of the public, despite travel that regularly took her around the world. The board's minutes show that Louise took on administrative duties like negotiating with a worker to fix the front steps. She apparently taught some classes and made very sure that things went as they should at the settlement. She was an important presence but not the controlling force she would become. Much later in life, Louise Marshall seemed a little resentful that people thought Alice Hegan Rice had a major role in founding the Cabbage Patch. But in the 1920s, Alice Rice was a mature, confident, experienced leader. Miss Marshall was still maturing, toughening, and learning. She needed the support she got from Alice Rice, and there's nothing in the record to suggest that Louise didn't welcome the help.

In March 1920, with Louise back from France, the board finally yielded to the Central Civic League, changed the Cabbage Patch Settlement's iconic name, and ordered new signs identifying it blandly as the Ninth and Hill Settlement.[145]

---

144. Cabbage Patch Settlement House fund-raising letter, 1919, CPSHR, FHS.

145. Minutes, Cabbage Patch Settlement House Board of Directors, March 11, 1920, CPSHR, FHS.

In the 1920s, efforts to gentrify the Cabbage Patch area straightened winding streets but didn't improve the homes—although a newspaper columnist complained that the Cabbage Patch's charm had been ruined.

Courtesy of the University Archives and Records Center, the University of Louisville Archives and Special Collections

The Mothers Club gathered for a special occasion in 1924 in the same room where the boys played basketball. The building, known then as the Ninth and Hill Settlement, needed more space for its programs.

Courtesy of Cabbage Patch Settlement House Archives

The *Courier-Journal's* Homer Dye moaned in a full-page feature that the Civic League and "spirit of progressiveness" had "improved the Cabbage Patch" until most of its picturesque qualities were gone. Certainly, the streets were straighter and less dusty. However, Dye failed to notice that homes still lacked running water, bathtubs, and indoor toilets. Without sewers, wastewater was thrown into often overflowing vaults, yards, and streets, providing perfect breeding grounds for mosquitoes and flies, along with the malaria and other diseases they carried.[146] Everyone went to a public bathhouse for a hot bath, perhaps twice a week. Most families still ran bills at both of the groceries that gave credit, and boys went to work as soon as they could find it, an issue that put Miss Marshall at odds with the Progressive Movement's stand against child labor. She knew that families badly needed the income from children who worked.

Dye's article also conveniently overlooked children like Alice Probst who, at age five, had picked through the Seventh Street dump for whiskey bottles her father could sell to saloons for five cents each. Fortunately, by the time she was 12, Alice found her way to Miss Marshall's settlement house. "I just drifted in like the other kids," she would say years later. When Alice Probst got to the settlement, Miss Marshall's leadership was clear. Miss Marshall may have struggled with decisions on finance and policy, but her stand on values was absolute and put an unmistakable stamp on everything. The settlement emphasized character, Christianity, and quality. Even a little girl who went to sewing classes was expected to do "just perfect

146. Margaret Speed, staff report to the Board of Directors, Ninth and Hill Settlement House, April 1923, CPSH R, FHS.

work" and to participate in devotionals. Alice liked Miss Marshall "real much," but Miss Marshall *was* demanding.[147]

Homer Dye, the society columnist, listed the settlement house's programs as proof that the area's problems had been addressed. "It is all matter-of-fact science and the capable kind of helpfulness from people with knowledge and means," he wrote. Dye had also failed to notice that the settlement building, once so modern and spacious, had become too small and increasingly worn out with heavy use. Boys who went to the "cat house" (as they called it) to play basketball were frustrated because a high arching pass or shot would hit the meeting room's low ceiling.[148] The Cabbage Patch's new, unfamiliar name and the newspaper's suggestion that the area's problems had been solved must have made the already difficult task of raising enough money for the settlement house's growing needs only harder. In summer 1920, the treasurer held her breath until a check from the Cabbage Patch Circle (which had not changed its name) came in to cover a bank overdraft.[149]

All in all, it wasn't a good summer. Louise's other life, the one based on fashionable Ormsby Avenue, was also changing in ways that taxed and grieved her.

That summer of 1920, Louise suffered a stunning loss. Her old, dear friend Clem Spalding died. Clem had come

---

147. Alice Probst Scott, interview by Keith Cardwell, February 5, 1987, CPSOHP, CPSHR, FHS.

148. Ray Glur, interview by Keith Cardwell, February 4, 1987, CPSOHP, CPSHR, FHS; Dye, "Cultivating the Cabbage Patch."

149. Minutes, Board of Directors, Ninth and Hill Settlement House, October 4, 1922, CPSHR, FHS.

to Louisville's Medical College in 1901 from Centre College where, according to a news article, he had been captain of "the famous college football team" and "one of the most popular" students ever at the college.[150] Like the Marshalls, he attended Second Presbyterian Church and soon joined the crowd of young people who gathered in the Marshall parlor. He was a regular both in the parlor and at the Marshall dinner table where he was considered a "great friend."[151]

Clem had also been a protector of Louise, who was eight years younger than he was. Clem had accompanied the teenaged Louise when she pulled young Ben Hynes out of the stable and sent him back to school. Clem brought flowers when he escorted Louise, by then an attractive young woman, to the theater for a Cabbage Patch fund-raiser. Before the war, at Sallie Ewing's wedding, Dr. Clem Spalding sat at the bride's table with Louise. We don't know if friendship had melted into romance, but Clem's death had to have been a jolt for Louise. He'd gone to Danville in apparently perfect health to spend the weekend with friends. There he was stricken with indigestion, and a surgeon was called from Lexington to operate for appendicitis. Clem, himself a surgeon, never regained consciousness after the surgery. He was only 40.

"News of the death came as a surprise to Louisville friends," the *Courier-Journal's* obituary reported with masterful understatement.[152]

---

150. "Illness Fatal to Dr. Spalding," *Louisville (KY) Herald*, August 31, 1920.

151. Elizabeth Johnson Haynes, telephone interview with authors, February 16, 2013.

152. "Dr. C. B. Spalding Dies Suddenly," *Louisville (KY) Courier-Journal*, August 31, 1920.

For Louise Marshall, fresh holes appeared in the familiar fabric at home, too. Sallie Ewing had, of course, married and started her own home. Over the pre-war years after his wife died, Grandfather Richard Veech had established himself as part of the picture at 422 Ormsby, gradually moving there from his Indian Hill farm so his favorite daughter, Lizzie, could care for him in his final years. He had died at the age of 85 in September 1918, just before Louise and Elizabeth left for Paris.[153]

Young Burwell, dapper despite his limp, had finished high school, then went off to Centre College where, according to a classmate, he "stirred things up" with friends.[154] He eventually studied at the University of Virginia and Columbia University, a sequence designed to fulfill his father's wish for a son who would follow in his footsteps as a lawyer.[155]

At home, that left Elizabeth, who was two years older than Louise and thoroughly a spinster by Victorian standards, which placed no value on her legal education, career, or work in her father's law office. Her parents had long since decided that Elizabeth, who had always worked so hard to comfort them, would remain a single woman living at home. At least, that's the way things stood when the family gathered for Christmas dinner in 1920.

At the end of the meal, Elizabeth dropped a bomb. "Lewis Johnson and I are going to get married next Sunday,"

---

153. "R. S. Veech Dies at a Ripe Age," *Louisville (KY) Evening Post*, September 18, 1918.

154. Walter N. Haldeman II to his grandfather, February 4, 1919, Haldeman Family Papers, FHS.

155. Burwell K. Marshall III, PI, March 16, 2012.

she said as the family finished eating. Her parents were dumbfounded and distressed. "They thought mother had given up the idea of marrying and that she was going to stay home and take care of them," said Elizabeth's daughter, Elizabeth Johnson Haynes. "Why they didn't know her better than that I don't know."[156]

In fact, Lewis Johnson, who had been a regular in the parlor, had been working for years to get on the firm financial footing necessary to support a wife like Elizabeth Marshall. After years of work as a newspaper man, he'd gotten a good job as branch office manager for the American Surety Co. of New York in 1918 and had showed his skill as a civic leader by heading the Louisville Board of Public Safety.[157]

Elizabeth and Lewis Johnson arranged a simple ceremony at the Presbyterian Seminary on New Year's Day. The bride's father did give her away, despite the consternation at home. Louise was the maid of honor in a black velvet suit, a large black picture hat, and a corsage of her favorite pink roses.[158] The bride's mother, Lizzie Marshall, barely made it through the ceremony.

"Grandmother could hardly be gotten to go," said Elizabeth Haynes. "They left immediately after the ceremony, and Daddy said they practically had to hold her up."[159]

---

156. Elizabeth Johnson Haynes, PI, March 1, 2013.

157. "Lewis Y. Johnson, 88, Bank Director, Dies," *Louisville (KY) Courier-Journal*, October 17, 1967.

158. "Marshall-Johnson/ Miss Elizabeth Veech Marshall and Mr. Lewis Yarborough Johnson Married Yesterday," *Louisville (KY) Courier-Journal*, January 2, 1921.

159. Elizabeth Johnson Haynes, PI, March 1, 2013.

Elizabeth's marriage left another enormous gap at 422 Ormsby, where no one had to point out that Louise was the remaining spinster.

Miss Marshall didn't have time to worry about that. Problems at the settlement were coming to a head quickly. Behavior—among both boys and girls—was increasingly a problem. The all-female board called on male leaders from the YMCA and Boy Scouts to advise them on boys. A first aid class and talks by prominent men with engaging personalities were suggested as possibilities to engage boys. A gymnasium and paid boys workers seemed like necessities. The women approved a plan to pay a boys worker $600 a year. The first four men offered the job turned it down.

The behavior problem wasn't limited to the Cabbage Patch. In the eyes of some elders, post-war moral standards had plummeted even as women's skirts edged ever up. Indeed, the Southern Baptist *Review and Expositor* moaned that girls, "by their dress and conversation" were tempting boys.[160] The problems came together at the settlement's weekly dances, which were attracting unladylike girls and young men who carried flasks and smelled of liquor. The board decided to limit the dances to twice a month and require those who attended to have admission cards issued by the settlement. By the year's end, the board would have to ask the police for help with the boys' gambling and drinking.[161]

---

160. Mark Sullivan, *Our Times: The United States 1900–1925, vol. 1, The Twenties* (New York: Charles Scribner's Sons, 1935), 578–580.

161. Minutes, Board of Directors of Ninth and Hill Settlement House, December 1922, CPSHR, FHS.

Giving plays was a staple activity for the settlement's children. In 1923, the boys produced a play, "Robin Hood and His Merry Men," to raise money to buy a tent for summer camping. *Courtesy of Cabbage Patch Settlement House Archives*

Miss Marshall's views on how to deal with such moral problems remained consistent throughout her life: She attacked sin one sinner at a time by living her faith and showing children she cared about them. Surviving records show little about how Miss Marshall spent her time at the settlement in those days, but there is considerable evidence that she was doing what she believed. Ollie (Alice) Probst Scott remembered Miss Marshall kindly teaching sewing, values, and things girls needed to know, like Bible stories—"good stories," Ollie called them. Children yielded to Miss Marshall's demanding standards and insistence on devotionals because the settlement also meant pleasures, including Christmas programs and presents. Ollie Scott remembered her own desperate, impossible longing for roller skates one Christmas.

When people at the settlement asked what she wanted for Christmas, she told them about the skates. "I just knew it was wishful thinking," she said, but on Christmas morning, the skates appeared on her doorstep. She used the skates to race up and down the fine pavement on Third Street. "You'd pass a wagon once in a while," she said, "but those roller skates were the best thing that ever happened."[162]

Miss Marshall's empathy and gift for working with children were all well and good, but the settlement needed leadership and decision making on the three difficult, interrelated problems: bad boys, the inadequate building, and finances. None of the problems say much about Miss Marshall's personality, but her response to them does.

Boys had tested Miss Marshall from the first, of course. They came to the settlement wearing caps on their heads, but frequently no shoes on their feet. They came prepared to disrupt or to play sports or, on occasion, to be lured into another activity if Miss Marshall and her colleagues, who finally included a part-time, paid boys worker, could capture their fancy.

March 1923 was a banner month that illustrated both the settlement's strengths and challenges. The settlement had record attendance that month because the boys, who needed money, decided to stage a play, *Robin Hood and his Men*, that they researched, wrote, and produced themselves. The Conservatory of Music provided coaching; the boys dragged in trees, logs, a huge stone, and grass for scenery. What the trees lacked in leaves, the boys provided with paper. The play raised the money the boys needed to buy a tent for their

---

162. Alice Probost Scott, interview by Keith Cardwell, February 5, 1987, CPSOHP, CPSHR, FHS.

summer camping trip, and provided public recognition; a newspaper published a picture of the successful production. Perhaps softened by their own success, the 15-, 16-, and 17-year-old boys later gave polite attention to little children saying Bible verses during a program for the sewing school. Resident worker Margaret Speed reported both events to the board with enormous relief.

That evening's success was tempered by a cold night's basketball game that pitted the settlement's older boys against a team from the Ormsby neighborhood a few blocks away. The game was played in the settlement's assembly room, the same one that served as a theatre for *Robin Hood* and as space for the library, sewing room, clubroom, and entertainment hall as well. The teams changed into their playing clothes and began a hard game, firing passes that cracked the plaster when the ball hit the walls. By the end of the half, the 38 non-too-washed bodies streamed with perspiration. The boys were thirsty, but the building lacked drinking fountains. All 38 of them drank from one cup.

"Then," wrote Margaret Speed, "they played on. At the end of the game, they went upstairs, warmer, if possible than before, and put their clothes on over damp bodies . . . and went out into one of the coldest nights we had this winter." The settlement had done "splendid" work, Speed wrote to the board, but "we are hampered at every turn for lack of space and equipment. I feel we are plowing our ground with a stick. We need a new, up-to-date American plow if we wish to meet the needs of the Community."[163]

163. Margaret Speed, report to the Board of Directors, Ninth and Hill Settlement House, March 1923, CPSHR, FHS.

In 1925, the Lion Cubs basketball team posed with their coach outside the Ninth and Hill Settlement House. The team still used a soccer-style ball with laces. *Courtesy of Cabbage Patch Settlement House Archives*

Everyone agreed: In order to meet the needs of boys and men, the settlement needed a real gym. It needed showers. It needed meeting space.

No one had to tell Miss Marshall or the board members that the settlement needed a new building. The problem—always—was money. As a step toward financial stability, the board had established a budget, but they had also accepted a $200 loan in July to meet expenses. An effort to repay the loan with a picture show had to be scrubbed because it violated guidelines of the Charities Endorsement League. Maybe joining the Community Chest would help; the board wasn't sure.

The situation required strong leadership and decisive decision making. It didn't get either. Miss Marshall and her board spent years struggling with the issues, even as they continued to build programs and services, adding boys' activities and male staff members that drew ever more people to the already crowded and crumbling settlement house. The settlement's growth was apparent to everyone. The growth within Miss Marshall was more subtle.

There is no record that Louise Marshall ever talked to her Cabbage Patch friends—or anyone else—about what happened in her life during the summer of 1923 as the Cabbage Patch struggled with success and shortage. However, it appears to have been an important summer for her for an unexpected reason. Since before the war, some of Louisville's most prominent churchmen (some of them Presbyterian) had been working to lure famous evangelist Billy Sunday, an ordained Presbyterian minister, to Louisville for a crusade. In 1923, he finally came for a six-week, 78-sermon crusade that dominated the news and raised the summer temperature in a wooden tabernacle on Broadway. By then, Sunday was past the zenith of his fame and the powers that caused the leaders to invite him, but that wasn't reflected in his welcome by Louisville's mayor and 1,500 others who gathered at the train station to greet him. We don't know if Louise was among them, but she could not have failed to notice. Day after day, the *Courier-Journal* devoted much of its front page and full inside pages to coverage of the Sunday campaign, including complete texts of his sermons. The tabernacle, constructed for 7,000, couldn't hold the 20,000 people who turned out at the first Sunday service to watch Billy Sunday climb on a table and swing a chair in a breathtaking display of his trademark "acrobatic preaching."[164]

---

164 "Billy Sunday, 'Ma' and Retinue Arrive in Louisville to Grapple with Satan . . .," *Louisville (KY) Courier-Journal*, April 22, 1923.

Louise and her sister, Sallie Ewing Dosker, had certainly never seen that kind of preaching at the staid Second Presbyterian Church of their youth, but they did go to watch Billy Sunday coax sinners by the hundreds down the sawdust trail to salvation. Sunday's preaching and acrobatics were supported by local financial offerings and talented local Christians. The *Courier-Journal* reported that the Cabbage Patch Settlement sent the Smiley Brothers quartet, four young black brothers, to perform at the crusade. The Smileys wowed the crowd by singing spirituals with such feeling that Billy Sunday's song leader, Homer Rodebeaver, shouted "amen" and invited the brothers back for another appearance later in the crusade.[165] Cabbage Patch founder Miss Marshall seems unlikely to have missed the performances.

We don't know exactly what Louise heard when she went to the services. To the modern ear, Sunday's sermons tended to be disjointed and overwrought, sometimes contradictory, strings of folksy stories and dramatic denunciations of sin and evils—like the theory of evolution. His themes, however, spoke even to staid Presbyterians like Louise and Sallie Ewing: He preached a fundamentalist faith, the power of prayer, the ability of God to "save the vilest sinner." Perhaps most important for Louise was Sunday's "insistence upon Christian men making religion a reality in their lives."[166]

Some of what Sunday preached meshed with what Louise already believed. "Everything that is done for the benefit of

165. "615 March Up Sawdust Trail," *Louisville (KY) Courier-Journal*, May 23, 1923.

166. "Billy Sunday's Evangelistic Campaign in Louisville, Kentucky," *Louisville (KY) Christian Observer*, May 9, 1923.

humanity, all charity, it all comes through the principles of Jesus Christ," Sunday said at one service. Character is "the grandest thing in the world," he proclaimed.[167] In a sermon delivered only to women, Sunday advised them not to marry except for love. "Don't worry if you don't marry," he said. "There are worse things in the world than being an old maid, and one of them is marrying the wrong man."[168]

Whatever Louise and Sallie Ewing heard at Sunday's crusade, "It just blew them away," their sister Elizabeth told her own daughter later. "My mother said that they were swept away by the evangelical fervor—somewhat to the disgust of the rest of the family." Both Louise and Sallie Ewing were "easily swayed by powerful emotional trends and currents," their niece Elizabeth Johnson Haynes said. "They got converted, though how they could have become any more converted, I couldn't tell you. Louise, especially, became committed with the requirement of service," Mrs. Haynes said. "I would say that that was really the key note that set her on that path."[169]

Rigidly Presbyterian though they were, public emotion certainly was not Burwell and Lizzie Marshall's style. But the impact on Louise was major and lasting, said Mrs. Haynes. When Louise was moved, she didn't waste time on emotion. "She got up and did something about it."[170] What Louise did

167. "Sunday Calls Character the Grandest Thing in World," *Louisville (KY) Courier-Journal*, May 12, 1923.

168. "Evangelist Declares Too Many Girls Marry for Reasons Other Than Love . . .," *Louisville (KY) Courier-Journal*, May 27, 1923.

169. Elizabeth Johnson Haynes, PI, July 11, 2011.

170. Elizabeth Haynes, telephone interview with authors, February 16, 2013.

was rededicate herself to the Cabbage Patch. She had finally made an absolute decision about the course of her life; she would marry her work at the settlement. The marriage was rooted in love, and, she believed, made in heaven. Like all good marriages, Louise's required hard work and compromise.

In that post-Victorian age, solving the settlement's problems required help from men, a truth the board women acknowledged slowly, first by asking male advice, then by hiring boys workers, and finally by adding two men to their board. The succession of men who tried to provide financial security always attached troublesome strings to their offers. One of the most important—and revealing—offers came in 1924 when Dr. John Vander Meulen, president of the Louisville Presbyterian Theological Seminary, presented a possible solution—and a decision-making test for Miss Marshall. He offered the settlement two funds, totaling $15,000, "which under certain conditions might be put at our disposal." The funds were a sweetener for a proposition that Miss Marshall would struggle with over the years: The settlement would become a Presbyterian organization.

Miss Marshall's esteem for Vander Meulen bordered on adoration. Bucking him on an issue so important must have been difficult, but the board didn't want to give up control. They made a counteroffer: They would accept the money, but only if they could hold open the possibility of applying for Community Chest (later known as United Way) membership, administer the funds themselves, and maintain the status quo in the settlement's operation and management. Louise Marshall and Alice Rice were appointed to negotiate with Vander Meulen. Negotiations went back and forth.

Finally, Vander Meulen persuaded Miss Marshall to link the settlement to the presbytery, the ruling body for local Presbyterian churches.[171] Things then fell into place quickly. The board gave in and received the money. Vander Meulen promised to encourage Presbyterian churches to support the work. Alice Rice led a committee to conduct a speaking campaign in Presbyterian churches. The board established a building fund. And the presbytery elected a permanent committee of five Presbyterian ministers to "have oversight" of the Ninth and Hill Settlement House. Burwell Marshall Sr. made it all legal by revising the settlement's articles of incorporation to reflect the change.[172]

The settlement's new fund-raising folder introduced Presbyterians to "our New Presbyterian Mission . . . adopted by the Presbyterian Church in the United States June 4, 1924 for definite Christian Service." The folder listed the settlement's programs beneath a picture of its "Banner Daily Vacation Bible School" class. The class included a girl who won a citywide contest by memorizing the words and music for 15 "famous old hymns of the church." The folder ended with a quote that Miss Marshall believed from the bottom of her heart: "God will provide all our needs."[173]

Indeed, Miss Marshall announced at a meeting of Louisville Presbytery that "a new building will be erected at

---

171. Lewis Marshall Johnson, telephone interview with authors, July 18, 2011.

172. Minutes, Louisville Presbytery, a regional governing body of the Presbyterian Church of the United States, June 4, 1924.

173. Pamphlet, "This is to Introduce You to Our New Presbyterian Mission, the Ninth and Hill St. Settlement," 1924, CPSHR, FHS.

once to provide facilities for carrying on the work."[174] In fact, the settlement's need for a new building was not answered for another five years.

In 1925, Louise's mother, Lizzie Marshall, broke her hip. Then she contracted pneumonia ("the old people's friend," Dr. Annie Veech called it) and died after only a week's illness. Louise may not have been close to her mother, but she had always been very touched by her parents' devotion to each other.[175] Lizzie's death devastated Burwell. He returned from his wife's funeral, went to bed, and refused to get up. He stayed there for a week before the family took action. Burwell Marshall Sr. was inarguably a strong character, but, as Louise told the story to her friend Dr. Jim Cooksey later, her Aunt Annie Veech was his match.

"Dr. Veech went in and said to him, 'Mr. Marshall, if you don't get out of that bed, you aren't going to die. You're just going to be an invalid, and other people are going to have to take care of you." Burwell Marshall got out of bed and went to work, his daughter said.[176]

As for Louise, she went back across the Atlantic on a cruise, always a sure way to rest and renew her energy. After the war, as she returned from France, Louise had picked up—and kept—a folder for the Fabre Line's Mediterranean cruise.

174. Keith Cardwell, "In the Beginning: A History of the Cabbage Patch Settlement House in the Early Years" (unpublished manuscript), July 24, 1987, CPSHR, FHS.

175. Lewis Marshall Johnson, telephone interview with authors, July 28, 2011; "Wife of Lawyer Here Succumbs," *Louisville (KY) Courier-Journal,* November 2, 1925.

176. Dr. James J. Cooksey, PI, July 14, 2011.

It promised a "sun-kissed azure sea . . . luxurious vessel . . . a glorious passage," and an "excellent table"—all at a "very moderate cost."[177] After Lizzie's death, the time for Louise to take that trip had come.

Miss Marshall attended the settlement's February 11, 1926, board meeting, where she voted to launch a building fund drive and to form a men's committee to help. Then she quietly left for the kind of trip she loved. The board minutes make no mention that she was gone. The board simply didn't meet again until she got back in the spring.

New York's winter gloom hung over the three-stack liner *Providence* until it hit the Gulf Stream's warm water.[178] From then on, balmy weather coaxed passengers out for promenades and deck games. The ship touched on the Azores, then cruised the Mediterranean, offering extended land excursions, including visits to Jerusalem and Egypt, places Louise had read about in the Bible. On March 27, 1926, the line issued her a certificate testifying that she had traveled 9,000 miles by sea and 800 miles by land, qualifying her to be considered a "trusty old salt" in the "Domain of Neptunus Rex."[179]

The "old salt" returned to Louisville ready to launch the Cabbage Patch Settlement into a new era that would test her again.

---

177. Louise Marshall's World War I scrapbook, CPSHR, FHS.

178. "The Southern Atlantic Route," 1926, YodelOut! Travel website, http://travel.yodelout.com/the-southern-atlantic-route/ (accessed April 12, 2017).

179. "Domain of Neptunus Rex" Certificate, Louise Marshall correspondence, 1922, CPSHR, FHS.

CHAPTER 8

ENDURING THE DEPRESSION

By the time she returned to Louisville in 1926, Louise Marshall's career path and character were firmly set. She was 38 and married to her work in the Cabbage Patch. From her father, she had inherited a tendency to be legalistic and pugnacious, demanding, controlling, and penny pinching. She also shared his relentlessly high expectations. None of those qualities endeared her to a long line of Cabbage Patch employees who resigned in anger and despair. But Louise had another side, too, one that children and Cabbage Patch clients saw, a compassionate side that led her to listen, love, and care deeply about them. Her belief that she was serving God drove her to work to exhaustion and beyond to ease the suffering she saw all around her. She was courageous—except when it came to decision making. And every year she got quirkier in ways that made people shake their heads. She would be sorely tested during the 1930s. The qualities that made her remarkable would not make her the leader the settlement seemed to need.

The first test was finding a site for the new settlement house. Miss Marshall appears to have returned from her

117

cruise in spring 1926 with a renewed sense of purpose for doing just that. She went to the first board meeting armed with an option to buy a site and a proposal to add two men to the board. The board was ready for that kind of leadership. It empowered an executive committee—one that included men and Miss Marshall—to purchase property. Then the sense of focused resolution evaporated. By September, the executive committee wouldn't act without hearing from the full board. The full board wasn't sure what to do. Every site the members considered had a problem. The Cabbage Patch neighborhood, squeezed by expanding industries, rail lines, and new construction, lacked open land for the big new settlement house, gymnasium, playground, and garden the women envisioned. The board flirted with simply renovating its old, worn-out building. The debate went on and on. New committees were formed, only to fail.

Finally, in January 1929, the board focused on some modest Sixth Street homes, not far from the Ninth Street building, that the settlement could buy and renovate for its programs. The property included enough land to build a proper gymnasium with a little space to spare. The board bought the houses and work began, although the building fund didn't have enough money to pay for the work and pledges weren't coming in as promised. (Even Alice Hegan Rice, who had been hospitalized for "wear and tear on the nerves & muscles," had an outstanding $500 pledge.)[180] Miss Marshall was authorized to borrow construction money, just as the nation's pre-Depression bubble prepared to burst.

---

180. Boewe, *Beyond the Cabbage Patch*, 274.

The board decided to sell the old Ninth Street Settlement building to raise money, then reversed itself and decided not to sell it just yet.[181] That typically tortured decision turned out to be important.

There was a certain in-your-face quality to the board's decision making. In its new location, the settlement house, with all its rowdy children, would be back-to-back with St. James Court, separated by no more than an alley from the elegant homes, including those where some board members lived. The board also voted to change its name back to the Cabbage Patch Settlement, the name that defined it before the Central Civic League asked for change. Despite the league's efforts, St. James Court had lost some of its glitter by the late 1920s, as wealthy homeowners moved to trendy new neighborhoods east of Louisville. The settlement's arrival in the neighborhood appears to have encouraged the decline. The Patch's new Sixth Street neighborhood was still home to doctors and others who prospered. They were less than welcoming.

"They moved out," said Bertha Weikel, who worked at the Cabbage Patch. "They didn't like it at all when the settlement bought that property—which is snobby."[182]

The wealthy didn't have much time for snobbery. New York's stock exchange crash on October 29, 1929, would plunge many of them into hard times, too. Some of them would even look to the Cabbage Patch for help

181. Minutes of the Ninth and Hill Settlement House Board, May 13, 1926–December 13, 1929, CPSHR, FHS.

182. Bertha Weikel, interview by Andrew Chancey, October 1, 1987, CPSOHP, FHS.

before the 1930s ended. In the meantime, Miss Marshall and the board did not appear to pay attention to either the neighbors' slights or the stock market's crash. They were busy moving into the new, still unfinished buildings, even as their programs served more and more people. The crash that launched the Great Depression also signaled the Cabbage Patch's greatest test so far.

The Cabbage Patch's 1929 fund-raising brochure called the new buildings "a dream come true."[183] Ray Glur, whose arching basketball passes no longer hit the ceiling, recalled that "it was like being in heaven at the new Cabbage Patch and playing over there and having our own club room."[184] Despite that giddy joy, most of the wonderful new space was in a brick building, built as a house, with only seven rooms devoted to programs serving hundreds of people. A 1930 diagram of the layout showed that 11 different organizations for men, women, and children shared space in the Mothers Club room. In the small Boys Club room, people of all ages waited to be seen at the clinic, and eight other activities met, including the Gangbusters Club. The head resident lived in a separate building known as the cottage, in partial compensation for a staggering workload. The gymnasium had a real stage and, perhaps most gloriously, shower rooms for both boys and girls.[185] To reach the activity rooms, children

---

183. Cabbage Patch Settlement House fund-raising brochure for 1929, CPSHR, FHS.

184. Ray Glur, interview by Keith Cardwell, February 4, 1987, CPSOHP, CPSHR, FHS.

185. "1930 Cabbage Patch Settlement: Its Layout and Activities," CPSHR, FHS.

would go down a little corridor that was always dark, "a maze that a child could get lost in," said Margie Blanford. It was a "fun place," "a good place," and a very, very busy place that was crowded from the first.[186] Attendance soared. In the first year alone, even before the formal dedication, the number of people using the small library grew from 68 to 210 and that was only a small part of the growing operation.[187]

By 1947, the Cabbage Patch Settlement complex on Sixth Street included a "cottage" at left for resident workers, a larger house for activities and offices, and the house, at right, with game rooms, purchased from the Optimist Club in 1944. The gymnasium with its basketball courts and stage is visible in the background. *Courtesy of Cabbage Patch Settlement House Archives*

186. Margie M. Blanford, interview by Andrew Chancey, September 24, 1987, CPSOHP, CPSHR, FHS.

187. Cabbage Patch Settlement House fund-raising brochure for 1929, CPSHR, FHS.

Summer vacation Bible school drew a crowd of young people to the Cabbage Patch Settlement during the Great Depression.

Courtesy of Cabbage Patch Settlement House Archives

As their expressions suggest, students took their roles very seriously in a vacation Bible school pageant performed on the Cabbage Patch Settlement House's new gymnasium's stage in 1931.

Courtesy of Cabbage Patch Settlement House Archives

Newspaper coverage of the "new $50,000 Cabbage Patch Settlement House" at 1413 South Sixth Street, was distinctly modest compared to the opening of the original Ninth Street building, but some things had not changed. Both the *Louisville Times* and the *Courier-Journal's* coverage of the January 30,

1930, dedication once again misdirected credit for the original Cabbage Patch program to "the late Gen. Bennett H. Young." One account did acknowledge that Alice Hegan Rice and the "women's class of the Second Presbyterian Church" had a role in organizing the original settlement. Miss Cornelia Steele, the head resident, got early mention for supervising the staff: one full-time assistant, five part-time assistants, and 30 volunteer social workers. Miss Louise Marshall, as president, was listed with the settlement's officers.[188] There's no record of how the team of women who had invested so much of their own money, time, and spirit in the Cabbage Patch reacted to the slight. Clearly, Louise Marshall, the Cabbage Patch Settlement's real founder, lacked the penchant for self-promotion that propelled Jane Addams of the Hull House into the media and the history books. That's the way Miss Marshall thought it should be. "True greatness exists only in unselfish service," she would write later.[189] In 1930, there were more important things for her to worry about.

What the new settlement location lacked in playground space, it gained in proximity to Louisville's Central Park, just half a block away. The park was a magical place for children,

---

188. "Cabbage Patch Settlement Open," *Louisville (KY) Times,* January 30 and 31, 1930; "Cabbage Patch Plant Opened," *Louisville (KY) Courier-Journal,* January 31, 1930; and "Opening of a New Cabbage Patch Settlement . . .," *Louisville (KY) Courier-Journal,* February 2, 1930. Bennett Young, a Confederate colonel in 1904, seems to have been given an honorific promotion.

189. Louise Marshall, letter to the editor of the *Louisville (KY) Courier-Journal* republished in memorial booklet, "The Reverend John Marinus Vander Meulen," June 7, 1936, E. M. White Library, Louisville Presbyterian Theological Seminary.

ringed by a double row of towering (to children, at least) mock orange bushes. Children had formed tunnels and trails beneath the drooping branches where they could play Tarzan of the jungle, stalk imagined wild animals, and circle the entire park without ever being seen. The park had real dangers, too. The most obvious—to a child—was the occasional mad dog that police had to shoot.[190] The much more dangerous and less visible hazards were human predators, men and women who were ready to use the Cabbage Patch's vulnerable children for pleasure or profit. There was little that Miss Marshall wouldn't do to protect her children from such people.

One fall, a 26-year-old woman who lived near the park began luring young teenage boys to her home "for immoral purposes," Miss Marshall wrote. "It has been difficult to locate her, more difficult to get proof." Then the mother of a 14-year-old found a letter the woman had written to her son. That provided a break in the case. The letter gave all the information needed to prosecute her, but the woman couldn't be found. Police were called but said they'd never heard of the woman. That wasn't good enough for Miss Marshall. As she did again and again when her children were threatened, Miss Marshall took matters into her own hands. For three nights, she searched for the woman. Finally, she found a boy "who was anxious to talk. He gave all the necessary information to locate her—the house, the floor, the room." On a Saturday night, Miss Marshall summoned plainclothes police to the house. They caught the woman with a child. That's what wrenched Miss Marshall's heart.

190. Margie Blanford, interview by Andrew Chancey, September 24, 1987, CPSOHP, CPSHR, FHS.

"She has taken this child and made of him a thief and liar. How shall we help him? He is so young and helpless." She used the story to plead for contributions to expand boys' programs at the Cabbage Patch. "Life is a battle and the forces of evil must be matched with the most aggressive and vitally attractive forces for good," she wrote in a fund-raising letter.[191]

The park's hazards threatened girls, too, and Miss Marshall wrote about them as well. "One day, this summer, an awful thing happened," Miss Marshall began the story of a 15-year-old girl. "Someone gave this child a drink. Then she hardly knew what happened—but it did happen."

"What must she do?" Miss Marshall asked when she wrote about such girls for the newsletter. "Where shall she go? . . . Shall there be no second chance for her?" Those weren't rhetorical questions for Miss Marshall. If she didn't have answers, she created them.[192]

The park spelled trouble for so many girls. Dorothy Parle's mother warned Dorothy not to go to Central Park, but it did no good. A group of her girlfriends wanted to go to the park, Dorothy said, so she went, too. "That's where I met my old man." Two months later, Dorothy was married. Her baby arrived the following summer, when she had just turned 16.[193]

Miss Marshall settled Dorothy, her husband, and new baby in one of the rough, two-room wooden apartments

---

191. Louise Marshall, "Tramp! Tramp! Tramp! The Boys Are Marching?" fund-raising letter, November 1936, CPSHR, FHS.

192. Louise Marshall, fund-raising letter, November 1960, CPSHR, FHS.

193. Dorothy H. Parle, interview by Andrew Chancey, September 23, 1987, CPSOHP, CPSHR, FHS.

carved in the old Ninth Street Settlement building. The rent was minimal. Dorothy continued to participate in Cabbage Patch activities, and at Christmas, in a masterstroke of casting, she was given a starring role in the Christmas play. "I was Virgin Mary," she said with pride 50 years later. Despite Dorothy's best efforts, her fretful infant daughter was denied the role of Jesus. Dorothy had to lay a doll in the manger. From time to time, Dorothy's husband helped Miss Marshall at the Cabbage Patch and, on one occasion, he arrived showing evidence of drinking. Miss Marshall, still a tiny five foot, four inches tall, locked him in a room, away from his wife, until he sobered up.[194]

As the Depression crushed the Cabbage Patch, the Ninth Street building proved a blessing, both for homeless families sheltered in the upstairs apartments and for hungry people who could buy groceries at cost—or less—from the commissary established downstairs.

The Depression may have eased into some parts of the country, but it washed over the Cabbage Patch neighborhood and its settlement house fast and hard. The settlement, always strapped for money, faced the same problems as everyone else after the banks failed in 1930. The settlement's endowment, deposited in one of the banks that failed, produced no income. Miss Marshall couldn't refinance the debt on the new building. Donors, who were strapped themselves, didn't give as they used to. The only bright light was that Louise's father, Burwell Marshall, gave his last major gift to the Cabbage Patch just before the banks failed: $700 to reduce the debt on the new

---

194. Dorothy H. Parle, interview by Andrew Chancey, September 23, 1987, CPSOHP, CPSHR, FHS.

buildings. Still, by July 1931, the Cabbage Patch didn't have enough money to pay its bills—at the worst possible time.[195]

The Depression didn't just bring more of the Cabbage Patch's usual problems with poverty. It brought a new problem that Presbyterians, well schooled in serving women and children, hardly knew how to address: unemployed, able-bodied men. Most Cabbage Patch households traditionally had a man, one who worked but didn't make enough. Now it had hundreds of men who couldn't find work at all.

"The public has gotten the impression that the Government is taking care of all the unemployed," wrote Miss Marshall. "This is not true . . . The numbers are appalling." In a single month, she wrote, one nearby industry had laid off "about 600 men, another around 700, a third 900."[196] The men were desperate to feed their families, humiliated at the prospect of seeking charity, and near breaking from the struggle. Eventually their health gave way, and many sought the only solace they could find, drinking.

Preserving self-respect was as important to Miss Marshall as saving bodies and souls. The Cabbage Patch Settlement would not give charity. "For what doth it profit a man, if he gain an order for food, or clothing or shelter, if he lose his own soul," wrote Miss Marshall, paraphrasing Jesus, whom she considered "the Great Social Worker."[197]

---

195. Minutes, CPSH Board of Directors, July 1930–December 1931, CPSHR, FHS.

196. Undated typescript filed among CPSH fund-raising letters from the Depression years (page 2 labeled "CABBAGE PATCH SETTLEMENT"), CPSHR, FHS.

197. Louise Marshall, fund-raising letter, Winter 1934, CPSHR, FHS.

The Cabbage Patch did take some of the government's WPA workers for its nursery school, an arrangement Miss Marshall found somewhat unsatisfactory. Her own answer to unemployment was to form her own employment bureau and to hire Bertha Weikel to run it.[198] The program trained men who had always worked in factories to work in homes, cleaning and doing odd jobs for Cabbage Patch supporters and Presbyterian Church members. Miss Marshall begged her supporters, "If you are planning to help someone in need . . . let them do a job for you, or someone else, instead of giving them charity." The Cabbage Patch had 585 men ready to do anything that needed doing around the house.[199]

Louise and her sister, Elizabeth Johnson, who had always used paid help to do their own housework, taught the men to wash woodwork, scrub and polish floors, and clean wallpaper. When the men had been trained, Miss Marshall would take them five at a time to the gym, give them scrub brushes, and line them up, each with a bucket of soapy water on one side and rinse water on the other. The man who did the best work on the gym floor would get the next job that came into the employment bureau.[200]

Men who registered with the employment bureau were paid 30 cents an hour, plus carfare and lunch. Men got their

---

198. Louise Marshall, Report to the CPSH Board of Directors, February 8, 1943, CPSHR, FHS.

199. Undated typescript filed among CPSH fund-raising letters from the Depression years (page 2 labeled "CABBAGE PATCH SETTLEMENT"), CPSHR, FHS.

200. Escue and Geneva Tomerlin, interview by Carolyn Kline, April 2, 1987, CPSOHP, CPSHR, FHS.

pay in script, cards they could use to pay for food at the commissary that had been opened on the first floor of the old Ninth Street settlement building. That was Miss Marshall's way of ensuring that they didn't spend their earnings on alcohol. In the worst of times, the commissary stocked only day-old bread and milk, sold for perhaps a penny. When possible, the commissary offered pale government surplus butter, beans, and canned goods, too. (It did not carry soap. At four cents a bar, no one could afford soap.) Everyone paid something for what she got. If a woman didn't have even a penny, she could sweep the settlement floor or wash towels for the cooking school. The same rules held true for the Cabbage Patch's monthly rummage sales. A person could get a big basket of clothing for 25 cents—but nothing was free. The settlement house's floors were very, very well cleaned—often four or five times a day.[201] The Cabbage Patch "did not give men charity, but a chance to live and keep their self-respect," Miss Marshall wrote.[202]

The means to support life was always uncertain in the Cabbage Patch of the 1930s. Hunger and its companion, disease, were rampant. Without any social safety net, starvation was a real threat—especially for children. As winter 1932 closed in, the Cabbage Patch Settlement opened a soup kitchen and cafeteria.[203] Churches helped pack Thanksgiving

---

201. Bertha Weikel, interview by Andrew Chancey, October 1, 1987, CPSOHP, CPSHR, FHS; Escue and Geneva Tomerlin, interview by Carolyn Kline, April 2, 1987, CPSHR, FHS.

202. Louise Marshall, fund-raising letter, winter 1934, CPSHR, FHS.

203. "Settlement to Open Soup Kitchen," *Louisville (KY) Courier-Journal*, December 15, 1932.

and Christmas baskets with the makings of a real meal for each Cabbage Patch family, but it was never enough. At one Christmas party, Santa Claus had to take an unscheduled break to go into a back room to cry. He'd just held a 10-year-old girl on his lap who weighed only 50 pounds. After the party, he arranged to pay for her to have a quart of milk every day.[204]

During the Depression, Cabbage Patch mothers were stressed and thin and their children were often hungry. Miss Marshall provided help with a large helping of self-respect; everybody paid a pittance or worked for what they got. *Courtesy of Cabbage Patch Settlement House Archives*

---

204. Eleanor Starks, CPSH fund-raising letter, 1939, CPSHR, FHS.

The girl would live and thrive because she got the milk and Miss Marshall's other major weapon against malnutrition, cod liver oil. Miss Marshall believed in cod liver oil. She gave it to children in the nursery school and recommended it to mothers with children at home. The mere mention of "that horrible cod liver oil" was enough to wrinkle the faces of old women 50 years later.

"God, Miss Marshall got Mother started on cod liver oil for us," Margie Blanford said. "I don't know what happened to vitamin supplements at the time, but I wish they had discovered them sooner... We lived on oatmeal, milk, bread, cod liver oil."[205]

Even in old age, other former Cabbage Patch children never stopped thinking they tasted cod liver oil when they drank perfectly good fruit juice like they had used to wash down the cod liver oil forced on them in response to Miss Marshall's dictum.

Mothers listened to Miss Marshall because of the quiet strength she radiated and her readiness to listen to them. Margie Blanford recalled trying to blend into the background so she could eavesdrop when her mother and Miss Marshall talked. Every so often Miss Marshall would reach out to touch or pat her mother. "It's going to be all right," she would say. Or perhaps, "Don't you think you could do this, or how about doing so and so." The scene was repeated to stressed women in barren kitchens all over the Patch. "The Lord only knows how many people she touched," Margie Blanford said.[206]

---

205. Margie Blanford, interview by Andrew Chancey, September 24, 1987, CPSOHP, CPSHR, FHS.

206. Margie Blanford, interview by Andrew Chancey, September 24, 1987. CPSOHP, CPSHR, FHS.

Miss Marshall believed in visiting people at home, visits that took her to back rooms and stables and filthy hovels of all kinds. Just when she thought nothing could surprise her, one of those home visits would. That's what happened when she went to visit a man who had come to the settlement with a modest request for help finding work. He had had a good job, a wife, three children, and no idea that he would even have to ask anyone for help. Miss Marshall found the family living in two small rooms in the back of a cottage. The wife had run the family into debt, then left her husband and children for another man. Her youngest child was five. The woman's young daughter, an honor student who had won second place in the school spelling competition, had stepped into her mother's place. In the three years that he had been unemployed, the man had sold all the family's furniture to buy food. All that remained was a bed, couch, and stove. The family used wooden boxes for chairs. In one corner, four paper cartons, one for each member of the family, held all the clothing they had left, carefully washed, ironed, and folded by the girl.

"Everything looked neat as a pin and spoke of better days long ago," Miss Marshall wrote. No one had suspected that the family was destitute. "The pathos of it all gripped me," she wrote. It didn't help that the five-year-old silently clung to Miss Marshall's coat. She promised to be his friend always. The vision of "hungry children silently pleading for bread" haunted Miss Marshall. She pleaded with her supporters to send the money she needed to help.[207]

---

207. Louise Marshall, "A Little Child's Cry," CPSH fund-raising letter, July 1938, CPSHR, FHS.

For Miss Marshall, the hard times were going to get only harder—at home and at the Cabbage Patch. On July 1, 1932, a Friday morning, Burwell Marshall Sr. died. He was 75 and had been in declining health for some months, the *Courier-Journal* said. A week later, the newspaper reported that Marshall had left an estate of $100,000 to be divided among his five children, with his son Burwell Jr., by now a lawyer, as executor and heir to the Marshall law books and office.[208] The inheritance would prove to be a mixed blessing for his children, but the will spoke eloquently about Burwell Marshall Sr.

Marshall wrote the will in February 1926 with a nontraditional opening, "IN THE NAME OF GOD, AMEN." Then, for the next five years, he added codicils to balance fairness and practicality. Clearly, he wanted to support Louise. He left her $10,000 in bonds that were to be distributed among his other children when she married or died. But Marshall's love and character showed most clearly in his provisions for his wayward oldest son Richard, Richard's wife, Helen, and their four children, including twins named for Burwell and Lizzie Marshall.

Age and family responsibilities had done little to improve Richard's record for reliability from the day he stormed out of his father's house. However, the intervening years had made his father wiser. Another father might have cut his son off without a dime. Marshall placed Richard's share of the inheritance in a trust fund, administered by Louisville

---

208. "B. K. Marshall Funeral Today," *Louisville (KY) Courier-Journal*, July 2, 1932; "Marshall Estate $100,000," *Louisville (KY) Courier-Journal*, July 8, 1932.

bankers, to benefit Richard, Helen, and their children. The trust included a house Marshall had purchased for Richard's family in Kirkwood, Missouri, apparently to provide the family with more security than Richard's work as a wandering soap salesman offered.

Burwell's concern for the family didn't end there, despite Richard's bad behavior. After Burwell wrote the original will, Richard left his wife and children for another woman and went to live in the St. Louis area. It was the sort of action that must have hurt his father deeply. As a moral issue, Burwell Marshall emphatically did not believe in divorce. Marshall changed his will to provide for Helen and the children, whether she was married to Richard or not.[209] During the coming Depression, that would provide Helen Marshall with a small, steady income and money for the children's medical expenses.[210]

The will hardly suggested Marshall's full legacy to Louise. He had, of course, been a good friend to the Cabbage Patch, quietly supporting it with money, legal services, advice, and male gravitas since the very beginning. The "meanest man in town" was arguably the one who had made the Cabbage Patch, an adolescent girl's crazy idea, work. His other final bequests were a more mixed blessing. Louise inherited a one-fifth share of the family home. With her father's death, his harsher personality traits—a tendency to combativeness, his controlling nature, and his penchant for austerity—seemed

---

209. Burwell K. Marshall Sr., last will and testament, filed with Jefferson County (Kentucky) Circuit Court Clerk, July 7, 1932.

210. Periodic Settlement of Accounts of Lincoln Bank and Trust Company, Trustee for Richard and Helen Marshall, October 23, 1934, Jefferson County (Kentucky) Circuit Court Clerk.

to take hold of her with a new vigor. Burwell also left his daughter with a friend whose impact on her life and fortune would be positive and substantial, Adella E. Latta.

Burwell Marshall had represented Mrs. Latta in one of the sensational cases growing out of the bank failures that triggered Louisville's Depression. The widow of an investor, Mrs. Latta became owner of Wakefield & Co., a stock and bond brokerage, and she became a pioneering female stockbroker. As the Depression closed in, Mrs. Latta was caught up in the court proceedings surrounding BancoKentucky Company's president, James B. Brown, who was at the center of the banks' collapse. It was a complicated case and involved towering sums of money that had gone through Mrs. Latta's company. Mrs. Latta cooperated with the investigation and she was eventually cleared of all wrongdoing.[211] She was free to be Louise's friend and, for many years, the investment advisor who handled Cabbage Patch's limited securities and the investments that made Louise Marshall rich.[212] (Miss Marshall never accepted any salary for her work at the Cabbage Patch.) Mrs. Latta was also the only person trusted by both Louise and her brother Burwell. That was important because not long after their father died, Louise and Burwell stopped speaking to each other. The silence would last for the rest of their lives.

Burwell Marshall Jr. never explained what happened, not even to his own son, but the dispute between Burwell and Louise certainly flared over the house where they had grown up. In his role as executor, Burwell Jr. asked a real estate

---

211. *Louisville (KY) Courier-Journal's* coverage of the "Banco Case," 1931–1934.

212. Staff reports to the CPSH Board of Directors, June 16, 1975, CPSHR, FHS.

agent and fellow Presbyterian, Bruce Hoblitzell, to help determine what should be done with the house. Hoblitzell polled the five siblings. Everyone but Louise seemed willing to do whatever everyone else wanted. Louise said the best thing for everyone would be to sell the property at auction immediately. Hoblitzell met with an auctioneer who said that, in the middle of the Depression, the property wasn't likely to bring much.[213]

What happened next is not entirely clear. Burwell and Louise apparently bought their siblings' shares of the house. Louise decided to turn it into apartments and to oversee the work herself. Burwell was to pay workers out of an account the two had established. Then, for three years, they exchanged letters that are remarkable for their failure to communicate and for their rising frustration and, eventually, bitterness. In the beginning, for example, Burwell would write what seemed a benign question about whether a worker should be paid in full. Louise's reply would be a defensive, even pugnacious, suggestion that he was being critical. Burwell, who was trying to run his own law practice, found himself engulfed in disputes between Louise and the workers. He and Louise seemed unable to understand anything they tried to communicate. Burwell preferred talking to Mrs. Latta.

In February 1935, Burwell wrote a conciliatory letter that began, "My dear Louise, I am sorry to hurt you in any way . . . I have always tried to be more than fair with my three sisters and brother's estate in spite of the fact that they have

---

213. Bruce Hoblitzell Sr., letter to Mrs. Nicholas Dosker, Mr. Burwell K. Marshall, Miss Louise Marshall, Mrs. Lewis Y. Johnson, Mr. Richard V. Marshall, December 22, 1935, CPSHR, FHS.

not always given me credit for trying to do so." Burwell went on to explain what he had done and concluded the letter, "Affectionately yours."[214]

Louise exploded. "My dear Burwell," she wrote, "'Affectionately yours' are surprising words coming from you after these 8 unhappy months." Louise rehashed old issues, then wrote a paragraph that clearly hurt Burwell deeply. "I am realizing more and more that you are not to blame for always wanting your own way." She recalled his childhood struggle with polio. "You were a sick little boy who suffered so terribly yet so courageously and how we all loved you so and longed so to relieve your pain that we all gave into you." It was no wonder, she said, that Burwell still expected to have things his way. The letter went on for two painful pages before it ended, "God bless you and make you happy."[215] Burwell didn't read that part. His reply said he'd stopped after the first two paragraphs.[216]

Soon after, the bank account for work on the house ran dry, and Burwell told Mrs. Latta again that he wanted, finally, to either buy out Louise's share of the property or to sell her his. He said he would accept "exactly $1,000 less than I have invested," if Louise wanted to buy the house. In a letter that began, "My dear Louise," Burwell set a deadline for a

---

214. Burwell K. Marshall to Louise Marshall, February 26, 1935, CPSHSR, FHS.

215. Louise Marshall to Burwell K. Marshall, February 28, 1935, CPSHR, FHS.

216. Burwell K. Marshall to Louise Marshall, February 28, 1935, CPSHR, FHS

decision.[217] Of course, Louise didn't make a decision by the deadline. The disputes over details of the house went on for years, building bitterness and sorrow.

The dispute with Burwell is telling and presaged other disputes Louise would have in years ahead—with tradesmen, Louisville city officials, Presbyterian churchmen, contractors for the Cabbage Patch, and Cabbage Patch employees. In the correspondence that survives, Louise rarely acknowledged that she had made a mistake or gave credence to someone else's complaint or criticism. More often, she responded to criticism with new and sometimes startling complaints of her own. Giving ground under fire was not in her genetic makeup.

Bertha Weikel knew and understood that side of Louise Marshall as well as anyone. Mrs. Weikel not only ran the Cabbage Patch employment bureau; she was also Miss Marshall's "general flunky" and assistant through 10 of the Depression years. There was no doubt in Mrs. Weikel's mind about where Miss Marshall got her sterner qualities: Burwell K. Marshall Sr.

"Oh, I won't forget him," she said many years later. "He was the meanest man alive . . . He was mean to his children . . . There is many a person that is strict that is not mean. I think he was mean."[218]

Somehow, Mrs. Weikel was able to get along with Miss Marshall when a long line of other staff members could not, although the tensions took their toll. Often the people Miss Marshall hired had strong credentials and worked very well

217. Burwell K. Marshall to Louise Marshall, April 13, 1936, CPSHR, FHS.

218. Bertha Weikel, interview by Andrew Chancey, October 1, 1987, CPSOHP, CPSHR, FHS.

with the children, but the real test was whether they would do exactly what Miss Marshall wanted.

"None of them lasted very long," Mrs. Weikel said. "Before they left, they got a dozen red roses from Miss Marshall. Whenever you got a dozen red roses from Miss Marshall, you knew you were going to get fired."[219]

Miss Marshall's work habits were also becoming both odd and irritating to her staff. She would come into the office and work for two or three hours in the morning, then leave and return just before five p.m.—when Mrs. Weikel was scheduled to leave. She would keep Mrs. Weikel working with her until six or six thirty "until I got tired of it," Mrs. Weikel said in an interview. "At five, I closed up my desk and said, 'I am leaving.'" Somehow, Mrs. Weikel could get away with that. Others could not. Or, with work in short supply, they could not afford to quit.

Frances Dover lived and worked at the Cabbage Patch as the resident director in the late 1930s and, for a time, her husband, William, was a coach for the boys. Mrs. Dover started work at nine a.m., and, when she was ready for a supper break with her family before the settlement's evening activities began, Miss Marshall would arrive and want something done immediately. "She worked. She worked," Mrs. Dover said. But Miss Marshall worked on her own schedule and expected her staff to be ready to help.

"Every time I crossed the street, I wished a car would hit me!" Mrs. Dover said. "That was the only way I saw of getting out."

---

219. Bertha M. Weikel, interview by Andrew Chancey, October 1, 1987, CPSOHP, CPSHR, FHS.

Finally, as the Depression eased, the Dovers bought a house and, without telling Miss Marshall in advance, Frances Dover told the board she was resigning. "They were a little distressed."[220]

Indeed the board was distressed. At that same special meeting, called October 23, 1940, (which Miss Marshall did not attend), Louise Marshall and Bertha Weikel also resigned. The board promptly and unanimously rejected Miss Marshall's resignation and begged Mrs. Dover and Mrs. Weikel to reconsider or, at least, to stay temporarily "until matters in questions could be readjusted." Mrs. Dover left.[221] Mrs. Weikel stayed until 1942, when she left because the doctor said she could never get pregnant amid the tensions at the Cabbage Patch. (Her baby was born one year after she left.)[222]

Not everyone knew that during many of the hours when she wasn't at the Cabbage Patch office, Miss Marshall was renovating the Ormsby house, using several workers from the Cabbage Patch. She paid them the going employment bureau rate, plus 50 cents for a good lunch, and taught them new skills.

"She would hire me to go up there and paint," said Escue Tomerlin. "I didn't know one paint from another, but she taught me." Miss Marshall taught him the difference between enamel and semi-gloss, between finishing enamel and undercoat, and how to care for the equipment.

220. Frances Dover, interview by Keith Cardwell, March 7, 1987, CPSOHP, CPSHR, FHS.

221. Minutes, CPSH Board of Directors, October 23, 1940, CPSHR, FHS.

222. Bertha M. Weikel, interview by Andrew Chancey, October 1, 1987, CPSOHP, CPSHR, FHS.

"Keep your paint brushes clean, Tomerlin!" she would command. House painting clearly wasn't part of a Victorian girl's education, but Miss Marshall learned to do it so she could teach. "If I don't know how to do something, I ask someone who does," she once said.[223]

As she worked beside the men, Miss Marshall taught Escue Tomerlin about more than paint. "She'd always say, 'Save, save enough. I want you to buy a home. If you're not able, I'll make you able." Tomerlin worked hard, at two or three jobs when work was available. When he was ready to buy a house, Miss Marshall helped find one and walked the Tomerlins through the whole confusing web of real estate agents and financing. Tomerlin and his sons painted their new house themselves. "Sometimes you're afraid to take that first step," he said, "but she gave us the courage to do it."[224]

As Louise worked on converting the house where she had always lived into apartments, her alternate living arrangements became increasingly odd—even alarming—to her family.

"Anybody that knows Aunt Louise knew that she had an unusual schedule," said Elizabeth Dosker Chambers, Sallie Ewing's daughter. As a young teenager, Elizabeth was willing to bend to Aunt Louise's schedule. The two were close, and Elizabeth often spent time with her Aunt Louise at the Cabbage Patch—but not without tucking an apple

---

223. Escue and Geneva Tomerlin, interview by Carolyn Kline, April 2, 1987, CPSOHP, CPSHR, FHS; Eleanor Leuenberger, PI, January 9, 2015.

224. Escue and Geneva Tomerlin, interview by Carolyn Kline, April 2, 1987, CPSOHP, CPSHR, FHS.

into her suitcase so she wouldn't go hungry before the next meal came. Elizabeth would sit quietly with a book while her Aunt Louise dealt with business. When the telephone rang, it would often provide Miss Marshall with an opportunity to talk to a potential donor about something the settlement or its clients needed, perhaps a load of coal or blankets. After such conversations, the coal or blankets would arrive the next day, Elizabeth said. Often Elizabeth got to meet the people she heard about. She would help line up the nursery school children for their walk to Central Park to play and helped serve them the lunches that kept them from starvation. She vividly remembered the mothers who couldn't afford to buy milk for their children. "They'd have a baby and a three- or-four-year-old, nursing them both." The mothers were thin, subsisting on cabbages and potatoes, sometimes in dirt-floored carriage houses where people with no furniture lived on the ground. "They were hovels," said Elizabeth.[225]

At the end of a very long day, Louise would switch worlds and take Elizabeth to a downtown cafeteria, such as the popular Miller's or Blue Boar, at the last possible minute before the eatery closed.

"We would be always the last to walk in," said Elizabeth, "and they'd be doing the dishes when we left." On those occasions, Elizabeth was allowed to get anything she wanted to eat. "She was very generous to me," Elizabeth said.

After dinner, the two would switch worlds again and return to the settlement house to sleep there rolled in old Army blankets without sheets on cots in a room illuminated

---

225. Elizabeth Dosker Chambers, interview by Mrs. William Harvin, March 19, 1987, CPSOHP, CPSHR, FHS.

by a bare electric bulb hung from the ceiling. Miss Marshall kept a toothbrush and nightgown in her overly large purse. Her coat served her as a robe and her shoes as slippers. She washed whatever needed washing in a sink. She had a navy dress for summer, a black dress for winter.

"She wasn't spending any money she didn't have in her purse," Elizabeth said. "If she did, she'd spend it in her mind 10 times before it left her purse." That was Aunt Louise's way of making sure she got her money's worth. Before they slept, Miss Marshall would always walk through the settlement, with her big key ring, making sure all the settlement's many doors were locked, a prudent step in that neighborhood and time.[226] Hungry people were turning to crime.

In January 1937, as the Cabbage Patch's people stretched the last scraps of food and coal from their Christmas baskets, rain began to fall on Louisville's frozen ground and simply would not stop. It caused a disaster still respectfully called the 1937 Flood, a time when danger and disease threatened people already beset by unrelenting misery. The cold water rose until its pressure in the sewers sent manhole covers sailing into the air and washed sewage, industrial waste, and dead animals down streets and into houses across the city. Slightly higher islands like the Cabbage Patch were the only refuge for more than 75,000 refugees. The settlement house had water in the basement, and it was completely surrounded by the flood. Wave after wave of people rescued from their homes in western Louisville spent the night on cots in the Cabbage Patch gym, ate a meal and waited for military trucks to take

---

226. Elizabeth Dosker Chambers, interview by Mrs. William Harvin, March 19, 1987, CPSOHP, CPSHR, FHS.

them to high ground to the east. Alice Hegan Rice reported that the settlement "fed and bedded 147 in the gymnasium until the furnace pipes broke," but the crisis did not end then. "Wheweeeee," said Mrs. Weikel. "I didn't leave that place for a week and a half. I never had my clothes off."[227]

When the refugees from the flood stopped coming, the Cabbage Patch gym housed Pennsylvania police officers sent to keep order. Then the Red Cross sent workers from places like California to process claims for flood damage, often unknowingly and maddeningly giving benefits to people who filed bogus claims for houses untouched by the flood. When the water and the flood of strangers receded, both the Cabbage Patch buildings and its staff were worn out.

The Cabbage Patch's leaders had started the decade with wonderful new quarters and the hope that the settlement's programs could make a difference for countless children. They staggered to the end of the decade, sinking ever deeper into debt with both the building and its workers ready to crumble. As 300 children crowded in for vacation Bible school in June 1937, the flood's legacy to the settlement house became increasingly apparent. Seven times after the flood, heavy rains had made the basement "a perfect swamp of filth" as the sewer backed up through the washbasins and toilets. As the swamp drained, the stinking remainder had to be shoveled into buckets and carried to street-level garbage cans. The dampness remained for a long time, Miss Marshall wrote, an invitation to termites that were ravaging

227. Alice Hegan Rice, *The Inky Way* (New York: D. Appleton-Century, 1940), 258; Bertha M. Weikel, interview by Andrew Chancey, October 1, 1987, CPSOHP, CPSHR, FHS.

the buildings' underpinnings. A leak in the new gym roof also puddled, then rotted the floor. Repairs were likely to cost $2,500.[228]

Still, the community needed help as much as ever. A 1939 fund-raising letter noted that Cabbage Patch workers visiting in homes found that "most of the families are just existing, heroically holding on until times are better, until the factories open, until 'Pop' and the boys can get back to work."[229] The Cabbage Patch Settlement kept struggling to help, although Miss Marshall admitted that she sometimes felt as if her ship was sinking under the unrelenting demands and growing debt.

"Some of our friends are telling us how exhausted we look and are urging us to go away and rest awhile," she wrote. "We are exhausted, [but] we cannot go. We will not go, until the ship is saved."

Miss Marshall rarely wrote about being happy, and the end of the 1930s seems like an unlikely time for her to do that. But, as an exhausted captain standing at the bow of her beleaguered ship, that's what she did. For one thing, her life's ambition—to live in a way that showed non-believers God's love—was bringing results; people were turning to religion. Giving oneself took a toll but brought a reward, she wrote. "Oh! the joy unspeakable that we are getting in exchange. One of our workers said it was impossible to remain at the Cabbage Patch for any length of time and not be happy."[230]

---

228. Louise Marshall, "The Bee Hive?" CPSH fund-raising letter, July 1937, CPSHR, FHS.

229. Eleanor Starks, CPSH fund-raising letter, 1939, CPSHR, FHS.

230. Louise Marshall, "Sinking?" CPSH undated fund-raising letter (probably 1939), CPSHR, FHS.

Miss Marshall may have been happy, but she could not rest. She had new challenges ahead.

CHAPTER 9

ANOTHER WAR AND A MAN TO SAVE THE BOYS

Like the rest of the country, the Cabbage Patch Settlement suffered through World War II, doing what it could to support both the war effort at home and to dig out of the Depression that somehow never seemed to leave the Patch. Although there was hardship enough to go around, the war years seemed to hit the Cabbage Patch's boys the hardest. With the best of the nation's young men off at war, the boys found more than the usual opportunity to get into trouble, often serious trouble, that Louise Marshall seemed powerless to stop.

After the war, as an aging Miss Marshall struggled with boys and money problems, nothing hinted that the settlement was about to move into its glory days when the city would marvel at its programs for boys. Certainly, no one saw good times coming when Miss Marshall closed down the boys' programs, just when the boys needed them the most. And no one would have guessed that an ordinary teen dance would foretell great things. Miss Marshall prayed for blessings, however, and she never doubted that God would provide— even when things looked darkest for her beloved boys.

Miss Marshall hadn't wanted to close the settlement's program for boys, but she had to do it. She wasn't about to stand for their fights and vandalism. She ordered the boys out of the settlement and discontinued the popular teen dances. Some people said it was because she didn't have men to provide leadership and keep order, but that's wrong. Plenty of men were willing to help. Miss Marshall didn't have the right man.

For weeks while the settlement was closed to them, the boys hung out in Central Park, wishing they could return to the Patch. Miss Marshall saw them there, and grieved and prayed. When the answer to her prayers arrived, no one was more excited than Miss Marshall, who honked her car horn to announce that boys were welcome back. Soon after, when she scheduled the first teen dance in a long time, everyone knew it was a test of whether the Patch could have a dance without a fight that would close things down again. Some people didn't think a peaceful dance was possible. Some people planned to make sure a peaceful dance didn't happen.

The Cabbage Patch's teens gathered for that Friday night dance with enough excitement and tension to lure 12-year-old Joe Burks (too young to go to the dance) to watch from the street. He didn't have long to wait for excitement. A car bearing three young toughs, spoiling for a fight, pulled up Sixth Street and stopped in front of the settlement. The thugs pulled on black gloves as they headed back to the gym's alley door.

"Oh, no! Here we go!" said Joe. Trouble was coming.

Sure enough, Joe heard scuffling inside. Then the toughs reemerged, propelled by two enormous University of Louisville football players. One of the players had one of the thugs in a headlock under one arm; the big man's other arm held another troublemaker in a vice grip, and the third tough was in the equally tender care of the other big man, a football center, (Joe reckoned him to be about six feet, five inches tall and 275 pounds).

Police arrived and packed the uninvited guests off to the police station. One of the big men—Joe came to know him as Lloyd "Pappy" Redman—waited for 10 or 15 minutes. Then he got into his car, drove to the police station, and had the troublemakers released so he could bring them back to the settlement for a conversation. That was the end of the trouble.[231] The Cabbage Patch had finally found the answer to its problem with bad boys: The right man using Miss Marshall's mix of love and discipline.

As usual with difficult Cabbage Patch problems, that solution had come slowly and painfully with many false starts. For all 36 years of the settlement's history, boys had posed special challenges—ever since the early days when young Miss Marshall had offered apples to the boys who threw rocks at her. But as the 1930s eased into the pre-war years, the problem had gotten ever more serious. Boys formed gangs that broke the law, burglarized homes, destroyed property— and disrupted the settlement's activities—for fun. Too many of the boys wound up in jail—beyond the settlement's ability to help them very much.

Part of the problem was numbers; the settlement's annual attendance had soared past 70,000, but everyone acknowledged that the program was not offering enough to counter the temptations boys faced. One estimate suggested

---

231. Joseph Burks Sr., PI, July 8, 2011.

that 500 boys needed the constructive activities and "highest ideals" that the Cabbage Patch offered. By the late 1940s, the number of boys who needed the Patch would grow to more than 600.[232] That count did not include the growing numbers of black children whom the settlement did not serve in an era when both custom and law separated the races.

Another part of the boy problem grew from the changing nature of the neighborhood itself. In the 1920s, the L & N Railroad, which employed many of the neighborhood's men, finished moving its operations out of the railroad shops bordering the Cabbage Patch. Its workforce followed their work to the new location. The huge, sprawling industries that replaced the railroad covered the old truck gardens planted by the upwardly striving immigrant families who initially settled in the Patch. The new industries employed thousands of low-wage workers when business was good and laid them off in hard times. The Depression left more big families with one parent, little income, and no one to look after the children. More and more of St. James Court's grand houses had become seedy apartment buildings. In some cities, settlement houses responded to such problems by moving to the suburbs with their neighbors. The Cabbage Patch Settlement did not. The Cabbage Patch neighborhood still needed what the settlement offered.

As close-knit neighborhoods with shared values collapsed, crime became a part of some families' cultures. Too many boys sat at home listening to fathers and brothers talking about life in jail. Too few men provided good role models. The Cabbage Patch fund-raising newsletter complained

---

232. Cabbage Patch Settlement fund-raising letters, 1939–1944, CPSHR, FHS.

again and again that boys were going to prison for want of the wholesome, character-building programs the settlement wanted to provide—if only it had enough money and manpower. The Cabbage Patch wasn't alone. Juvenile delinquency was soaring across the country, on its way to becoming what some called the "defining social issue of the decade" in the 1950s. According to some scholars, settlement houses had gone "into a tailspin during World War II," just when communities' children needed them.[233]

Beginning in 1930, the Optimist Club, founded as an international men's organization to serve and instill values in youth, had helped the Cabbage Patch Settlement with some of the boys. The men provided mentoring, clothing, and school supplies, first for one boy and eventually for 25 boys selected by Miss Marshall. In 1939, the Optimists purchased a house next to the Cabbage Patch to serve 550 boys with activities, including a game room to be open six nights a week with a supervisor paid by the Optimists. For a while, that helped. However, fostering partnerships with other organizations was never among Miss Marshall's strengths. Conflicts developed over her belief that the Optimists were undermining Cabbage Patch ideals by giving the boys things they hadn't worked for or earned through good behavior. The underlying issue seems to have been control of the boys' program that the Optimists had fostered and paid for.[234]

---

233. Fabricant and Fisher, *Settlement Houses under Siege*, 47, 52.

234. Louise Marshall to John Hession, October 26, 1942; to Optimist Club, February 12, 1943; and to My dear Fellow Board Members, February 26, 1943, CPSHR, FHS; "Optimist Club Plans Game Room for 550 Boys of Cabbage Patch," *Louisville (KY) Times,* November 24,1939.

Miss Marshall launched a flood of correspondence that followed the usual escalating pattern of her disputes. Since beginning their "unholy alliance" with the settlement, the Optimist Club members had undermined and destroyed the good the settlement was doing with the boys, she reported to the Cabbage Patch Board in February 1943. The club's "influence is so insidious and so far reaching" that the considerable amount of money they had given couldn't compensate for the harm they were doing, she contended.[235] Miss Marshall's letters to the Optimists attacked their character, intentions, and actions, but because Louise had her mother's Veech ethic that always demanded courtesy, she generally ended such letters pleasantly. After four pages of blistering accusations, Miss Marshall closed one letter, "I thank you for your many kindnesses for which I am eternally grateful."[236]

Finally, in 1943, the Cabbage Patch board sent the Optimists a letter "accepting their withdrawal from the Boys work at the Cabbage Patch."[237] A year later, the Cabbage Patch board purchased the Optimists' cottage, thus expanding the settlement's space on Sixth Street. The Optimists moved their work with boys to a sparkling new building that was theirs alone in another neighborhood. In keeping with her practice with fired employees, Miss Marshall sent roses when the Highland Park Optimists opened their new clubhouse in 1946. The Optimists, who

---

235. Louise Marshall to CPSH Board of Directors, February 26, 1943, CPSHR, FHS.

236. Louise Marshall to Optimist Club, February 12, 1943, CPSHR, FHS.

237. Minutes, CPSH Board of Directors, March 8, 1943, CPSHR, FHS.

wouldn't have understood the irony, responded that the roses were "very much appreciated."[238]

Conflict with the Optimists coincided with the galaxy of problems World War II brought to the Cabbage Patch. Miss Marshall believed that men bound for war left their families in the settlement's care. Crowds of war workers also jammed into the neighborhood's always-inadequate housing, bringing many children and "greater insecurity, less stability and more irresponsibility," the settlement's fund-raising letter reported. Entire families lived in single rooms where some parents left their children alone during the day. According to the fund-raising newsletter, too often, child care was provided by "some inefficient, careless" girl who had been thrown out of school because she had head lice.[239] Soldiers who found themselves in Louisville on a weekend wandered through town lonely, depressed, often drunk, and without a place to stay. Miss Marshall saw all those people as victims of a terrible war. Money and manpower were scarcer than ever, but she was determined that the Cabbage Patch would serve them all. Her motto was "whatever the need," the Cabbage Patch would try to meet it.[240] With so many divergent problems coming together, that was a tall order.

Miss Marshall had seen what war did to young men during World War I, and her heart went out to the often very young soldiers she encountered as the United States plunged

---

238. Minutes, CPSH House Board of Directors, February 7, 1946, CPSHR, FHS.

239. "Victims of War!" CPSH fund-raising letter, October 1943, CPSHR, FHS.

240. Margaret Pleune Harvin (Mrs. William), interview by Keith Cardwell, February 20, 1987, CPSOHP, CPSHR, FHS.

into World War II. In 1942, the Cabbage Patch put up cots in the gym for 120 servicemen every Saturday night. By October 1943, 9,274 servicemen had spent the night there. The staff squeezed cots into the gym for 200 men but often admitted even more soldiers who needed a place to stay.[241] The vilified Optimists supplied 60 of the cots; Cabbage Patch friends provided the rest. Even with volunteer help, the Cabbage Patch staff groaned under the job of making up all those cots every week, finding blankets for them all, and storing the bedding again when the soldiers had gone. The gym had to be ready for children to use on Monday.

The service to soldiers was not without problems—some of which Miss Marshall pinned directly on the Optimists and their paid boys worker, a hapless seminary student she referred to as Mr. Grant. Mr. Grant allowed some of the teenage boys from the game room to show soldiers—drunk and sober— to their cots, she charged. And, when Grant failed to pay attention (she conceded that he might have been running a Scout meeting), boys also took to climbing onto the roof of the shower room. There the boys jammed shoes and cans into the downpipe from the gutter, leaving storm water to flood the shower room and toilet area below. Soldiers had to wade through puddles in order to use the necessaries.[242]

Come Sunday mornings, churchwomen rallied to serve the servicemen breakfasts that ranged from donated sweet rolls and coffee to real breakfasts financed by contributions from businesses. On March 12, 1944, for example, the men

241. Cabbage Patch Settlement fund-raising letter, October 1943, CPSHR, FHS.

242. Louise Marshall to Optimist Club, February 12, 1943, CPSHR, FHS.

in uniform awoke to the smell of 14 pounds of bacon and 19 dozen eggs, served with butter, milk, tomato juice, and six pounds of honey.[243] The ladies and their breakfasts brought the soldiers great joy, Miss Marshall wrote.

In 1942, Miss Marshall decided that she had to combat a notion that the Cabbage Patch had ceased its good work and turned its facilities over to the Optimist Club to provide a social center for soldiers.

"This is not the case at all," she wrote in a letter to the editor of the *Courier-Journal*. The Optimists had "nothing whatsoever to do" with management of the Cabbage Patch, she wrote. Indeed, the settlement still offered more than 50 activities a week, and the services to soldiers represented only a small part of its work.[244] Still, during the war years, the Patch's boys suffered. The boys needed men, and the men were off at war. The people who later attributed the boys' problems to the war were at least partly right—but there was more to the story.

In "the swing from war to peace" in the fall of 1945, the Cabbage Patch joyfully hired five new part-time boys workers, all seminary students, to supplement the solitary longtime employee who had served the boys during the war. Miss Marshall was confident that they would provide "the highest caliber" leadership necessary to teach boys to "obey the laws of God and man."[245]

---

243. Unsigned letter to R. T. Seay, March 20, 1944, CPSHR, FHS.

244. Louise Marshall, "To the Editor of the *Courier Journal*," September 29, 1942, CPSHR, FHS.

245. Louise Marshall, "From Childhood to the Death Cell," CPSH fund-raising letter, October 1944, and "Moving at Full Speed," October 1945, CPSHR, FHS.

Her faith in the seminary students was misplaced.

"They were good guys and all that, but they didn't know how to handle the type of kids of the area," said Joe Burks, the boy who had lived near the settlement. Burks suspected that the students were well tutored in religion but not in dealing with street-tough boys. The boys took pleasure in turning off the lights in the game room while they tore the place up. When the lights came back on, the seminarians wouldn't know who had taken the pool balls or done damage that the Cabbage Patch couldn't afford to repair. The "preachers" didn't last.

"They weren't very tough," said Burks. "The kids chased them out." Miss Marshall quickly got tired of that. She closed the programs for boys. It grieved her to do it, but she wasn't about to let the boys get by with that kind of behavior.[246] The boys returned to the street and to Central Park and to the probability that they would get into more serious trouble.

In November 1946, Miss Marshall asked the Cabbage Patch board members to join her from eight thirty to nine each morning to pray "for divine guidance in choosing a consecrated person for our work."[247]

The answer to her prayers was 23-year-old Lloyd Redman, a self-described "big old, over-grown country boy" who served as a chief petty officer in the Navy during the war. He came home to play center for the University of Louisville's

---

246. Joseph Burks Sr., interview by Keith Cardwell, January 31, 1987, CPSOHP, CPSHR, FHS; Joseph Burks Sr., PI, July 2011.

247. Minutes, CPSH Board of Directors, November 4, 1946, CPSHR, FHS.

"War-studded Eleven," veterans who carried their fighting spirit onto the football field. U of L's 1946 football roster listed Redman as six feet tall and 205 pounds, but when boys like Joe Burks looked up at him that night at the dance and for years after, they saw a near giant. Lloyd Redman was not about to put up with trouble from Cabbage Patch boys, not at the dances and not anywhere else.[248]

Miss Marshall was thrilled. Joe Burks heard the news as he walked down the street and someone attracted his attention by blowing a car horn. It was Miss Marshall. "We're going to open the Patch. We're going to open it back up," she said. "I've hired a guy who is a football player at UL, and he's going to see if he can't get things straightened out." Miss Marshall blew her horn all over the neighborhood, telling every boy she could find the good news.

On Redman's first day, the boys were all on the steps of the Patch waiting when Redman drove up. "Okay, guys," Redman said. "You all can come in if you act right. If you don't act right, you're going out that door faster than you came in."[249]

"Who you?" a 14-year-old Italian kid asked.

"I'm the new boys worker," said Redman.

"Huh," said the kid. "We'll run your ass off next week."

As the rest of the boys watched, Redman walked over, grabbed the kid's jacket, and pulled the kid up to him.

"Buster," he said, "you ain't running my ass off."

Both Redman and the boy stayed at the Patch. The boy, Mike Defazio, played guard on the football teams Redman

248. Football game program, University of Louisville vs. Georgetown, October 25, 1946, University of Louisville Archives.

249. Joseph Burks Sr., PI, July 8, 2011.

started. "He'd have died for the Cabbage Patch," Redman said much later. "He'd have died."[250]

"Lloyd, he turned out to be a real good fella," Defazio said many years later. "He kept a lot of kids out of the penitentiary."[251]

Redman believed that even tough kids like Defazio were pretty much like everyone else. "They can be reached."[252] Redman and Miss Marshall agreed on that. Neither the churches nor the schools were reaching what Redman called the "borderline kids," kids like Defazio and Joe Burks, who could "go either way." To reach them, Miss Marshall and Redman believed, the settlement needed programs, from woodworking to football, that would make every kid want to come to the Patch. Maneuvering around his school classes and university football practice schedules, Redman went to work building programs for the boys. He asked the Cabbage Patch Circle to give him $500 to start a football program, and he bought good helmets. Then he went to the city's public and Catholic high schools to beg the other equipment he needed to start football and basketball programs that would become legendary. Soon the city's high schools begin jockeying to get players trained at the Cabbage Patch.

250. Lloyd Redman, interview by Keith Cardwell, February 12, 1987, CPSOHP, CPSHR, FHS.

251. Michael Defazio, oral history interview by Sasha Caufield, March 17, 2008, University of Louisville Department of History project, University of Louisville Archives and Special Collections. Defazio and Redman became lifelong friends. Even after Redman retired and had a stroke, Defazio visited him at home once a month.

252. Lloyd Redman, interview by Keith Cardwell, February 12, 1987, CPSOHP, CPSHR, FHS.

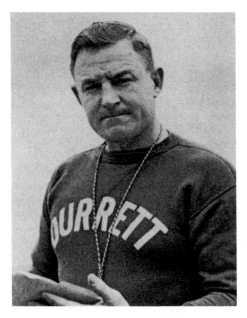

After serving in the navy during World War II, Lloyd Redman returned to the University of Louisville, where he played football, earned Bachelor of Science and master's degrees, and worked as the boys worker at the Cabbage Patch Settlement. Later "Pappy" Redman, as he was known, became a high school football coach and a respected school administrator. He was named "Jefferson County Football Coach of the Year" in 1959, the year his Durrett High School team won the Jefferson County football championship. *Courtesy of Jefferson County Public Schools Archives and Resource Center*

Finding boys who would become those gifted players wasn't hard. One day, Redman heard someone holler, "Pappy, come to the gym!" When Redman got there, he saw a 13-year-old standing over a 19-year-old who was out cold on the floor. The kid had decked him.

"I knew right then that I had an athlete, and I knew I had a problem," Redman said. After playing for the Patch, the kid, Jimmy Sedbrook, went on to lead both his high school basketball team and his college football team to championships.[253]

Those kinds of results made every boy want to be part of the Cabbage Patch and gave Redman and Miss Marshall the tool they needed to shape character. While the Cabbage Patch peppered all its programs with Bible readings and devotions, the most important teaching often happened when children did something wrong. Bad behavior, even in seemingly small things, wasn't tolerated. Some kids, for example, thought it was fun to take the eight ball off the pool table. Redman would say, "No more pool. We'll close the game room until the eight ball shows up."

"That ball would show up, even if they [the boys] had to chip in and buy one," said Burks. Usually Redman would discover who did it, and "nine times out of 10," it was a kid who was new to the Patch. "That was a chance for Cabbage Patch personnel to work with him and show the kid what he did was wrong," Burks said.[254]

For Cabbage Patch regulars who broke rules, justice was predictable and certain; breaking a rule meant you couldn't come back to the Patch until Miss Marshall or Redman said you could. There were "no beatings, no fussing, no nothing like that—just a simple statement," Margaret "Peg" Harvin, a Cabbage Patch board member, said years later. "It was pitiful to see some of them standing out on the sidewalk, walking up and down, waiting to come back in. Miss Marshall would

---

253. Lloyd Redman, interview by Keith Cardwell, February 12, 1987, CPSOHP, CPSHR, FHS.

254. Joseph Burks Sr., interview by Keith Cardwell, January 31, 1987, CPSOHP, CPSHR, FHS.

always tell them that we still loved them, but they had to do this because it was unfair to everybody else for them to act that way."[255]

"She talked always with love," Peg Harvin said. "That was her big deal. We just love you all . . . They just thought she was wonderful."[256]

Redman, who seemed so old that the boys called him "Pappy," became a revered father figure who taught boys how to live as well as how to play. He called all the boys "son."[257] For an unsportsman-like act, Redman might chew a boy out "up one side and down the other." For a boy who simply wouldn't respond to language, Redman was known to have taken off his belt and hit him—an approach the board probably didn't know of or approve. The boys, however, understood and respected him.[258]

"I was hired to see that peace was kept," Redman told an interviewer later, "and peace was kept!"[259]

The boys problem was in hand, but by 1947, Miss Marshall thought the girls were being "sadly neglected," at a time when money was in such short supply that she wasn't sure that the

---

255. Margaret Pleune Harvin, interview by Keith Cardwell, February 20, 1987, CPSOHP, CPSHR, FHS.

256. Peg Harvin, PI, June 16, 2011.

257. Ruth Tomerlin Chaffins, interview by Carolyn Kline, April 4, 1987, CPSOHP, CPSHR, FHS.

258. Joseph Burks Sr., oral history interview by Chris Petzold, March 2, 2008, University of Louisville Department of History project, University of Louisville Archives and Special Collections.

259. Lloyd Redman, interview by Keith Cardwell, February 12, 1987, CPSOHP, CPSHR, FHS.

settlement would be able to pay its existing staff in October. Some programs, such as the electric woodwork shop, had to be closed for want of money, but ever-increasing numbers of people packed into the Cabbage Patch, a total of 132,928 visits between August 1947 and August 1948 for the library, sports programs, health services, classes, movies in the gym, nursery school, hot showers, game room, field trips, and more.[260] The Cabbage Patch needed more staff, not less. Hiring women to do home visits and to work with girls was at the top of Miss Marshall's wish list. But there simply was no money.

Miss Marshall felt as if she were at a dead end, an image that recurs again and again in her writing. "We feel as if we were in a blind alley, not knowing which way to turn with these heavy expenses and a great desire to serve our young people," she wrote in 1947. There were so many hundreds of "hot, dirty boys and girls," and she wanted to reach all of them.[261]

Miss Marshall had believed in the importance of home visits since her teenage visits to her Sunday school boys. She told her supporters often that a child's bad behavior could usually be explained by a visit to the home. Was it any wonder, she'd write, that a teenage girl who shared a bed with siblings of all ages and suffered abuse and neglect from her parents then got pregnant by the married man who lived across the alley from her home? How could anyone expect a boy whose home was empty of everything but filth and poverty to stay off the streets and out of trouble at night? The staff needed

---

260. Louise Marshall, "The Crowds are coming to the Cabbage Patch Settlement!" CPSH fund-raising letter, October 1948, CPSHR, FHS.

261. Louise Marshall, notebook (possibly drafts for fund-raising letters) dated April 1947, CPSHR, FHS.

that vital information to reach those children, and it could be gotten only by home visits. Miss Marshall felt the need of a home visitor so strongly that she decided to hire a worker and to pay the woman's salary with her own money.[262]

Help for buttressing the girls program came sadly, with the death of Alice Hegan Rice, the writer who had made the Cabbage Patch neighborhood famous and provided the settlement's board with leadership for so long. Alice Rice's leadership and support of the Patch's programs never wavered, even as her international fame allowed her to travel broadly and as she published more books. In addition to her long service as a settlement board member, Mrs. Rice had taught Cabbage Patch classes for women and girls for as long as her health and schedule allowed. Even during the Great Flood of 1937, despite pain from lumbar, sciatic, and heart problems, Alice Rice had gone to the Cabbage Patch to encourage workers who were working around the clock.[263] Although her health continued to fail in the years that followed, Mrs. Rice's ability to tell stories did not. Alice Hegan Rice continued to write newsletters full of stories intended to wring the hearts— and wallets—of settlement supporters almost to the end of her life. Alice Hegan Rice died February 10, 1942, depriving the Cabbage Patch of one of its most devoted friends but prompting an infusion of memorial contributions. The board decided to use the initial round of memorial gifts to improve the settlement's well-used library; that seemed a fitting tribute for a writer. Later, board members decided to honor Mrs.

---

262. Minutes, CPSH Board of Directors, May 1948, CPSHR, FHS.

263. Boewe, *Beyond the Cabbage Patch*, 322.

Rice—and to trade on her popularity—by establishing an endowment to pay a worker for the Cabbage Patch girls Mrs. Rice had so loved.[264]

Miss Marshall once told her good friend and board member Peg Harvin that she especially liked working with boys because of the way they thought; they "weren't devious."[265] But she also had a gift for mentoring girls. She developed an approach that worked for both sexes: When she saw a child with special needs or promise, she hired the youngster to work in the office or to do odd jobs around the settlement. She'd use the contact to teach and encourage young people to stay in school, to aim for excellence, and to work hard. She helped uncounted young people with college expenses. However, there was an important difference in her expectations for boys and girls. She expected the girls to marry. She expected her chosen boys to return to the Patch to help run the settlement, unencumbered by other loyalties. Over the years, that expectation would lead to considerable anguish.

Two of the girls Miss Marshall identified for special attention were Escue Tomerlin's daughters, Dorene and Ruth. Tomerlin had five children when Miss Marshall taught him to scrub, paint, find work, and buy a house during the Depression, and all those children, Dorene and Ruth among them, found their way to Cabbage Patch activities. Dorene was drawn to vacation Bible school, then sewing classes, fast-pitch softball, and basketball. When Dorene was 14, Miss Marshall asked her to work in the office for 50

---

264. Minutes of the CPSH Board of Directors, March 9, 1942; April 24, 1944; January 20, 1947, CPSHR, FHS.

265. Margaret Pleune Harvin, PI, June 16, 2011.

cents an hour answering the phone and updating the three-by-five-inch cards kept to record each child's involvement with the Patch.

Dorene Tomerlin also helped Miss Marshall with the banking. Miss Marshall always wore black gloves for banking and had Dorene count the money "because money was dirty," Dorene Tomerlin Stopher said years later. Then Dorene would fill out the deposit slip, and the two would go to the bank together. On two memorable occasions, Miss Marshall took Dorene out to dinner, a very big deal for a girl from a poor family. For those occasions, Dorene dressed up in the grey-striped suit that she'd made in the sewing class and worried about which fork to use and whether to eat chicken with her fingers or a fork. When she approached high school graduation in need of a real job, Dorene's high school business teacher gave her a letter from a lumber company that needed a secretary. Dorene applied, went for an interview, and got the job. She didn't learn until later that the company's executives had connections to Miss Marshall and the Cabbage Patch.[266] Miss Marshall had a way of quietly using such connections to make sure her young people got jobs.

Miss Marshall sometimes said she knew Dorene's younger sister Ruth since before she was born. Ruth's long history with the Patch started with the well baby clinic. She was a graduate of the Cabbage Patch nursery school, a young patron of the library and the game room, a student in the sewing school, and a participant in the devotions.

---

266. Dorene Tomerlin Stopher, PI, September 3, 2011.

"I just generally worked my way in," Ruth said. No matter if Miss Marshall had known Ruth forever, Ruth was subject to the same discipline as anyone else—as she learned the day she said, "Damn!" in the game room. "Miss Marshall would have a conniption," if she'd heard the word, Ruth said later, but Pappy Redman (who'd been known to use such words himself) was nearby.

"Sis, come over here," he said.

"He explained to me that wasn't a very lady-like word to say and I could go home and think about it for a couple of days before I could come back in," she recalled. "That stayed with me quite a while."[267]

Character development was only a part of Miss Marshall's agenda. She wanted her children to know the world beyond the Cabbage Patch, so from the beginning, she made sure they went on field trips to new places: the Coca-Cola bottling plant, a potato chip factory, swimming in public pools. Even the city's suburban parks—Cherokee and Iroquois—held charms and surprises for children raised in treeless housing projects and crowded slums. Cabbage Patch volunteers would pack picnic lunches and take children out to parks to look for leaves and wildflowers, climb trees, and hike up and down hills. The children loved it.[268]

As the settlement matured, its camping program also became more formal and elaborate. Large numbers of boys and girls went to campgrounds in Kentucky and Indiana where

267. Ruth Tomerlin Chaffins, interview by Carolyn Kline, April 4, 1987, CPSOHP, CPSHR, FHS.

268. Anita C. (Mrs. John R.) Green, interview by Andrew Chancey, September 24, 1987, CPSOHP, CPSHR, FHS.

they slept in tents or cabins, had vespers around a campfire, and took responsibility for camp chores like cleaning up after dinner. Miss Marshall, who was 60 in 1948, didn't camp with them, but sometimes she would drive out to check on how things were going. Once, when Ruth Tomerlin was 10 or 12 years old, Miss Marshall asked her to ride with her to check on the campers at Cumberland Falls, 175 miles southeast of Louisville in the rugged hills of Appalachia. Miss Marshall's erratic driving would later become the stuff of legend, but, for Ruth, a car trip was a rare pleasure, and she remembered only that it was very pleasant on the road. Miss Marshall and Ruth talked, and Miss Marshall asked Ruth's opinion on the things they discussed.

"I felt very honored," Ruth said many years later.

They spent the night in a pleasant country inn, then went on to Cumberland Falls where Ruth joined the rest of the group for her first real camping experience with "tents and cots and all the good stuff that goes with it."[269]

The children who knew Miss Marshall well recognized that she had two sides. When she "hollered" at children or barked orders, she used a sharp voice that sounded mean and inspired fear and awe. "But she had a beautiful laugh. She just had a way of smiling at you to kind of defuse what she'd said," Ruth Tomerlin Chaffins remembered. There was a reassuring predictability about Miss Marshall, too. She always explained why she told a boy not to climb a fence or demanded perfection of a girl working in the office. And always, Ruth recalled, "You could tell how much she really cared and wanted things for the kids there."

---

269. Ruth Tomerlin Chaffins, PI, July 6, 2011; Ruth Tomerlin Chaffins, interview by Carolyn Kline, April 4, 1987, CPSOHP, CPSHR, FHS.

Miss Marshall's approach to working with children and to settlement work was studied and well considered. She went to national social work conferences where she took careful notes. She didn't approve of all she heard. At a National Conference of Social Work in Minneapolis, she noted that the trend in both settlements and churches was to follow people as they moved, often into the suburbs, "instead of taking care of neighborhoods." She believed in keeping ahead of changes in the community and in studying the "community mind."

"There is a community mind just as there is a mind in the individual," she wrote. "Is the community changing—disappearing, enlarging, specializing? Often issues are economic rather than racial."[270]

After endless efforts to attract trained social workers from universities in other states, Miss Marshall developed her own approach. She identified local people, who knew their community, to work at the Patch. And she began growing her own social workers. Lloyd Redman, the football player, was the start of a remarkable line of men whom Miss Marshall identified and mentored. She identified most of them when they were very young. She employed them when they were teens and sent them to college, often at her expense. She expected those young men, thus steeped in her values, to return to help run the Cabbage Patch. Joe Burks, the neighborhood kid who began under Redman's guidance, was the next of those men—and his experience would show both the benefits and the flaw in her plan.

The need to ensure the Cabbage Patch's future grew increasingly urgent as Miss Marshall grew older. Her

---

270. Louise Marshall, undated notes from National Conference of Social Work in Minneapolis, CPSHR, FHS.

dedication to the settlement's people didn't dim, but there was no denying that both she and the neighborhood were aging.

Central Park, especially, had become a source of considerable civic concern. The *Courier-Journal* reported that "wine-heads" had taken to sleeping there, making the park a "hobo jungle" that frightened women and children. More alarming, the park was increasingly becoming a mecca for illicit sexual activity. The female prostitution there was hardly new, but society was struggling to come to grips with homosexuality, which was still considered a sin, a crime, and, possibly, an illness. Of acute concern were the loitering "sexual psychopaths" who preyed on children. The city parks department tried to make the park less welcoming to loiterers by cutting back the bushes where the children had loved to play Tarzan. Police conducted sweeps of the park using plainclothes detectives. A grand jury indicted two men from the area for "improper conduct" with small boys, a double tragedy because such boys were too often committed to an institution and required to testify in open court. The grand jury's report also recommended a list of steps for dealing with "sexual psychopaths" who were, by definition, a danger to others.[271]

Some of those who were very much in danger were Cabbage Patch boys. One boy's genitals were injured by a homosexual. Then Redman discovered that the Cabbage Patch boys figured in a much bigger scheme involving a

---

271. *Louisville (KY) Courier-Journal*, "Wine-heads Get Bum's Rush," June 16, 1951; "Police Renew Central Park Checkup Drive," July 1, 1951; "Grand Jury Says It's Concerned," June 7, 1952; "Jury Favors Special Place for Sex Misfit," July 3, 1952; and "(Judge) Jull Suggests Law Covering Sex Offenders," August 14, 1951.

mysterious "Fi Fi LaRue" and a group of men who had rented a "posh" apartment near the park for sex parties involving teenage boys. The story began to emerge one night when Redman took a sports team to Central Park to practice. The boys kept talking about Fi Fi. A boy named Marvin promised to take everyone over to Fi Fi's after practice. Finally, Redman called Marvin over.

"Marv, what are you talking about? Who is this girl Fi Fi?"

"Oh, Pappy," Marv laughed. "You know about Fi Fi?"

"No," said Redman. "Who is she?"

So Marvin laughed and explained: Fi Fi LaRue was a man who invited boys to his apartment near Central Park for country ham sandwiches and beer, good food and lots of it. Redman suddenly understood very well what was going on. "What do you think a 15- or 16-year-old boy is going to do if he can walk over there and get all that good food, and he doesn't eat half the time?"

Redman and Miss Marshall called police and cut a deal with the lieutenant who listened to Marvin's story: Police agreed not to arrest any of Redman's boys, but they did raid Fi Fi LaRue's apartment. They questioned 17 boys found at the apartment, but, true to their deal, did not arrest or identify them. Seven men, including Fi Fi, were arrested.[272]

That was not enough to clear the park of pedophiles. Police were so undermanned that they eventually considered

---

272. Lloyd Redman, interview by Keith Cardwell, February 20, 1987, CPSOHP, CPSHR, FHS; *Louisville (KY) Courier-Journal,* October 28, 1949. The newspaper covered the trials, legal proceedings, and public debate through the end of December. "Fi Fi" was convicted and sentenced to a long jail term.

asking for volunteers to help patrol the park.[273] Miss Marshall didn't wait for the invitation. One night she got Lloyd Redman to go to Central Park with her. They carried sticks and beat gay men in an indiscriminate effort to chase pedophiles out of the park.[274] Later generations would call that a shameful act of homophobia, but pedophiles in the park were hurting children. Miss Marshall would not stand for that.

The neighborhood no longer felt like a safe place to live for Miss Marshall, who had settled into one of the Cabbage Patch cottages. She was somewhat insulated from danger by the people she had helped over the years. "Toughies," hardened men who had done prison time despite Miss Marshall's best efforts, came to see her after they got out of jail and would tolerate no disrespect from others when they were near. But the protection was not complete. The wrong kind of people knew that Miss Marshall was rich. One night about nine thirty, as Miss Marshall crossed the porch of the cottage, someone grabbed her purse. She fought, but he got it.[275]

A few minutes later, staff members playing basketball after closing time looked up to see Miss Marshall on the gym's stage with her clothes torn and blood over one eye.

"Somebody just robbed me, and he headed to Central Park," she said.

The basketball players dashed out of the gym and plunged into the blackness of Central Park. One of the staff members,

273. "Volunteers Might Police," *Louisville (KY) Courier-Journal,* July 16, 1960.

274. Lewis Marshall Johnson, telephone interview with authors, July 18, 2011.

275. Dr. James J. Cooksey, PI, July 14, 2011; Joseph Burks, interview by Keith Cardwell, January 31, 1987, CPSOHP, CPSHR, FHS.

Russell Gibson, was "scared to death," reduced to shaking, in Miss Marshall's presence, but he wasn't about to let anyone hurt her and get away with it. Only as the park's pitch dark surrounded the group did Gibson raise an important question: What are we going to do if we catch him? The pursuers retreated. The episode only raised Gibson's awe of Miss Marshall. "She was so tough," he said later. "So tough."[276]

The dates and sequence of events are not entirely clear, but Miss Marshall's family and friends convinced her that she had to move. So she moved—nominally—to the Puritan Hotel, a pleasant, gracious residential hotel only half a mile from the Cabbage Patch and just around the corner from the old Marshall family home on Ormsby.

"Her sister said that she just perched there because she just slept there, really," said Louise's friend and board member Peg Harvin. She might have moved, but Miss Marshall continued to keep her clothes in the Cabbage Patch cottage, and she frequently paid her hotel bill one night at a time for a room that was small and spare.[277] The move would not protect Miss Marshall from future violence, but it quieted her sisters for the moment. In summer 1952, Louise Marshall was 64 years old and tired. It was again time for her to take the kind of break she loved.

The 1950s would boost post-war prosperity and bring threats of godless communism and nuclear annihilation

---

276. Russell Gibson, oral history interview, March 16, 2008, by Victoria Groce, University of Louisville Department of History project, University of Louisville Archives and Special Collections.

277. Margaret Pleune Harvin, interview by Keith Cardwell, February 12, 1987, CPSOHP, CPSHR, FHS.

to the country and more change to what remained of the national settlement house movement. The years would also begin a new era for Miss Marshall and her Cabbage Patch Settlement. As she had before, Miss Marshall ended one era and began the next with a voyage to Europe.[278]

---

278. US passport issued to Louise Marshall, June 18, 1952, CPSHR, FHS.

CHAPTER 10

THE TALES FROM
TWO LIVES

For a person who did not want to be known in her own right, Louise Marshall was remarkably memorable. For one thing, she inspired strong emotions: awe, adoration, intimidation, hate, hurt, gratitude, love, and admiration, often at the same time. For another, she approached her life, work, family, friends, and Cabbage Patch patrons in ways that were utterly her own. None of those people—even those who knew her better than anyone else—completely understood. To explain what they knew—or thought they knew—of Louise Marshall, almost everyone in both of her lives tells stories that provide the best windows we have into Louise Marshall and how she worked her magic. The picture the stories suggest is, at best, a complex, contradictory puzzle. Maybe she was a courageous, committed pioneer. Maybe she was crazy. Maybe she was God's hands on earth.

There is one point on which everyone agrees: At the Cabbage Patch, Miss Marshall was "The Boss." The window of her office gave her a broad view of everything that happened in front of the settlement. She could holler out the window, and the kids outside would straighten up. Through her office door, she could see everyone who entered the building and went down the hall. From her desk chair, she could stop anyone cold by barking his last name. And, somehow, from that office, she could know everything that happened anywhere in the Patch. How she did that was a matter of special wonder to errant boys.

Louise Marshall's appearance never hinted at her strength. She was not a large or striking woman. By the time she turned 60, her appearance was unimposing in every way. Her hair was roughly chin length and an ordinary brown, usually held back by a ribbon. Her eyes, behind thick, plastic glasses, were hazel, her height five feet, four inches at her tallest. Her dress was navy in the summer and black in the winter, with pearls, gloves, and a nondescript hat for going out. She changed her sensible shoes only to climb over the chain-link fence to one of her favorite pastimes, tending the Cabbage Patch garden. She changed her glasses often, depending on what she needed to see. Although she spent her life in Kentucky among those who mutilated Standard English and spurned the manners of polite society, she never modified her cultured Virginia accent or lost her Victorian bearing. And yet, even in her 60s and 70s, Miss Marshall— as everyone at the settlement called her—had a command presence that could wither police, punks, drunks, or soldiers. She could wade into a fight between big, tough boys. She could get a drunk home to his wife. She could command— and receive—absolute commitment from her staff—at least for a while. If staff members weren't committed, they quit or she fired them.

In the 1950s, Louise Marshall, by then in her 60s, launched into a new era at Cabbage Patch with a new passport photo and a trip abroad. Her appearance belied her strength. *Courtesy of Cabbage Patch Settlement House Archives*

As she aged, that staff was increasingly made up of men she had tapped and nurtured as boys. Much later, the Cabbage Patch would call what she did with those boys a "leadership development program." In those days after World War II, Miss Marshall simply said she worked to develop character, the most important attribute a boy would need. She would put boys, and the occasional girl, to work at the Patch, encourage (and sometimes pay for) their education, help them discover their gifts, and give them jobs at the Cabbage Patch where they, too, would become legends. In time, those young people, especially Lloyd Redman, Joe Burks Sr., Jim Cooksey, Roosevelt Chin, and Charles Dietsch put their own stamps on hundreds of other children.

Miss Marshall's "boys" came from various backgrounds. Redman was a 23-year-old World War II veteran at the University of Louisville when Miss Marshall discovered and hired him. Joe Burks and Jim Cooksey grew up as Patchers. Roosevelt Chin was the son of Chinese immigrants (and the grandson of a Chicago Chinese gang leader) who moved to Louisville and discovered the Cabbage Patch as a teenager. Charles Dietsch was playing on the Cabbage Patch football team in 1949, the year his father died. Miss Marshall took him under her wing.[279]

If the boys had a common trait that attracted Miss Marshall's attention, it was probably a willingness to work. If she had a plan for how to develop their other gifts, that was known only to her. The way things unfolded at the Cabbage Patch, her plans just seemed to happen.

Joe Burks's story shows, as well as any, how Miss Marshall worked her magic. Burks said that he was born "exactly 14 houses" up Sixth Street from the Cabbage Patch, close enough to watch other kids going there to have fun while he waited for his father to say he could cross the street alone. When he was nine or ten, Joe plunged into the Cabbage Patch clubs, the Wednesday and Friday puppet shows, and the game room with its ping-pong and pool tables. He loved playing in the gym, but, for as long as he could, he fled the mandatory showers that followed.[280]

---

279. Lloyd Redman, interview by Keith Cardwell, February 12, 1987, CPSOHP, CPSHR, FHS; Charles Dietsch, telephone interview with authors, December 31, 2014.

280. Joseph Burks Sr., interview by Keith Cardwell, January 30, 1987, CPSOHP, CPSHR, FHS; Joseph Burks Sr., PI, July 8, 2011.

During those years, Joe, like the other boys, knew Miss Marshall only as a stern presence with the ultimate power; she could bar you from the Cabbage Patch. When she told someone to do something, it happened. The boys had watched Miss Marshall when she walked into the game room and saw the toughest guy there doing something wrong. "Straighten up or leave," she had told him to his face. They had seen police chasing a boy into the Cabbage Patch, only to be faced down by Miss Marshall.

"You're not coming in here," she told the officers. "You are not going to get that boy until we find out what he did. Then, you *might* have him." The police did not come in.

"We knew that we had a person here who would protect us, and we knew it was Miss Marshall," Joe Burks said later.[281] The Cabbage Patch became Burks's second home. He was going to need it. When Joe was about 14, his mother died. His father's neighborhood grocery faltered, and his father had to take a night job. Joe was free to roam the streets at night, to play a rough game called buckity-buck with large bands of boys in Central Park and to sit on the corner to "tell jokes and holler at people." When the Cabbage Patch was closed, some of the boys liked to go to pool halls or steal quarters so they could play pinball at a neighborhood bar. Burks could have done that, too, but the Cabbage Patch got Joe off the street. At the Patch, he could earn a little money by cleaning the gym or painting. And he had standards to meet there, Miss Marshall's standards.

"Burks, that's not right," she'd say if he erred. Then she would quote scriptures.

---

281. Joseph Burks Sr., interview by Keith Cardwell, January 30, 1987, CPSOHP, CPSHR, FHS.

The dark chain-link fence in front of the Cabbage Patch Settlement was a major tool of discipline and education. Errant boys repainted it repeatedly on orders from Miss Marshall as punishment for their misdeeds.

Courtesy of Cabbage Patch Settlement House Archives

Sometimes Miss Marshall's expectations seemed utterly unreasonable. Burks once figured that a boy tired from doing the painting Miss Marshall had assigned should be able to take a break if Miss Marshall wasn't around.

"And, there she was," said Burks.

"Burks. What are you doing?"

"Miss Marshall," he replied. "I got so tired. I had to rest for just a minute."

"Well, I can't have you sitting around."

Miss Marshall believed in work. She used it as a reward, a punishment, a teaching tool. Even the chain-link fence in front of the settlement provided useful lessons. When a boy had gotten in trouble, he might have to work his way back into Miss Marshall's good graces by painting that fence with its endless little spaces that could only be properly covered by tedious effort. Years later, when Joe Burks's Cabbage Patch friends were old men, they all remembered that fence. "We all had to paint it," Burks said, and if anyone failed to do it right, "She'd get on us."[282]

Joe Burks grew up under Miss Marshall's eye with Lloyd Redman as his coach and mentor. When Joe was 16, Redman asked him to help coach the younger boys, an important step for Burks and for the boys who learned from him.

"Without the influence of the Cabbage Patch, I might have been a wino, or I may have been a bum, or I might have been anything," Burks would say much later. Because of the Cabbage Patch, he became a respected teacher and coach, a Christian, and the husband of Kathleen Hornback. As with so many things at the Cabbage Patch, Joe and Kathleen's meeting seemed an accident. It wasn't. When Kathleen was 15, she started playing softball at the Patch, and Redman soon knew what had to happen.

"She was a cute, pretty little old girl—an athlete—and I just had to get those two together," Redman said. When Redman organized a hayride for all the kids, he made sure that Joe and Kathleen were on it. "That's where they first met," Redman said. "They're two of the finest people I've ever known."[283]

A cycle was beginning that would be repeated over and over. Miss Marshall was constantly looking for people—especially men—who would share her commitment and

---

282. Joseph Burks Sr., PI, July 8, 2011.

283. Lloyd Redman, interview by Keith Cardwell, February 12, 1987, CPSOHP, CPSHR, FHS; Joseph Burks Sr., PI, July 8, 2011.

vision and remain at the Cabbage Patch to carry on her work. When Miss Marshall was about 65, she asked Joe Burks—by then a coach—to send one of the boys he was coaching to help her plant some bushes. James Cooksey, age 14, who had been a Cabbage Patch kid since his baby roll days, volunteered— Army style, he said later. Miss Marshall and Jim Cooksey got to know each other that afternoon while planting bushes to Miss Marshall's precise specifications.

"I remember thinking, 'this is the pickiest person I have ever seen in my life,'" Cooksey said much later. He kept that thought to himself. Miss Marshall liked the way he planted bushes, so they got along very well. To his delight, she asked if he would like a job doing maintenance at the Patch. Like Joe Burks, Roosevelt Chin, and Charles Dietsch, Cooksey would work at the Patch through his years at college, and prepare for a career continuing the Cabbage Patch tradition.[284]

"She'd get the right people working for her," Burks said. The problem is that they wanted to marry and have families, and Miss Marshall didn't want that. "She wanted them fully dedicated like herself," said his wife, Kathleen Burks. "No distractions."[285]

Miss Marshall also made plans for girls, but she seems to have been more yielding when they wanted to choose something else. After seeing the Tomerlin family through the Depression and helping Dorene Tomerlin get a job, Miss Marshall planned for Ruth Tomerlin to go to college, study social work, and return to the Cabbage Patch to work and

---

284. Dr. James J. Cooksey, PI, July 14, 2011.

285. Kathleen and Joe Burks, PI, July 8, 2011.

marry Patcher Charles Dietsch, who would also continue his work there. Ruth didn't buy that plan.

"She's just too funny," said Ruth, much later. When Ruth told Miss Marshall she didn't want to go to college, "She got a little irritated with me. 'You've got this great opportunity and I can't believe . . . .'" For Ruth, Miss Marshall's irritation blew over. Ruth married someone else and worked for more than 50 years as the beloved secretary of Highland Presbyterian Church, where Henry Mobley, a longtime member of the Cabbage Patch board, was a longtime pastor.[286] She continued to volunteer at the Patch and helped build a tradition of breathtakingly ambitious camping trips for Cabbage Patch children.

Bucking Miss Marshall didn't work as well for the men she groomed for Cabbage Patch service. When Lloyd Redman graduated from the University of Louisville, Miss Marshall announced happily to the board that he would work full-time for the settlement and move his wife and small daughter into the settlement's cottage. Rent-free residence in the cottage was partial compensation for a man who was promised a full-time, around-the-clock job for $3,000 a year and no benefits. Living in the cottage also put Redman within Miss Marshall's reach any time she wanted him, an arrangement that put a considerable strain on his family. Miss Marshall thought the money raised for the Cabbage Patch should be used directly for its programs—not its staff. But she was grateful for Redman and tried to find other ways to show her gratitude.

With the war over, Miss Marshall bought herself a new car, a Mercury. Redman, who didn't own a car, admired it.

---

286. Ruth Tomerlin Chaffins, PI, July 6, 2011.

Not long after, the dealer who had sold Miss Marshall her car knocked on Redman's door and handed him a set of keys.

"There's your new car," he said.

"I don't have a car, mister," Redman replied. "You've got the wrong one."

The dealer insisted. Finally, when Redman started to get mad, the man explained: Miss Marshall had bought the car for him.

"I guess I should have taken it," Redman said much later. "I wouldn't do it."

Still, he added, "That meant a lot to me in my life for that woman to love me that much. And I loved her in return." He did get angry with her, however, even hated her. And there were days when he had to wonder about her priorities.

On one of those days, an angry father, a huge man with a beer belly, stormed into Redman's office to complain that his son had been ejected from the Cabbage Patch for fighting. "He was just cussing and carrying on," said Redman. Then the man pulled out a knife and threatened Redman. A brand-new Royal typewriter sat on Redman's desk. Redman heaved the typewriter at the man and sent him backwards into the hall and through a glass door.

Miss Marshall came running. "Oh, my word, Mr. Redman," she exclaimed. "My new Royal typewriter!"

"'My Royal typewriter, hell!" responded Redman. "What about me?" Redman muttered about that for years.[287]

In time, Redman moved his family out of the cottage, and he began a teaching career in the semi-rural suburb

287. Lloyd Redman, interview by Keith Cardwell, February 12, 1987, CPSOHP, CPSHR, FHS.

where his extended family lived—and where Miss Marshall couldn't reach him so easily. For years, Miss Marshall tried to get Redman back full-time. He worked for the Cabbage Patch, sometimes part-time and occasionally full-time for short spurts, but he was destined to become a legendary coach for the public school system, using the skills he had developed at the Cabbage Patch to shape wave after wave of other children. Many years later, he would wonder if he had done the right thing in leaving the Cabbage Patch to climb a career ladder in the school system. It might have been a mistake to leave, he concluded, but he hoped to have another chance in the hereafter.

"I just want to be at her right hand someday," he said. "Boy, she was a saint . . . She was a great, great woman. She might be crazy, but she was great."[288]

The Korean War interrupted plans for some of Miss Marshall's boys, but afterward, two more of Miss Marshall's protégés, Joe Burks and Charles Dietsch, returned to the Patch and to Miss Marshall's magnetic plans for them. By then Joe and Kathleen had married as Redman had planned. They moved into the cottage with their small son, Joe Jr., with the understanding that Burks would give "every bit of time" he wasn't in school to the work of the settlement.[289] They soon discovered that all those who lived in the cottage also had to follow Miss Marshall's rules, whether or not they received a paycheck.

---

288. Lloyd Redman, interview by Keith Cardwell, February 12, 1987, CPSOHP, CPSHR, FHS.

289. Board of Directors, Cabbage Patch Settlement House, to Joseph Burks Sr., August 24, 1956, CPSHR, FHS.

Miss Marshall didn't think women should wear pants. She certainly did not wear them. Girls had to wear skirts to the Cabbage Patch, even during the emerging feminism of the 1970s.[290] Miss Marshall even protested when her sister Sallie Ewing Dosker showed up to volunteer wearing fashionable slacks. So, when Kathleen Burks wore pedal pushers to take little Joe out in his stroller, Miss Marshall made her feelings clear.

"I don't think I pushed the stroller in britches anymore," said Kathleen Burks. "I think I found me a dress."

Even three-year-old Joe was subject to Miss Marshall. One day she looked out her office window when Joe was playing in the little fenced yard and saw the tot break a small branch off a forsythia bush. "Oh, she came right out," said Kathleen Burks. Miss Marshall gave Joe a little speech about how she didn't like what he was doing. The next time Miss Marshall looked out, she saw little Joe trying to plant the branch he'd broken. As usual, Miss Marshall had made an impression.[291]

Miss Marshall encouraged Burks to finish his education, even when his father wanted his help in the family grocery, and she finally got Burks to return to his work at the Cabbage Patch. Burks worked at the Patch part-time or full-time for years, long enough to put his stamp on hundreds of children who played for Cabbage Patch teams. Joe Burks intended to work at the Cabbage Patch forever.

"That was my vocation," Burks said later. "That's what I wanted to do. But it didn't work out that way. Miss Marshall, she was hard to get along with. Hard to get along with."

---

290. Dr. James J. Cooksey, interview by Andrew Chancey, October 15, 1987, CPSOHP, CPSHR, FHS.

291. Kathleen and Joseph Burks Sr., PI, July 8, 2011.

The player jumping at right in this basketball tipoff was Joe Burks, who coached football and basketball and taught lasting life lessons. Players who didn't have sneakers wore their socks, never street shoes, on the Cabbage Patch Settlement's gym floor. *Courtesy of Cabbage Patch Settlement House Archives*

Among other things, the Burks family was growing, and the Cabbage Patch's low wages weren't supplemented by health insurance or other benefits. Burks went to see Miss Marshall and told her he was going to have to leave.

"What do you mean?" she said.

The lack of benefits was a problem, Burks explained. He needed security. "I have three kids."

"Go on and get out," said Miss Marshall, "and don't come back again."

"Okay," said Burks. "I'll leave."

Miss Marshall meant what she said. When Burks came back later in the week to play basketball with some old friends in his new role as an "ordinary guy," his old friend and former coworker Charlie Dietsch was on duty. "Burks, you can't go in," Dietsch said. "Miss Marshall doesn't want you to come in."

Burks's first response was anger. "Who's going to throw me out?" he responded. The hurt went deep. "I left, and I didn't come back."[292] He became a teacher, a job that allowed him to continue to see—and continue to shape—children he had served at the Cabbage Patch.

There was no opposing Miss Marshall. Jim Cooksey, her next protégé, would discover that, and so would members of the Cabbage Patch board of directors. Even those who admired her best qualities bristled at Miss Marshall's determined control of her settlement and her people.

On the surface, at least, meetings of the Cabbage Patch Settlement Board of Directors were pleasant, perfunctory, and followed a set pattern dictated by Miss Marshall. First, the board members would have lunch together. Then the board would meet. "Miss Marshall would tell us what was going on and asked us if we approved of this, and that, and the other thing," said Peg Harvin, Miss Marshall's friend who served on the board for 20 years. "Of course, we always did."[293]

There was more to the board's placid operations, of course. It was Miss Marshall's board, no matter what the settlement's agreement with the Presbyterian Church said about the presbytery having the right to approve board members. Miss Marshall handpicked board members who then served at her pleasure—for 25 years and more, if she

292. Joseph Burks Sr., PI, July 8, 2011.

293. Margaret (Peg) Pleune Harvin, interview by Keith Cardwell, February 20, 1987, CPSOHP, CPSHR, FHS.

liked them. Then she sometimes drafted their children to succeed them on the board. Dr. Peter Pleune and Martin Sweets, for example, both served for 20 years or more and encouraged their daughters, Peg Pleune and Meme Sweets, to be Cabbage Patch volunteers. Miss Marshall mentored both girls, then drafted them for their own long service on the board.

Other directors had no idea why Miss Marshall tapped them. As a young, newly married woman, Lynn Gant attended Second Presbyterian Church and regularly sat a couple of rows behind Miss Marshall in the balcony. "One day she turned around and pointed her finger at me and said, 'I want you to be on my board.'" A surprised, awed, and honored Lynn Gant said yes.[294] Everyone knew that Miss Marshall had given her own life to the Cabbage Patch. It was hard to say no to anything she asked.

The result was a board of "very competent people who had accomplished rather remarkable things in their own lives," said Jim Cooksey. "But there was always Miss Marshall masterminding what she wanted to do."

Over 50 years, Miss Marshall's leadership skills and decision-making ability had matured. When she could, she started months ahead, planting seeds about new ideas with board members, taking them out to dinner one or two at a time, and asking their opinions. She'd have marathon phone conversations that would last for hours with each member of the board.[295]

---

294. Lynn Gant March, PI, June 14, 2011.

295. Dr. James J. Cooksey, interview by Andrew Chancey, October 15, 1987, CPSOHP, CPSHR, FHS.

"She would say, 'What do you think of this? If we did it this way, what would you think of that?'" said Anne Raley. "She'd just go on and on and on about things," said Thames Palmer-Ball. "I guess that's how she somehow worked them out in her mind, was to talk to somebody about it."[296]

Board meetings were carefully orchestrated with staff reports that only included what Miss Marshall thought the board should know and with board members prepared to make the points Miss Marshall wanted made. She omitted "all those awful things that happened" and talked instead about children's needs, success stories, and her vision of what the Cabbage Patch needed to do and be. "She had a magnificent mind," said Anne Raley, who served on the board for 32 years.[297]

Thus, even potentially controversial decisions were taken without any to-do. In the early days, when Cabbage Patch boys were frequenting pool halls, Miss Marshall called Peter Pleune, a Presbyterian minister who served on the board, to ask how churchgoers would react if the settlement installed a pool table to lure the boys from the pool halls' bad influences.

"Louise," he said, "give them the pool table and keep your mouth shut." She did.

For years, the board meetings were held in the Mothers Club Room where lunch was served on card tables meticulously set up for the occasion.

"I mean she was a fanatic," said Rod Napier, now the Cabbage Patch's director of programs and facilities. In those

296. Thames Palmer-Ball, interview by Andrew Chancey, September 18, 1987, CPSOHP, CPSHR, FHS.

297. Recorded conversation between Anne Anderson Raley and Margaret (Mrs. William) Harvin, February 24, 1987, CPSOHP, CPSHR, FHS.

days, he was the guy who set up the tables and put plastic covers on them under Miss Marshall's direction. "Every cover had to go on a certain table, and the tables had to go at a certain angle." Miss Marshall wanted board members to think that the Cabbage Patch did everything in a quality way. For her, details counted.[298]

Miss Marshall set the tables with sterling silver bearing her MLM monogram and prepared the lunch herself: fresh salad and canned cream of mushroom soup with a pat of butter on top. "Everything was so good, and we'd just eat our heads off," said Anne Raley.[299]

Board members would help clear the tables after lunch at their own peril. "She was wild about you losing one of her silver forks," said Thames Palmer-Ball. "She really didn't like anyone being out there supervising that scraping of plates . . . because she was afraid she was going to lose one of her silver forks."[300]

The issue in all things, of course, was that Miss Marshall insisted on being in control. She may have sought board members' opinions during phone calls, but during the board meetings, she expected them to support her. When they didn't, she took opposition personally. A board member who argued against a Miss Marshall position was certain to get a

---

298. Rod Napier, PI, June 22, 2012.

299. Lewis Marshall Johnson, telephone interview with authors, July 18, 2011; recorded conversation between Anne Anderson Raley and Margaret (Mrs. William) Harvin, February 24, 1987, CPSOHP, CPSHR, FHS.

300. Thames Palmer-Ball, interview by Andrew Chancey, September 18, 1987, CPOHP, CPSHR, FHS.

follow-up letter or call from Miss Marshall. The tone of the communication depended on how Miss Marshall felt about the member.

Peg Harvin, one of Miss Marshall's longtime favorites, opposed her once on a long-forgotten issue, but remembered the call she got a few days later. "She called me in great distress and wanted to know why I was against her," Mrs. Harvin said. "See, this was always a personal relationship."[301] Peg Harvin and Miss Marshall patched things up. For other board members with less enduring relationships, Miss Marshall would have expected a resignation—as more than one board member discovered during the difficult days in the 1950s and '60s.

All her life, Louise Marshall did a delicate dance back and forth across the line between her life of privilege and her life serving the people of the Cabbage Patch. Her closest associates at the Patch thought her family didn't understand her. Her family thought those at the Patch didn't know her either. They were probably both right. Miss Marshall kept her worlds apart. Cabbage Patch patrons knew she was wealthy, and some drove past the Marshalls' old Ormsby Avenue house and wondered about the life inside. Except for men like Escue Tomerlin who went there to work, Miss Marshall didn't invite people from the Cabbage Patch to her home. Not until the 1960s would she take her closest associates at the Cabbage Patch into her other world.

Board members and almost all of the Cabbage Patch's donors and patrons came from Miss Marshall's wealthier

---

301. Margaret (Peg) Harvin, interview by Keith Cardwell, February 20, 1987, CPSOHP, CPSHR, FHS.

world where people had lovely garden parties and served coffee from silver urns and trays. She could comfortably make polite conversation at parties in the city's most prosperous homes, and she worshiped on Sundays with the city's elite at Second Presbyterian Church. When the Cabbage Patch needed money for a camp, program, or equipment, those were the people she called. She spoke their language.

Since the settlement's early days, Louise's sisters had volunteered to teach classes and help with Thanksgiving baskets and Christmas parties, but they had husbands, children, and concerns of their own and didn't focus on Louise's mission or share her passion. The Marshall sisters, Elizabeth Johnson and Sallie Ewing Dosker, welcomed Louise to their homes. Louise forged close relationships with their children, and stayed with her family for respites and memorable holidays. When she was with her family, however, she couldn't control things as she did at the settlement. She could only take a position and refuse to compromise, which is what she did when dealing with the property the siblings inherited jointly. When Louise's brother, poor Burwell Jr., tried to execute bequests that benefited his siblings, Louise made her opinion felt—first with regard to the Marshall home on Omsby Avenue and then with 100 acres of prime real estate Grandfather Richard Veech had left to his daughter Lizzie and, eventually, to her children.

The Veech land was east of Louisville, its borders touching on the new Bowman Field airport, a main traffic artery, a city park, and a lovely stretch of Beargrass Creek. It was ripe for development in the late 1930s. The air board wanted to buy some of it for the airport, and the Standard Country

Club made an offer to buy some for a golf course. The Marshall siblings decided to divide the land into five, 20-acre parcels instead of selling it all at once. The division didn't go smoothly, and Burwell finally filed suit to settle the division. In the meanwhile, someone offered to rent the land for farming, a proposal that would have provided everyone some income while the suit dragged on. Louise refused. Richard needed the money, but Louise's refusal to rent the land blocked him—and everyone else—from getting the income. Litigation over the property—not all of it Louise's fault—went on for years. As always, Louise's letters were argumentative and unpleasant.[302] In the end, however, the land's sale would provide money for the investments that helped make her wealthy. The disputes also widened Louise's distance from her brothers.

The holidays generally followed a pattern. Louise stayed with her sister Elizabeth Johnson for several days, starting with Christmas Eve. When the family gathered for dinner on Christmas Eve, Louise was always memorably late. The family assumed she was out helping "some woman" get a drunk husband home.

"I have never known anyone who was as late," said her niece Elizabeth Johnson Haynes. "You never waited dinner for her. Never. We went ahead."

When Louise did arrive, she was exhausted—from driving herself too hard, her family thought. Often she'd go straight to bed. When Louise got up, there would be a fire in the fireplace, and the sisters would sit up late talking about "family, events, everything that was happening" in Louise's

---

302. Louise Marshall, various letters to her siblings regarding the Cannons Lane property, 1936–1940, CPSHR, FHS.

life, Elizabeth Haynes said.[303]

On Christmas Day, Elizabeth Johnson invited extended family to dinner, often including their brother Burwell Jr., despite the falling out between him and Louise. If the two found themselves in the same room on Christmas— something they avoided—they would sit on opposite sides of the room and simply didn't speak to each other.[304] Adding to the holiday spirit was the annual Christmas message from brother Richard, who the family believed had deserted his wife and four children to live with another woman in St. Louis.

"Uncle Richard would send really evil telegrams," said Elizabeth Johnson Haynes. "'I hope you all have a terrible Christmas and everything is bad and Hell gets you all.'" Each year the family knew the message was coming and braced themselves. "It bothered mother more than anybody," Elizabeth Haynes said. "We had to comfort her when it happened."[305]

After dinner, when the senior Johnsons went to an adult party, Louise stayed home with her nephew Lewis and niece Elizabeth for a delicious, outrageous outing they all looked forward to: They drove to White Castle, the nation's first fast food hamburger chain, to get supper. Established in a day when the purity of ground beef was suspect, White Castle clad its small restaurants with shining white enamel designed to look both pristine and like a castle. In the gleaming stainless steel interior, customers could buy only hamburgers, grilled

---

303. Elizabeth Johnson Haynes, PI, July 11, 2011.

304. Burwell Keith Marshall III, PI, March 16, 2012.

305. Elizabeth Johnson Haynes, PI, March 1, 2013.

on top of fresh onions, and Coca-Cola. The small, fat-soaked sandwiches (known for generations as sliders) were tucked into little cardboard boxes to keep them hot. Because they were small, customers generally purchased them by the bag for 10 cents each. Sliders inspired no nutritional respect, although the company had paid a medical student to eat them for a month with no reported ill effect. Elizabeth Marshall Johnson would never have advocated White Castles for her children. Aunt Louise added to the mischievous adventure by driving the children to the White Castle in her car that she dubbed "Leaping Lena."

"She was the world's worst driver," said Elizabeth Haynes. Louise and the children thought the outing was great fun.[306]

Elizabeth and Lewis would grow up visiting their Aunt Louise at the Cabbage Patch and helping with the work there. No matter what was going on between Louise and the rest of the family, Louise's young relatives never doubted that their aunt—or cousin—Louise cared for them very much.

"Cousin Louise wasn't a mush person," said Meme Sweets Runyon. "In her wonderful direct firmness, she was able to express affection."[307]

Indeed, there seemed little that could separate Louise from children, especially those she felt needed her care. Louise may have been unable to get along with her brother, Burwell, but when she decided that his son, Burwell Keith Marshall III, seemed isolated, she invited him to help Cooksey and Chin with Cabbage Patch camping trips where she believed

---

306. Elizabeth Johnson Haynes, PI, March 1, 2013.

307. Meme Sweets Runyon, PI, October 17, 2011.

he would find the acceptance he needed.[308] He helped with two trips to the Smoky Mountains and one camp in Indiana. Cooksey and Chin praised him in reports to the board.

"I enjoyed myself," Burwell recalled.[309]

People who still tell stories about Louise remember that she had a special sense about people's needs. After Meme Sweet's mother died, Miss Marshall always dropped what she was doing to listen as young Meme passed her office door. Anita Green was a fellow worshiper at Second Presbyterian Church when her husband was killed in an automobile accident. Miss Marshall sought out the young widow and asked her to work at the Patch, an important move for both Mrs. Green and the settlement. For many years, Anita Green helped build camping programs, classes for girls, and activities for elderly women. She recruited teenage girls as volunteers and became a key part of the settlement staff herself.

Even a teenaged waitress in a country restaurant was struck by Miss Marshall's unexpected kindness. At 15, Margaret Ann Drescher worked after school at Miller's Cafeteria in the semi-rural Buechel community south of Louisville. Miss Marshall came there often for the "best food in town," especially fried chicken. Margaret Ann would always wait on her, and Miss Marshall would talk to her. Margaret Ann Drescher Young remembered Miss Marshall as a no-nonsense person who was very nice, very polite, and very kind, especially to children. At Christmas, Miss Marshall gave Margaret Ann a silver thimble that Margaret

308. Dr. James J. Cooksey, PI, July 14, 2011.

309. Burwell Keith Marshall III, PI, March 16, 2012.

Ann kept for more than 50 years. Despite her unassuming lifestyle, Miss Marshall was known in the community as "a pretty outstanding person," Margaret Ann Young said.[310] In Louisville, Miss Marshall was a celebrity of sorts. Margaret Ann never forgot.

Louise was also very generous in other ways. She gave her young relatives silver wedding presents and expensive trips for big occasions. When Sallie Ewing's daughter, Elizabeth, graduated with a master's degree, Louise celebrated by taking her on a trip to French Canada for two weeks. "We had a gorgeous time," Elizabeth said later.[311] Louise's other niece, Elizabeth Johnson Haynes, drove with her Aunt Louise on an equally memorable—if sometimes terrifying—car trip to New York.[312] Fortunately, Aunt Louise turned most of the driving over to Elizabeth.

The stories go on and on, vivid memories that conjure a confusing, inconsistent picture of a woman who was eccentric (bordering on crazy), controlling, demanding, unreasonable, and inflexible—a real character. The remarkable thing about the stories is that they often don't focus on Louise's acts of caring and courage, her dedication to the settlement, her devotion to her faith, and her absolute commitment to helping people who would never be able to repay her with anything but gratitude. For the storytellers, that part of Miss Marshall was a given, the rock-solid assumption that

---

310. Margaret Ann Young, PI, January 16, 2012.

311. Elizabeth Dosker Chambers, interview by Mrs. William (Peg) Harvin, March 19, 1987, CPSOHP, CPSHR, FHS.

312. Elizabeth Johnson Haynes, PI, July 11, 2011.

underlay everything they said. The storytellers assumed that everyone knew about Miss Marshall's everyday good work and saintly qualities. Every morning, she got up ready to live her faith, to "follow the Master," and to "bring his love to the people" of the Cabbage Patch neighborhood said a woman Miss Marshall had touched.[313] That was the story they felt no need to tell.

313. Eleanor Gorin Leuenberger, email to Bill and Linda Ellison, October 24, 2014.

CHAPTER 11

RACE, FAITH, AND HISTORY

In the difficult 1960s, when the Cabbage Patch welcomed black children and white children separately, at different times, Ron Butler remembered what would happen when Miss Marshall went to the game room where black children were playing. The children would stop playing and run to greet her. "Miss Marshall, Miss Marshall!" Miss Marshall would throw her arms open to them. As the children crowded around, she would touch their shoulders, rub their heads, and call them by name. Sometimes she would stay a few minutes to play with them.

For a black boy like Ron Butler, that was a powerful image. "Here was a white lady showing all these little black kids affection, time," Butler said years later. "At that time, you didn't see that too often."[314]

Loving children was not hard for Louise. Wanting to embrace and help every child who needed the Cabbage Patch's care came naturally. But opening her settlement house to all the changes demanded during the new era of race relations was much, much more difficult. Integration's

---

314. Ron Butler, PI, May 15, 2014.

changes threatened the stability that the Patch's stressed children—black and white—needed at a time when their lives were hard and their community was split over race, communism, and the Vietnam War. Children who came for the safety and fun of the Cabbage Patch game room, activities, and sports teams didn't care about the historic context for all the civil rights conflict. But Louisville was a southern city, and Louise was a Victorian, upper-class child of the South. That history mattered—even when no one wanted to talk about it; even when the law demanded change; even when Miss Marshall's Presbyterian Church took activist stands that she found alarming on race, war, and social issues.

To the tangled racial values and attitudes born of history and culture, Louise Marshall brought a "pioneering spirit," a sharp, questioning mind, her usual pugnacious approach to differences, and five young men she had nurtured to help her lead the settlement. Lloyd Redman provided both an unclouded understanding of the hardships the Cabbage Patch's children experienced and a hard-nosed approach to demanding the best from them. Roosevelt Chin, who was Chinese-American, understood firsthand the ugly face of prejudice against Asians during World War II.[315] Jim Cooksey mixed a knowledge of conditions in the Patch's neighborhood with a psychologist's insights and an ability to use sports to instill life-changing values in children— black and white. Joe Burks brought his good heart and his experience as a street kid in a racially mixed neighborhood. Charles Dietsch brought an unshakable dedication to Miss

---

315. Roosevelt Chin, interview by Keith Cardwell, March 7, 1987, CPSOHP, CPSHR, FHS.

Marshall and her work. All those men shared a deep-seated belief with Miss Marshall that God had a job for them to do. Indeed, Miss Marshall believed that they were answers to her prayers for "consecrated leadership" of the Patch's important work.[316]

The problem they faced was figuring out how to do that work in a time when there was so much change and contention. Miss Marshall found what she hoped was insight in the National Conference of Social Work meetings, which she attended, despite her lack of formal, academic social work training. Settlement houses, which had long been segregated in both the North and South, were struggling with issues of race. Some found themselves serving an all-new, all-black clientele. Others followed their white clients to new neighborhoods. As the civil rights movement gained momentum in the 1960s, most settlements, especially in the South, still served only one race.[317] At a conference in Minneapolis, Louise was impressed by a speaker who discussed the challenges of understanding the dynamics of a particular community and its residents, rather than following waves of residents to new suburban neighborhoods.

---

316. Louise Marshall, Report to the Cabbage Patch Settlement House Board of Directors, March 11, 1957, CPSHR, FHS.

317. Paul H. Stuart, "The Kingsley House Extension Program: Racial Segregation in a 1940s Settlement Program," *Social Service Review 66 no. 1* (March 1992): 112–120; Judith Ann Trolande, "From Settlement Houses to Neighborhood Centers: A History of the Settlement House Movement in the United States," *Hundred Years of Settlement and Neighborhood Centres in North America and Europe*, ed. Herman Nijenhuis (Utrecht: Gamma, 1986), 41–56; Wade, "Settlement Houses," http://www.Encyclopedia.chicagohistory.org/pages/1135.html.

"Is the community changing—disappearing, enlarging, specializing?" she wrote in undated notes she saved in a notebook. "Often issues are economic rather than racial."[318]

On one level, that idea must have been comforting. The Cabbage Patch had plenty of experience dealing with economic issues. However, after World War II, many of the Patch's issues were undeniably racial. The crowds of black children at the end of the alley by the Cabbage Patch Settlement made that very clear. They would be there at nine at night when Lloyd Redman closed the gym—50 or so black young people outside a locked gate, waiting to fight the white boys who had been in the Cabbage Patch playing.

"There'd be the God-awfullest fights you'd ever seen," Redman said later. "An idiot would soon learn that you need to do something."[319] The Cabbage Patch learned, even if the lessons were sometimes hard.

In some ways, racial pressure was greater on the Cabbage Patch Settlement than on some other neighborhood organizations because, in the segregated Louisville of the 1940s, '50s, and '60s, Miss Marshall's Cabbage Patch neighborhood had both white and black families living close together. Families moved in and out as employers shifted and the city built housing projects, but children of both races lived within walking distance of the settlement. Children from both races faced problems of single-parent families and pervasive, soul-sucking poverty. Children of both races

---

318. Louise Marshall, undated notes for National Conference of Social Work meeting in Minneapolis, CPSHR, FHS.

319. Lloyd Redman, interview by Keith Cardwell, December 2, 1987, CPSOHP, CPSHR, FHS.

needed and wanted the fun the Cabbage Patch offered to white children. However, for most of its history, custom and law had prevented the Cabbage Patch from serving black and white families together.

Certainly, Louise's personal history offered little help on the subject of race. Gentrified white Louisvillians like the Marshalls did not consider themselves racists. Indeed, when 20th-century white Louisvillians considered their city's history of race relations, they labeled themselves moderates who had treated "Negroes" well.[320] To reach that conclusion, they brushed aside the city's heritage as a place where some citizens who were white had owned some residents who were black from the city's beginnings until the 13th Amendment to the US Constitution abolished slavery.

That heritage was still a fresh memory in the late 1800s when young Louise had visited her Veech grandparents for summer vacations at their Indian Hill farm. US Census records show that her grandfather, Richard Veech, had owned about eight slaves, as his father had before him.[321] Some of the African Americans who worked at Indian Hill when Louise visited as a child may well have been former slaves or would have remembered slavery. Indeed, her family's history as slave owners ran deep on both sides. Her Marshall kin in Virginia had also owned slaves.

Although slavery was legally a thing of the past when Louise was growing up, the attitude that black people were inferior and should live segregated lives survived, even in

320. Tracy E. K'Meyer, *Civil Rights in the Gateway to the South: Louisville, Kentucky, 1945–1980* (Lexington: University Press of Kentucky, 2009).

321. US Census 1860.

white households where black employees lived on the property and were treated with courtesy. The distinction showed in small and large ways. In Burwell Marshall Sr.'s household, for example, Lizzie Marshall referred to her husband as Mr. Marshall and to almost all white adults by title and last name. Even as an adult, Louise referred to her married sisters in public as Mrs. Johnson and Mrs. Dosker. But black adults were another matter; the Marshalls, Louise included, called their black employees by their first names. That paternalistic approach to race relations helped maintain the racial order upper-class whites valued.[322]

The condescension was not entirely a matter of personal choice for white residents in Kentucky. After the Civil War, the 13th Amendment abolishing slavery was passed in 1865. However, the Kentucky legislature quickly made it clear that blacks were not equal to whites under the law. The 14th Amendment, which soon gave all those born in the United States their full rights as citizens, didn't alter the white Kentucky lawmakers' determination to keep black citizens in "their place."[323] By the time Louise Marshall opened her Cabbage Patch Settlement, lawmakers and public officials in Kentucky had mandated segregation in schools and universities. Segregation practices not covered by state law; local ordinances, and public policy were set by individual businesses and enforced by deed restrictions and public

---

322. George C. Wright, *Life behind a Veil: Blacks in Louisville, Kentucky 1865–1930* (Baton Rouge: Louisiana State University Press, 1985), 1–10.

323. Marion B. Lucas, *A History of Blacks in Kentucky: From Slavery to Segregation, 1760–1891,* vol. 1 (Frankfort, KY: Kentucky Historical Society, 1992), 292–325.

pressure. Louise went to segregated schools, socialized at elite segregated clubs, skated at a segregated rink, and worshiped at a church that was resoundingly white (although some Presbyterian churches allowed the black servants of members to join the church and worship there). The laws mandating segregation of educational institutions might not have applied to Miss Marshall's privately funded settlement house, but there was no question about what white society expected: segregation. Integration would threaten the settlement's fund-raising, volunteer support, and attendance.

The Cabbage Patch's white children, who grew up without the benefit of private clubs and segregated skating rinks, started life without the same spirit of condescension. In the Patch's racially checkered neighborhood, racial distinctions dimmed when black children and white children went out to play—until adults intervened.

"I talked with them, ran with them, and we'd fight each other and everything in the neighborhood," Joe Burks, who is white, recalled. But if the black children and white children were caught playing ball together or walking through Central Park or sitting together on a bus, things changed. Police would break up the ball games and chase the black children out of Central Park.[324] Black girls knew where they had to sit on a bus, even if an uninformed white friend suggested that they sit together in front.

Miss Marshall established her settlement for white families, but it provided some services to black families from its early days. The Cabbage Patch mother-baby clinic

---

324. Joseph Burks Sr., interview by Keith Cardwell, January 31, 1987, CPSOHP, CPSHR, FHS.

provided medical care for both black and white babies, but as they got older, the black children could not move into the settlement's nursery school and other activities established for white children. Cabbage Patch rummage sales also provided inexpensive clothing for both white and black families, although probably not at the same time. Miss Marshall would have been unlikely to turn away black families who came to her in need, but the settlement didn't have programs or keep records for them. The settlement carefully kept file cards recording information on every white family who received services. No permanent files were kept for black families.[325]

World War II accelerated changing housing patterns and racial relationships in the Cabbage Patch as it did in the rest of Louisville. The Louisville NAACP pushed for equal salaries for both black and white teachers and won. Louisville elected its first black alderman. The NAACP pressed Kentucky to eliminate racial barriers in higher education and Louisville to open all its public libraries to black citizens.[326] Nationally, President Harry Truman endorsed racial equity in 1948 when he abolished racial segregation in the US armed forces, and the US Supreme Court began issuing opinions that weakened segregation's hold, including the historic 1954 *Brown vs. Board of Education*, which ended state-mandated school segregation. At the Cabbage Patch Settlement, as in broader society, change brought conflict.

---

325. "Method of filing" instructions for family participation cards, undated, CPSHR, FHS.

326. Mervin Aubespin, Kenneth Clay, J. Blaine Hudson, *Two Centuries of Black Louisville: A Photographic History* (Louisville, KY: Butler Books, 2011), 26–30.

One evening, shortly after dark, a 13-year-old white boy ran into the Cabbage Patch Settlement pursued by 20 or more rock-throwing black boys. White boys lined up inside the settlement wall. Black boys threw rocks over it.

"Great excitement prevailed," Miss Marshall wrote in a fund-raising letter to supporters.

An armed policeman pursued the black children back into the "black district" and fired his gun in the air. The black children scattered and disappeared. After an investigation, the settlement made it known that the white boy had been at fault.

"We went to work to make friends of the negroes and played softball with them," Miss Marshall wrote. "Justice and fair play settled what might have developed into a race riot."[327]

It's unclear how many times such scenes were repeated or when that particular event happened; Miss Marshall, who was clearly pleased by the outcome, included the story in two different newsletters in different years. Joe Burks, a Cabbage Patch kid before he became a member of the staff, remembered an event like that in the late 1940s when the black kids threw rocks and sticks as he left the gym. Lloyd Redman went out to talk to the black boys.

"Why can't we come in?" the boys asked. They just couldn't, Redman said, but he added, "You all have a ball team . . . we'll play you a game." Redman arranged to play at a University of Louisville athletic field, one of the few fields

---

327. Louise Marshall, "Do Your Part to Stop Crime/ Don't Let It Start!" Cabbage Patch Settlement House fund-raising letter, October 1946, CPSHR, FHS.

where a mixed-race game would be permitted.[328]

Those games didn't settle anything. The black children still wanted into the settlement. When the white teenagers had dances at the Patch, the black teenagers gathered outside and danced to music that spilled into the alley.

Louise's Victorian upbringing had not prepared her to deal with such problems. She had no problem with providing services to blacks and whites alike—they were all God's children, after all—but she struggled with the question of whether black people were inferior.[329] She also struggled with the idea of interracial relationships between girls and boys at the Patch where so many white romances had begun.

"I know what needs to be done," she said later, "but I don't know how to do it because of the way I was raised."[330]

"This was a problem with Miss Marshall," Redman said later. "We talked about this." For those born and raised in segregated white society, the conversations were hard. "I didn't understand enough about it myself for me to try to communicate this to Miss Marshall," Redman said. "This was a giant hurdle! She began to see."[331]

Fortunately, other men Miss Marshall had trained for her staff understood well what was happening and the problems that were ahead. Roosevelt Chin had grown up in the housing project at 13th and Hill when it had no black residents. That

328. Joseph Burks Sr., interview by Keith Cardwell, January 31, 1987, CPSOHP, CPSHR, FHS; Joseph Burks Sr., PI, July 8, 2011.

329. Dr. James J. and Anne Cooksey, PI, July 18, 2014.

330. Burwell Keith Marshall III, PI, March 16, 2012.

331. Lloyd Redman, interview by Keith Cardwell, December 2, 1987, CPSOHP, CPSHR, FHS.

racial mix was changing, and a phenomenon that social scientists called the "tip ratio" appeared to be taking over; when the black population reached 30–40 percent, all the white residents left.

"We could see the writing on the wall," said Chin. "If once we opened our doors, that would happen, and so we thought we'd better do it step by step."[332]

When the US Supreme Court acted to desegregate schools on May 17, 1954, the Cabbage Patch began to take those first steps quietly, quickly, and, perhaps, unofficially. As with many things at the Cabbage Patch, the sequence isn't at all clear.

The Cabbage Patch board minutes suggest that the board started discussing integration in June 1954—less than a month after the US Supreme Court's decision. Redman briefed the board on problems "concerning the Negro question." Then Miss Marshall's favorite nephew, board member Lewis Johnson, made a motion, seconded by Thames Palmer-Ball, that the Cabbage Patch "executive authority" look ahead to integrating the settlement's activities. The minutes don't record any action and probably didn't need to.[333] Lewis Johnson and Mrs. Palmer-Ball were two of Miss Marshall's closest friends and allies on the board. (Mrs. Palmer-Ball's mother, Ida Castner, one of Miss Marshall's good friends, had also served on the Cabbage

---

332. Roosevelt Chin, interview by Keith Cardwell, March 7, 1987, CPSOHP, CPSHR, FHS.

333. Minutes, CPSH Board of Directors, June 14, 1954, CPSHR, FHS.

Patch board.)[334] It is unlikely that they would have brought up such an explosive issue without talking it through with Miss Marshall first or that Redman would have started the conversation if she hadn't asked him to report.[335] In December 1955, Lewis Johnson and Mrs. Palmer-Ball made another motion, this time to register and admit "colored children" who applied for admission to the settlement. No vote was recorded, but Miss Marshall was directed to consult the staff about their feelings. The language in the minutes was vintage Miss Marshall.[336]

The city of Louisville was also moving haltingly toward desegregation in ways that made integration easier for the Cabbage Patch. In 1956, Louisville desegregated its parks, making Central Park, where Cabbage Patch teams practiced, a place where black and white children could play together without police intervention. Louisville public schools prepared to desegregate in the fall of 1956 by allowing black children to attend previously all-white schools. However, many private organizations, including churches and boys and girls clubs, moved slowly or not at all.

That lack of movement left black kids like 14-year-old Sherman Lewis in a bind. He and six or seven of his friends wanted badly to play football in the ninth grade, but public schools did not allow freshmen on their varsity teams. White ninth graders could play at boys and girls clubs spread about

334. Thames Palmer-Ball, interview by Andrew Chancey, September 17, 1987, CPSOHP, CPSHR, FHS.

335. Dr. James J. Cooksey, PI, July 18, 2014.

336. Minutes, CPSH Board of Directors, December 12, 1955, CPSHR, FHS; Dr. James J. Cooksey, PI, July 18, 2014.

the city, but those private organizations would not accept Sherman Lewis and his friends.

"You can't play here. Blacks can't play here," they were told at the Optimists Boys Club. But the Optimist they talked to added, "There's a place down on Sixth Street. It's called Cabbage Patch, and they play ball there." It seemed worth a try. So, Lewis and his friends trotted down to the Cabbage Patch. "They welcomed us with open arms," Lewis said nearly 55 years later. "They said, 'Come on out. You can play on our football team.'"[337]

That was an important moment in many respects: It made Louise Marshall and her Cabbage Patch pioneers in Louisville race relations. It may have helped smooth public school integration. It opened a renewed tradition of breathtaking success for Cabbage Patch sports. And it launched Sherman Lewis into a football career that included a spot on the 1959 Kentucky all-state football team as a running back for Manual High School; third place in the Heisman Trophy voting when he played at Michigan State University; and three NFL Super Bowl rings as an assistant coach for the San Francisco 49ers.

For Lewis, the fast, skinny black kid who showed up for Cabbage Patch practice, however, the important thing was that he was getting to play football with coaches who pushed and mentored him and with other kids who wanted to have fun and win. Integrated sports teams were new for the boys on the Cabbage Patch team that year, but, by all accounts, they had no problems because of race. In an era when other black teenagers were getting arrested for taking part in lunch

---

337. Sherman Lewis, telephone interview with authors, July 22, 2014.

counter sit-ins, Lewis and his friends knew that they, too, were pioneers who were breaking ground—at the Cabbage Patch and in Louisville.

"We were the first ones to walk through those doors," Lewis said. "We were aware of the fact that we were first . . . We tried to make sure we carried ourselves and represented our race in a very respectful manner. And we did."[338]

The coaches—Charles Dietsch and Joe Burks—made sure the boys on the team didn't segregate themselves or get different treatment in a world that must have seemed unfamiliar. The coaches' message to every Cabbage Patch player was the same: they were a team, not a bunch of individuals. That was true even if Sherman Lewis was the fastest kid around. Sometimes a coach would say, "Throw the ball to Sherman, and everybody else get out of the way." When they did that, Sherman would score six or seven touchdowns a game—enough to give the Cabbage Patch a record no one else could top.[339] But Burks and Dietsch kept drilling home the lesson.

"If we had success, it was because all 11 guys did their job," Lewis said. "If I was a running back and made a good play, it was because a lineman did his job." That was a lesson Lewis remembered for the rest of his life.[340]

After the games, the team would pile onto the Cabbage Patch's big, red truck and sing all the way back to the Patch. "It was just a happy, happy time," said Lewis.

---

338. Ibid.

339. Dr. James J. Cooksey, PI, July 18, 2014.

340. Sherman Lewis, telephone interview with authors, July 22, 2014.

Cabbage Patch Settlement football players recall good times on the "Big Red Truck," a used truck acquired in the mid-1950s. Having the truck for transportation opened new worlds of opportunities for activities, field trips, and camping trips. The folding-chair seats would never pass safety standards today. *Courtesy of Cabbage Patch Settlement House Archives*

The year was both happy and successful on many levels. The undefeated Cabbage Patch team won the city championship. Then, as the holidays approached, Lewis entered the "Turkey Trot," a race around Central Park for a live turkey in a crate. Fifty-five years later, Lewis still laughed about that day. "I won that turkey to take home," he says. "That was a great experience. That was a great time."

As the football season morphed into basketball, Lewis and the rest of the team, black and white, became basketball players for the Patch, then baseball players. Then the 14-year-olds on the Cabbage Patch team moved, more or less as a unit, to Manual High School where they would form the core of a state championship football team. Integration wasn't an issue at Manual, Lewis said. A core of the black and white teens who started high school that fall were already on the same team.

Lewis did well at football and track, although he was always small for a football player, just five feet, nine inches, and not much more than 160 pounds at his prime. Joe Burks, who coached the running backs at the Cabbage Patch, was short, too, but he had played successfully on the 1948 Manual High School championship team. He convinced Lewis that he could succeed, too. Cabbage Patch coaches became role models who made Lewis want to go into coaching. "I really admired those guys."[341]

Excellence and pride were two of the values Miss Marshall fostered in everything the Cabbage Patch did. Boys, black and white, flocked to the Cabbage Patch from all over Louisville to play for the best youth teams in town. Cabbage Patch coaches welcomed both the white, longtime Cabbage Patch kids and the street-hardened black players, who made the teams stronger.[342] Those integrated teams won so often that in 1958 the settlement had to install a trophy case.[343]

The teams also gave the Cabbage Patch its best opportunity for integration it could control. By February 1958, the first time black participation is listed in board minutes, the Cabbage Patch had 17 black boys playing football for the Cabbage Patch. Because kids had to try out for teams, the

---

341. Sherman Lewis, telephone interview with authors, July 22, 2014.

342. Lloyd Redman, interview by Keith Cardwell, February 12, 1987, CPSOHP, CPSHR, FHS.

343. Louise Marshall, report to CPSH Board of Directors, February 10, 1958, CPSHR, FHS.

coaches could use their cut system to make sure that every team had a white majority—and boys of both races who could get along together. The Cabbage Patch staff didn't like to use the word "quota," but that's what they had.[344] In 1958, the Cabbage Patch had decided that only one-third of any team could be black. That eliminated resentment by the white boys, Miss Marshall wrote in her report to the board.[345]

The white children's feelings were important to Miss Marshall. She didn't want white children who had grown up in the settlement and considered themselves Patchers to feel unwelcome or displaced as more black children joined activities. She wanted them to stay even as black children became more of a presence.

"How do we do this in a way that we get true integration?" she kept asking the staff and board. An all-black Cabbage Patch was no more integrated than an all-white one, she'd point out. And creating resentment among the white Patchers would only make race relations worse.[346] That position put her in the mainstream of white moderate Southerners, who favored integration but thought it should come slowly and peacefully, without all the shouting.

Black children were pushing to participate in other Cabbage Patch activities, the sewing school, Roosevelt Chin's crafts classes, and the game room among them. Eager black girls—41 of them—joined the popular sewing classes.

---

344 Roosevelt Chin, interview by Keith Cardwell, March 7, 1987, CPSOHP, CPSHR, FHS.

345. Louise Marshall, report to CPSH Board of Directors, October 20, 1958, CPSHR, FHS.

346. Dr. James J. Cooksey, PI, July 18, 2014.

"It has been difficult at times to get teachers who would work with them," Miss Marshall wrote. "Two teachers stopped coming because of them."[347] When new teachers did come, Miss Marshall welcomed them warmly with hugs.[348]

In all, nearly 100 black children were participating in Cabbage Patch activities by February 1958, including 23 in the craft classes. The numbers were a problem. The settlement didn't have enough staff, equipment, or money to handle everyone.

"The negroes are begging to come in and we would gladly have them if it were possible," Miss Marshall wrote to the board. With enough money, she suggested, the Patch could open its gym and game room at certain times "for negroes only." (Miss Marshall underlined the words.)[349] And that's what happened, very quietly at first, perhaps without the board fully understanding that the settlement had parallel programs for black and white children.

At first, as it edged toward serving black children, the Patch was open for its normal activities for whites from three to five in the afternoon. Then "from five to seven, it was known that the staff 'went to supper,'" Rod Napier said. "What they did was let the African American kids in the back way." The black children who filled the gym had two hours to play ball before the settlement reopened. "At seven, we opened up, and I would come in the front," Napier said. "I suspect a lot of people didn't know that was happening."

347. Louise Marshall, report to CPSH Board of Directors, February 10, 1958, CPSHR, FHS.

348. Patsie Peak, PI, July 28, 2014.

349. Louise Marshall, Cabbage Patch Settlement Report to the Board of Directors, February 10, 1958, CPSHR, FHS.

Even that small step took courage for Miss Marshall. If the word had gotten out, Napier said, a lot of people would have reacted badly. "She did it at risk of closing the Patch. That's how volatile tensions were in those days. . . . Miss Marshall said, 'It's the right thing to do.' She took, I think, a high risk because I think that's who she was."[350]

Eventually, Miss Marshall opened the game room just for black children for three days a week. Black children could play in both the gym and game room with a black staff member, Ron Johnson, there to supervise. Other activities followed the same segregated pattern. If Joe Burks and Charles Dietsch took a group of white children to Butler State Park for a day outing on a Monday, they'd go back again on Wednesday with a group of black children for the same experience. Sports teams and some specialized activities like crafts and sewing remained integrated, although crowding was a problem.

The integration would spread to other activities over the years, triggering an exodus of white children—1,945 white children left in a four-month period in 1964—until vestiges of segregation at the settlement were gone.[351] In the meantime, in the late 1950s and early 1960s, the settlement was taking a patchwork approach, integrating some activities and maintaining segregated but equal programs in others. Miss Marshall was proud of that approach, despite the US Supreme Court's assertion that "separate but equal is not equal." However, the settlement's approach raised questions,

---

350. Rod Napier, PI, June 22, 2012; Joseph Burks Sr., interview by Keith Cardwell, January 31, 1987, CPSOHP, CPSHR, FHS.

351. Dr. James J. Cooksey, PI, July 18, 2014; Louise Marshall, report to CPSH Board of Directors, March 16, 1964, CPSHR, FHS.

not from the courts or angry crowds, but from Miss Marshall's own Presbyterian Church, which was changing in ways that troubled many of its members. Miss Marshall's reaction to both the church's questions and to other changes in the church activated all the combative instincts she'd gotten from her Marshall and Veech forebears.

From the distance of time, the actual issues that brought Miss Marshall's blood to a boil in the late 1950s and early 1960s seem only slightly related to each other and considerably less explosive than they became for her. The Stuart Robinson Presbyterian Church, next door to the Cabbage Patch, wanted to forge a partnership with the settlement and presbytery to better serve the inner city. The Cabbage Patch board of directors, strapped for money, wanted to build broader Presbyterian support. The governing boards of the Presbyterian Church wanted to encourage racial justice and integration in church-related organizations, and the Northern and Southern branches of the Presbyterian Church began discussing a national reunion after a century of separation. Those were all red-flag issues for Miss Marshall.

Miss Marshall had never found partnerships workable (as the unfortunate Optimists had learned), and she didn't like being told what to do. When the Rev. Gerald Stone, the eager pastor of Stuart Robinson, asked a question about a routine matter, such as repairing broken steps, Miss Marshall took it as criticism. She saw threats to the future of the Cabbage Patch in questionnaires about integration from activist Presbyterian leaders. And all her protective instincts flared when willing, well-meaning new members of the Cabbage Patch board didn't observe the board's most important unspoken rule:

No one was to question or disagree with Miss Marshall. In that atmosphere, where everything seemed threatening to her, uniting Presbyterians into one national church could mean only one thing to Miss Marshall: The larger, more liberal northern church would seize control of the denomination and force new, liberal members on the Cabbage Patch's board to dismantle Miss Marshall's good work. Even Miss Marshall's close friends and staunchest supporters on the board had to agree with a former board member who pronounced the situation "just a mess" and said that the result was a "pitched battle." Because Miss Marshall often misinterpreted the issues, details of what actually happened seem less important than her reaction to them. The Cabbage Patch was her baby, and she was willing to hurt feelings, cut important ties, and attack anyone who seemed to threaten her life's work.[352] She apparently called her cadre of powerful friends into action, although what she asked them to do is not recorded, and she launched a salvo of sharp, self-justifying letters aimed at anyone who appeared to threaten the settlement.

May of 1959 seems to have been an especially hot month, ignited by a decision the Louisville Presbytery (the local Presbyterian governing body) made to strengthen the relationship between Stuart Robinson Presbyterian Church and the Cabbage Patch. The presbytery decided, in typical Presbyterian fashion, to appoint a committee to study the relationship.

Miss Marshall responded with a statement defining the Cabbage Patch as an inner-city mission of the Presbyterian

---

352. Margaret Harvin, interview by Keith Cardwell, February 20, 1987, CPSOHP, CPSHR, FHS.

Church, established in 1910 to "reach the people the church was unable to reach." Miss Marshall proudly reported new programs for white kindergarten children and white "Golden Agers."

"We have had a wonderful negro program for three years," she wrote and listed the programs that included black children. The letter went on for three pages, listing the Cabbage Patch's unsuccessful efforts to coordinate with Stuart Robinson Church and suggesting that the Presbyterian Church (excepting her own church, Second Presbyterian) had been stinting in its financial support of the Cabbage Patch. She ended by again touting the settlement's "unusually harmonious" work toward integration with an unmatched absence of problems. "I am sure there is nowhere else in Kentucky where a Sunday Service could be held with negroes and white people worshiping our Heavenly Father together, with such love and understanding," she wrote. Miss Marshall also produced a list of Cabbage Patch programs and statistics that she titled "An Inner-City Mission Where Religion is a 6 Day Week Affair." The settlement employed seven full-time and 10 part-time workers, used 51 volunteers, and served 89,726 clients a year.[353]

That much of the correspondence had been relatively informational and free of spleen. Next she went after individuals, starting with Stuart Robinson's pastor, "that cockey show off," Mr. Stone, who she said was "pathetically immature and emotionally unstable" and impossible to work with. The idea

---

353. "An Inner-City Mission Where Religion Is a 6 Day Week Affair," Louise Marshall response to a Louisville Presbytery Committee, May 1959, CPSHR, FHS.

that Mr. Stone's addition to the Cabbage Patch board would produce "harmony and co-operation for the sake of Christ is certainly an enigma to me," she wrote. Vigorous attempts to work with Stone over three and a half years had exhausted her, all for naught, she wrote to her board of directors. "The nicer I was to him, the more difficult he became."[354]

Even a committee formed to study the relationship between Stuart Robinson and the Cabbage Patch would damage the settlement and her life's work, she contended in a July 1959 letter to "Fellow Board members," although she didn't expect them to care. "Although I have literally spent my life in this work, I was given to understand at the May Board meeting that my opinion amounted to nothing, and that my word could not be taken."[355]

Miss Marshall had invited Dr. W. R. Clark, pastor of her own Second Presbyterian Church, to join the board to strengthen ties to the presbytery, but now she claimed that he was "working against" her when he did just what he had been asked to do. With considerable, pointed encouragement from Miss Marshall, a dazed Dr. Clark resigned, just six months after he was named to the board.[356]

Miss Marshall's longtime friend, Margaret "Peg" Pleune Harvin, who was named to the board at the same time as Clark, also found herself very much at odds with Miss Marshall, but the two managed to smooth the relationship. The board may

---

354. Louise Marshall to Dr. W. R. Clarke, June 4, 1959, CPSHR, FHS.

355. Louise Marshall to CPSH Board members, July 10, 1959, CPSHR, FHS.

356. Louise Marshall to Dr. W. R. Clarke, June 4, 1959; W. R. Clarke to Louise Marshall, May 20, 1959, CPSHR, FHS.

have still thought a closer relationship with the Presbyterian Church was a good idea, but it learned from the "mess."

"The board just kind of sank down and didn't make any gestures to do anything that she did not orchestrate," Margaret Harvin said.[357]

In fact, Miss Marshall's distrust of her Presbyterian Church continued to grow because the church was changing—on race and other issues—in ways she couldn't embrace. For the first half of the 20th century, Louise Marshall and her Southern Presbyterian denomination shared the belief that a minister's duty was to "preach the word" and the church's job was saving souls, one by one. Stands on social issues were not a part of the church's mission. But by 1958—at the height of conflicts over communism and race in the United States—there had been an "epochal change" in the church. Now many Christians believed they were called to "stand in the world in the name of Christ."[358] Indeed, Dr. Henry Mobley, pastor of Highland Presbyterian Church and a Cabbage Patch board member, used his pulpit and the Bible's Old Testament to lead his congregation's response to racism. Worse yet (in Miss Marshall's eyes), at Louisville Presbyterian Theological Seminary, where Mobley was also on the board, professors such as George Edwards and seminary students were taking to the streets during the 1960s demonstrating for causes such as open housing and an end to the Vietnam War. Some conservative Presbyterians wondered

---

357. Margaret Harvin, interview by Keith Cardwell, February 20, 1987, CPSHR, FHS.

358. Milton J. Coalter, John M. Mulder, Louis B. Weeks, eds., *The Confessional Mosaic: Presbyterians and Twentieth-Century Theology* (Louisville, KY: Westminster/John Knox Press, 1990), 7–10.

openly whether those professors were Christians at all. Some suspected that a spirit of communism had infected both the seminary and those professors who were training the next generation of pastors. Louise shared those suspicions.

In his role as chairman of the seminary board, Henry Mobley had to defend Edwards and the seminary. However— despite her consternation with the activism—Louise continued to maintain the kind of relationship with Mobley that she had with all her bad boys at the Patch. Mobley had a gift for defusing tension with his considerable charm and humor. He was a regular cutup at Cabbage Patch board meetings, offering a stream of irreverent commentary while Miss Marshall tried to run a meeting. Miss Marshall would just as regularly shush him. "That's enough now, Dr. Mobley. That's enough."[359] Sometimes, however, even Mobley would cross a line, as he apparently did in the 1960s when Louisville was throbbing with tension over black demands and demonstrations for an end to segregated housing.

Miss Marshall fired off one of her characteristic letters, full of escalating anger and accusation. She didn't take Mobley's horseplay at a board meeting seriously, she wrote, because she knew that seminary professor George Edwards "calls the tune" for many preachers, including Mobley, on issues such as open housing.

"This is just another evidence that the preachers in my denomination are no longer preaching the gospel of love but the gospel of Force," she wrote. If Mobley were sincere about racial equality, "you would move into a negro neighborhood

---

359. Dr. James J. Cooksey, PI, July 14, 2011.

and encourage your children to marry them." She ended ominously with a quote from the old King James translation of the Bible: "Whatsoever a man soweth, that shall he also reap."[360] Henry Mobley was undeterred; he would spend many more years on the Cabbage Patch board and preach at Miss Marshall's funeral.

If the letter failed to change Mobley, it is significant for what it showed about Miss Marshall. Like much of Southern society, her greatest fear about integration was intermarriage. Many white Southerners couldn't bear the thought of black men with their daughters, and 29 states had laws against interracial marriages with criminal penalties for the people involved.[361] Miscegenation was a rallying point for Southern extremists, who opposed all desegregation, and a deeply held fear even for whites who considered themselves moderates. Miss Marshall was no exception.

Miss Marshall had always worried about the chemistry between white girls and boys generally, said board member Lynn Gant March. "She was very afraid of girls having SEX-U-Al intercourse" (as Miss Marshall pronounced it).[362] Miss Marshall monitored the white teens carefully, worked to keep girls and boys at a respectable distance at dances, and, when

---

360. Louise Marshall to Dr. Henry Mobley (undated), CPSHR, FHS.

361. James R. Browning, "Anti-miscegenation Laws in the United States," *Duke Bar Journal 1*, no. 1 (1951): 26–41. Kentucky law prohibited a white person from marrying a person with one-fourth Negro blood. Children of an interracial marriage were considered illegitimate, and penalties included jail sentences of up to a year and fines of up to $5,000. The US Supreme Court voided such laws in 1967.

362. Lynn Gant March, PI, June 14, 2011; Joseph Burks Sr., PI, July 8, 2011.

her efforts failed and two 16-year-olds married, she thought it "absolutely sinful."[363] Having seen the problems sex could cause, Miss Marshall didn't want to add race to the already fraught dynamics between adolescents. At least early on, integrated activities for boys and girls ended when hormones started flowing in 12-year-olds.

"Miss Marshall didn't want the blacks and whites to mix. She was afraid of intermarriage," said Joe Burks.[364]

Over the years, that changed. Black teens, girls and boys, went on trips and campouts. Even teen dances began including black youngsters—although at first, the Patch offered folk dancing in place of anything that invited body contact. Then teen culture provided a solution: the twist, a dance craze that people enjoyed without any partner at all. In time, the dances disappeared, and the teens hung out together in the teen lounge, a space where teenaged boys and girls, black and white, could eat, listen to music, and play games away from annoying little kids. They all seemed to like that.

By 1963 and '64, the sports teams Terry Gibson coached as a young staff member were mostly black youngsters in desperate need of the Cabbage Patch's help.

"They lived a tough life," he said. "No structure in their life. No discipline in their life. Very seldom three good meals." The Cabbage Patch teams provided structure and discipline. Camps provided three hot meals a day, but too often, that wasn't enough to overcome the hardships. Terry Gibson stayed in touch with many of his players over the years, long

---

363. Ruth Tomerlin Chaffins, PI, July 6, 2011.

364. Joseph Burks Sr., PI, July 8, 2011.

enough to go to some of their funerals. "They died pretty early because life was just killing them," he said.[365]

Over the next decades, the initial harmony of integration at the Cabbage Patch would sometimes dissolve into interracial fights. Neighbors would complain about black children hanging around the neighborhood causing mischief. Cabbage Patch leaders would watch black attendance rise and white attendance drop. Court-ordered busing to integrate all public schools would force the Cabbage Patch staff to devise new schedules and new ways to reach children in the neighborhood.

In the meantime, children kept coming to the Cabbage Patch in near record numbers, absorbing its values and having fun. Those children, black and white, knew who Miss Marshall was: Miss Marshall ran the show. You didn't want to get on her wrong side. Her carriage suggested British royalty, goodness, and Christian spirit. When she passed black boys like Mike Carter in the hall, she would smile and nod. He would keep going. Mike's respect for Miss Marshall bordered on awe.

Boys like Sherman Lewis, who remembered the beginnings of integration, felt all that and something more: "I realized that she was the reason that we were there . . . She opened the door to everybody."[366]

---

365 Terry Gibson oral history interview by Victoria Groce, February 20, 2008, University of Louisville History Department project, University of Louisville Archives and Special Collections.

366. Mike Carter, interview by Keith Cardwell, January 18, 1987, CPSOHP, CPSHR, FHS; Sherman Lewis, telephone interview with authors, July 22, 2014.

CHAPTER 12

OPENING A DOOR
LONG CLOSED

Despite all the stress, Miss Marshall pronounced 1960—the Cabbage Patch Settlement's golden anniversary year—the settlement's best year ever. And that was just the beginning of an extraordinary decade for the settlement and its founder. Thousands of children, many of them children and grandchildren of original Patchers, came to the settlement for a memorable menu of sports teams, camps, trips, classes, and activities. They all left inoculated with lessons in faith and life that they would remember many years later. Miss Marshall also placed her stamp on an extraordinary group of teenage volunteers, young women from prosperous homes, who came to the Patch to help and left changed by the experience.

In the 1960s, the Cabbage Patch sports teams would establish such a record for winning that crowds chanting "The Cabbage Patch is going to lose" appeared suddenly from nowhere on the rare day when a Patch football team fell behind in the fourth quarter. In the 1960s, Cabbage Patch staff would load a bus with children who would jostle

and sing their way to such far-off places as the Grand
Canyon, Canada, New York City, and Washington, DC. In
the 1960s, 3,615 people, black and white, young and old,
enrolled at the settlement in just one 18-month period.[367] In
the 1960s, those numbers would grow and long lines would
stretch down the walk as children waited to go into a gym
packed with children, activity, and Miss Marshall's plans
for them.

When this picture was taken in the 1960s, Miss Marshall was in her 70s—a
good time for her and for her settlement. *Courtesy of Cabbage Patch Settlement House Archives*

---

367. Louise Marshall, Cabbage Patch Settlement House fund-raising letter,
March 1960, CPSHR, FHS.

Those were good years for Miss Marshall, too, for the most part. Some of the settlement's pressures had eased enough that she could have frequent meals with good friends and indulge her love of reading, gardening, and travel. In some ways, she was at the top of her career at the settlement. Her command of everything that went on there was complete. She had a loyal staff, committed to her ideals. And, if finances were always a problem, she had learned to both pinch pennies and to raise funds without the old anxiety. Indeed, a single phone call from Miss Marshall could raise $10,000 overnight for a special program or particular need. Quarterly reports on the settlement's activities, financial appeals to old (and sometimes wearied) friends, and prayers raised the rest. Help from the government or united charitable appeals—and the rules that went with them—were simply not acceptable to her.

In those days, when she was in her 70s, Miss Marshall also did something extraordinary. She opened the door between her two always-separate lives to the young men she had groomed to sustain the Cabbage Patch's work. She took them on very secret, very elegant cruises to Europe and to meals where the upper crust dined. She said the travel was a part of their education. The men theorized that she considered them family and that she was thanking them for long hours of underpaid work and devoted service. That was, no doubt, true; she did consider them her family. It's also possible that she was introducing them to the broader world they'd need to know to raise money and support for the Cabbage Patch when, as she planned, they would carry on her work. By the next decade, some of those expectations for the young men would be bitterly disappointed.

In the meantime, however, success was everywhere at the Patch, and nothing seemed more successful than the sports programs with their boys in ragged blue jeans and the Cabbage Patch's blue and gold jerseys. Confident boys on opposing teams, who first saw what they thought were unimpressive country boys, learned fast. Terry Gibson recalled that those shabby looking boys "whipped the tar" out of teams whose members thought they were pretty good. The opponents developed a new respect. The boys in blue and gold developed Cabbage Patch pride. Soon other boys from all over town, even rich kids, wanted to play for the Patch and to earn the prestigious Cabbage Patch jacket that would make them sought-after players for high school teams. Cabbage Patch teams seemed so invincible that even the prospect of a loss sparked excited attention.[368]

These Cabbage Patch Settlement football players were city champs in 1965. The settlement's many trophies required construction of a new trophy case.
Courtesy of Cabbage Patch Settlement House Archives

---

368. Terry Gibson, oral history interview with Victoria Groce, February 20, 2008, University of Louisville History Department project, University of Louisville Archives and Special Collections.

Ron Butler remembered the days when the Cabbage Patch went undefeated in football for one season after another. Then, one Saturday afternoon, that record seemed about to end. The clock showed one minute, 15 seconds left in the game and the scoreboard showed the Cabbage Patch behind by one point. The opponents had the ball. Butler looked up at the stands that had been half-empty when the game began. Suddenly they were full.

"Everyone wanted to see this moment when the Cabbage Patch got beat," said Butler. "The crowd was just going wild."

The other team fumbled, and a little guy on the Cabbage Patch team fell on the ball with 30 seconds left on the clock. The Cabbage Patch's quarterback went into the final huddle crying big tears that fell on the ground. One of the players smacked him on the side of the head. "Get it together and call the play." The quarterback threw a low pass near Butler's knees. Butler picked it up, ran, and scored. The Cabbage Patch's record was secure for that day at least, and the team left hollering and screaming. But that's not where the story ends. That's not even the story's point.

When they got back to the settlement, Coach Jim Cooksey, who'd once played for the Patch himself, gave a speech that surprised his team.

"This is just one game," he told jubilant players, who were expecting congratulations. "You have things you accomplish in life. You think you can be on the verge of losing, but if you just keep the faith, keep hope, things will turn out for you."[369]

---

369. Ron Butler, PI, May 15, 2014.

When James Cooksey coached in Central Park or in the locker room, he taught boys how to win in football and in life. *Courtesy of James Cooksey*

That was the point, of course. That was what Miss Marshall insisted on. "In all our activities, we try to emphasize the spiritual, believing that man's relationship with God is the most important thing in life," she wrote.[370]

Thus, before every game, the team would look at a plaque on the wall bearing the prayer every player had to learn: "Lord, I play this game with all my might and when I'm playing, keep me in your sight, that I may never say or do anything that gives offense to you." Fifty years later, Ron Butler remembered the prayer and understands. "It wasn't about the game. It was about the game of life itself." [371]

It didn't matter whether a child went to a sewing or a crafts class, a ball game or a field trip. No matter what the activity was, a devotional and prayer were part of everything Cabbage Patch kids did. Even at a Valentine party, Roosevelt Chin used the occasion to emphasize God's love and the need for the children to love everybody.[372] Miss Marshall wanted to reach the people churches weren't reaching. Some denominations started settlement houses to win people to their faith and to woo them to church. Miss Marshall wanted to build character in children, widen their horizons, and build hope. That was the purpose of all the fun; it was an opportunity for the staff to build faith and character in children so they could improve their lives. And nothing gave the staff a better chance to bond with the children and to

---

370. Louise Marshall, report to CPSH Board of Directors, March 13, 1961, CPSHR, FHS.

371. Ron Butler, PI, May 15, 2014.

372. Louise Marshall, report to CPSH Board of Directors, March 13, 1961, CPSHR, FHS.

instill values in them than camping and travel. So, in the 1960s, Cabbage Patch kids traveled as never before.

From the very beginning, Cabbage Patch kids had gone on short field trips, to a local business, perhaps, or to city parks. Miss Marshall loved travel herself and was determined that her children would have opportunities to see a bigger world. At first, Patchers camped in nearby Indiana or Kentucky state parks. In the 1960s, that program grew to provide adventure on a grand scale known as the camp-on-tour program. Other settlement houses offered camps and field trips—but none as ambitious and complex as the trips for children at Cabbage Patch. They weren't just trips; they were tools for forming character.

Roosevelt Chin's crafts classes were legendary; everyone wanted into them. Chin used them to teach both crafts and God's love.

The Cabbage Patch's camp-on-tour meant that 40 or so children and seven or eight adult volunteers and staff members would pile into a school bus (until the Cabbage Patch Circle donated a 60-seat bus) for a two-week trip across the country.[373] The children would cut grass, collect soft drink bottles, and do odd jobs to earn the $15 or so they needed to pay their share of the much more expensive trips. Then, they had to qualify for the trips with good behavior and report cards that showed attention to school work. At the Cabbage Patch, self-respect demanded that nothing was free.

Once they got on the road, the group would camp at night in tents with everyone taking a hand in housekeeping duties that taught responsibility. For city kids, the camps offered a new world of outdoors with hiking, wildflowers, swimming, and fishing. And, sooner or later, everyone had to go on a "snipe hunt" where the snipe was never, ever found despite a good deal of hilarity. You weren't a Cabbage Patcher until you'd been on one. The evenings would end around a campfire with vespers. Someone would lead a devotional, and maybe the group would sing a well-worn hymn like "Bringing in the Sheaves" or "Onward Christian Soldiers." Before meals, the campers gave thanks, and on Sundays, they had church services. Campers from varied religious traditions took part. There was no pressure. That's just how things were done at the Cabbage Patch. Staff members were Christians, and Miss Marshall figured that some of that "Christian influence . . . would rub off on the kids."[374]

373. Joan Kay, "Speaking of People: Cabbage Patch Founder Saluted at Charity Ball," *Louisville (KY) Courier-Journal*, February 8, 1970.

374. Joseph Burks Sr., interview by Keith Cardwell, January 31, 1987, CPSOHP, CPSHR, FHS.

The trips offered adventure, too. In the Shenandoah Valley, bears attacked the camp, tore the canvas off the Big Red Truck that hauled supplies, and ate all the campers' sweet rolls. On the way back from Canada, the bus broke down in a one-stop-sign Ohio town where friendly firemen opened a fire hose to shower sweaty, stranded campers. And when a New Jersey tollbooth operator refused to allow a school bus on the toll road, Jim Cooksey simply used masking tape to cover the word "school" on the side of the bus and drove on down the turnpike.[375] By the time Patcher Mike Caswell quit school in 10th grade to support his family, he had camped at two state parks, traveled to "Washington, DC, New York City, Canada, and two world's fairs, and he had met a vice president."[376]

Miss Marshall didn't travel with the campers, but sometimes she would meet them someplace like Washington, DC. On one memorable occasion, she gave everyone coins so they could experience eating at an automat—a cafeteria where diners fed coins into machines that dispensed each food they wanted. "We just thought that was the most wonderful thing," said Patcher-turned-volunteer Ruth Chaffins. Then, Miss Marshall went with the group to the US Capitol to meet Kentucky Senator Thruston Morton, who had a party for them with Cokes and cookies. Ruth Chaffins still has the picture taken in the senator's office that day.[377]

---

375. Mike Caswell, interview by Keith Cardwell, January 31, 1987, CPSOHP, CPSHR, FHS; Anita Green, interview by Andrew Chancey, September 24, 1987, CPSOHP, CPSHR, FHS; Ruth Tomerlin Chaffins, PI, July 6, 2011; Dr. James J. Cooksey, PI, July 18, 2014.

376. Mike Caswell, interview by Keith Cardwell, January 31, 1987, CPSOHP, CPSHR, FHS.

377. Ruth Tomerlin Chaffins, PI, July 6, 2011.

In 1966, Patchers on a camp-on-tour dressed up to visit the US Capitol, where they were photographed with Kentucky Senator Thruston Morton, who treated them to a party. Settlement staffers Roosevelt Chin (left) and Jim Cooksey (right) bracket the back row.

Courtesy of Cabbage Patch Settlement House Archives

Those camps may have provided better memories than experiences—at least for the staff. "These trips . . . were a horrendous way to see cities," Jim Cooksey said many years later. The days would be crammed with activities to maximize the children's exposure to monuments and museums that didn't interest them at all.

"We wised up after a while," said Cooksey. "We'd tour for a while, then we'd have a day of swimming and ball and relaxing."[378] A strong staff could solve those sorts of problems

---

378. Dr. James J. Cooksey, PI, July 14, 2011.

and make mid-course corrections. And, in the 1960s, Miss Marshall had a staff she could rely on.

A key part of that staff for many years was Anita Green, the young widow Miss Marshall had recruited from the Second Presbyterian Church congregation. While the men worked with the boys, Anita Green became the driving force behind the sewing school that helped shape character and gave girls practical skills and lasting pride. Anita Green also filled two rooms with Golden Agers on different days every week for lunch and sewing. She provided important support for the camping programs the men ran.[379] One of Mrs. Green's most important—and perhaps least noticed—contributions, however, were the teenaged volunteers, mostly girls, she recruited for work at the Patch. Many were members of Second Presbyterian Church, the offspring of affluent families who sent their children to the city's most expensive private schools where students had a reputation for snobbery. That wasn't permitted at Miss Marshall's Cabbage Patch.

Before volunteers could help with the camps, they had to attend training sessions that taught them not to judge people based on what they had. Those affluent teens had to absorb the Cabbage Patch virtues and rules that applied to everyone equally.

"It was like the Marines. You performed," said Meme Sweets Runyon. "You didn't just show up for work. There were standards."

A gruff, firm Jim Cooksey taught the standards and the ways to provide structure, boundaries, discipline, and love to

---

379. Anita Green, interview by Andrew Chancey, September 24, 1987, CPSOHP, CPSHR, FHS.

children who often didn't have fathers and the amenities the volunteers took for granted. The volunteers, he emphasized, could not patronize the children, who deserved to be treated with respect, high expectations, and love.[380]

Once on the job, the volunteers kept learning. Katherine M. "Kit" Davis learned about Miss Marshall's frugality when she taught city girls to fish at camp. The number of worms for fishing hooks was limited, so Kit found herself cutting worms into four pieces so everyone would have a worm for her hook. "Waste not, want not," was Miss Marshall's watchword. When Kit got back from camp, Miss Marshall had another lesson to teach. Miss Marshall sent Kit to do home visits for each of her campers so she could see the conditions in their homes.

"Every person she looked at as an individual and as one of God's unique creatures," Katherine Davis said nearly 50 years later. The lessons stuck and spread to the volunteers' private schools. The private Louisville Collegiate School, for example, began a Thanksgiving project that encouraged children to earn money to support the Cabbage Patch. Classes competed to earn the most, and to tell what they'd done to earn it. Asking wealthy parents for the money was not an option.[381]

Miss Marshall's impact on the young volunteers went deeper and followed them for years. She counseled the young women as they struggled with life's tug and pull and gave advice that suggested she knew something about hard decisions.

---

380. Meme Sweets Runyon, PI, November 4, 2011.

381. Katherine M. Davis, telephone interview with authors, September 27, 2014.

"My dear," she said to one young woman, "it is the hardest thing in life to be able to say, 'I am doing God's will.'"[382]

Some volunteers, like Meme Runyon and Katherine Davis, went on to serve long terms on the Cabbage Patch board. Some, like Eleanor "Bambi" Goren Leuenberger, graduated from college and became part of a Cabbage Patch staff united by the belief "that each person, each family served at the Cabbage Patch, should know that they were precious in God's eyes, that they had an immense value even if they didn't have that recognition in society's eyes."[383]

A strong staff meant that Miss Marshall could spend more time concerning herself with the children—although that's not always how it looked to them. The children saw her giving directions to staff members who would do exactly what she wanted. Then Miss Marshall would change into "little special shoes," put a band around her hair, and take tools and a stool to climb over the fence into the Cabbage Patch garden. When children arrived at the settlement in the afternoon, that's often where she would be, in her dark dress and headband, planting flowers or picking them, pulling weeds, and using scissors to cut ivy away from her rose bushes. She loved flowers and gardening. Sometimes the headband would be pink, and once in a great while, on a hot day, she would wear a yellow cotton dress.

The garden and her office window also gave Miss Marshall observation posts where she could keep an eye on things and holler at kids who got out of line—although it

---

382. Kimberly McConnell Schiewetz, email to Bill and Linda Raymond Ellison, September 25, 2014.

383. Eleanor Gorin Leuenberger, PI, January 9, 2015.

didn't take much to prompt her to wrench open the window and set someone straight. One day, it was the sight of a little five-year-old girl who was quietly swinging on the Cabbage Patch's front gate. The office window opened, and Miss Marshall leaned across her desk to bark a command: "You there! You! Go home and do something constructive." The startled child took one look at Miss Marshall and disappeared down the street at a run.[384] More often Miss Marshall would stop a child so they could have a talk. "What's going on in your life?" she would ask, and even big, tough kids would open up and tell her. She would listen without saying a thing—although she might have plenty to say later.

Miss Marshall knew all the children, their names and family histories, and whether they were having trouble in school. Woe to the youngster who came to the Patch chewing gum or who got a bit too big for his breeches. After a few minutes with Miss Marshall, he'd be saying, "Yes, ma'am; no, ma'am" and find himself out of the Patch for a few days—or as much as two weeks. Being cocky or stubborn did no good at all.

"She was probably just as stubborn—or more stubborn—than anybody else about getting you in line and helping you," said Mike Caswell, one of Miss Marshall's favorite bad boys.[385]

Mike Caswell had crossed wills with Miss Marshall since he was four years old, too young to participate in Cabbage Patch activities for big kids but small enough to slip under

---

384. Kimberly McConnell Schiewetz, telephone interview with authors, September 30, 2014.

385. Mike Caswell, interview by Keith Cardwell, January 31, 1987, CPSOHP, CPSHR, FHS.

a back gate. He would regularly be escorted out the front door with instructions to wait until he was six. Caswell's father had died, leaving a wife with eight children to raise. For 15 years, Caswell went to the settlement every day— except for the regular instances when he was excluded because of misdeeds. Sometimes Miss Marshall would talk to Mike as she walked through the settlement doing her usual checking up on everything. Sometimes she would call him into her office to ask how he was doing. When he had a problem, Miss Marshall's door was open. When a fire set by neighborhood children burned the Caswell house down, Miss Marshall and the Cabbage Patch staff were there, providing the family with dishes, clothing, and food and helping them find a new place to live, just half a block from the settlement. Other boys in the neighborhood may have cut school, sniffed glue, drunk wine, or smoked pot. Mike Caswell never did; he was always at the Patch where the counselors kept him busy and Miss Marshall loved him dearly and kept him in line.[386]

When she wasn't ordering people around, Miss Marshall talked on her black rotary telephone. Miss Marshall's telephone style was remarkable for both her approach and its effectiveness. She considered herself a charmer of men, and when she was on the phone, she turned the charm to full voltage.

"Oh, my dear, yes," she'd say to a man on the other end of the line. "Oh, that would be lovely of you to donate those cans of hams." When she was done, she'd simply hang up without a good-bye. "Oh, all the men just love it when they

---

386. Ruth Tomerlin Chaffins, PI, July 6, 2011; Mike Caswell, interview by
Keith Cardwell, January 31, 1987, CPSOHP, CPSHR, FHS.

talk to me," she said once after abruptly hanging up. Who could deny it? The hams and other things the settlement needed kept arriving as promised.[387]

With a strong staff in place, Miss Marshall could take time to have lunch or supper with longtime close friends, Adella Latta and Helen Norton among them. Like Miss Marshall, both were strong, independent women. Both were also members of Second Presbyterian Church.[388]

Adella Latta was a widow whose relationship with the Marshalls had been forged when Burwell Marshall Sr. defended her in a complicated court case during the Depression. The relationship had been tested when Louise and her brother Burwell Jr. were at odds in the 1930s. In those days, Adella Latta was the only person both Burwell and Louise could trust and talk to and so became a go-between. Mrs. Latta had done some volunteer work in the settlement office, helping with thank-you notes and checking donor lists.[389] Mostly however, Adella Latta was a busy, savvy, successful financial advisor, a rare status for a woman of her day. Some people thought Mrs. Latta didn't look the part.

"She was a sweet little charming lady who just looked like she should be somebody's grandmother fixing tea and

---

387. Kimberly McConnell Schiewetz, telephone interview with authors, September 30, 2014.

388. Second Presbyterian Church, originally situated in the Marshalls' neighborhood near downtown Louisville, burned in 1956. The congregation moved its services to a mission chapel it had built in the prosperous suburbs east of Louisville and later relocated there.

389. Minutes, CPSH Board of Directors, November 15, 1965, CPSHR, FHS.

cookies," said Jim Cooksey. "She was the sweetest person you can imagine."[390]

Adella Latta and Louise were very close. Like Louise, Adella loved public affairs and stayed up to date on everything. Before leaving for lunch with Louise, she would always check the latest ticker tape reports in her office. When she was with Adella, Louise didn't discuss the Cabbage Patch. The women talked about news and financial affairs and what might lie ahead.[391] Mrs. Latta managed the money Louise had accumulated from the property she inherited. With Mrs. Latta's financial management, Louise, who had never accepted pay for her work at the Cabbage Patch, was becoming a millionaire, a very wealthy woman in that day.

In Helen Norton, Louise had a different kind of friend, a soul mate who shared her passion, her faith, and her sometimes-contentious disposition. Louise and Helen had grown up as friends in the same neighborhood and had gone to the same Presbyterian church. Helen had "let one boyfriend slip away." Then she married her work as a social worker. Eventually, she became the longtime director of the Home of the Innocents, a residential institution that embraced children who couldn't—for one unfortunate reason or another—live at home. Miss Norton lived in an apartment over a garage behind the Home of the Innocents where she showed a stronger domestic side than Louise did. Helen delighted in decorating her living space attractively with antiques, and she had a reputation as a cook, especially for her fried chicken and

---

390. Dr. James J. Cooksey, PI, July 18, 2014.

391. Ibid.

caramel cake. Like Louise, Helen Norton showed the world two sides. One was kind and compassionate, the other "very cantankerous." With Helen, Louise could talk shop. When they didn't meet for lunch, they talked on the phone. Their passions and problems were very much the same.[392]

In the mid-1960s, Miss Marshall—by then in her mid-70s and perhaps slowing down a bit—seems to have made a decision. The five boys she had groomed to succeed her were all grown college graduates. Two—Lloyd Redman and Joe Burks—had already deeply disappointed her by leaving the Cabbage Patch for teaching, a profession that would feed their families and provide financial benefits their Cabbage Patch jobs lacked. The other three men, Charles Dietsch, Roosevelt Chin, and Jim Cooksey seemed fully committed to her, the Cabbage Patch, and their work. About the time Cooksey graduated from the University of Louisville and committed to full-time work at the Patch, Miss Marshall seems to have begun training the men for a time when she wouldn't be running things. Some of that training was entirely predictable. Some involved their leaving the settlement for study toward advanced degrees or to work in private industry. (She had absolute faith that they would return.) Some of the preparation was nothing short of astonishing.

In 1962, as a modest start, Miss Marshall took Dietsch and Chin to a settlement conference in Cleveland as her guests. Then, beginning in late 1963 and early 1964, Chin, Dietsch, Cooksey, and sometimes staff member Anita Green,

---

392. Rob King, telephone interview with Linda Raymond, July 28, 2014; Frances Laughton King, telephone interview with authors, 28 July 2014; Dr. James J. Cooksey, PI, July 18, 2014.

began having lunch with the board of directors before their meetings and started giving reports to the board.

None of that foreshadowed the very odd item that appeared in Miss Marshall's report to the board of directors on July 20, 1964. The notice said that Dietsch, Chin, and Cooksey were all taking two weeks of vacation and another two weeks of unpaid leave and would be gone the entire month of August. Nothing much seemed to happen in August anyway, Miss Marshall wrote. Miss Marshall said she had been unwell for over four months and so would take a month-long vacation, too.

"I have been on the job so long with very long hours six days a week, and I don't feel that I can continue without a rest," she wrote. She cautioned the board not to tell anyone about her absence. She said she didn't want the cottage, where she kept her possessions, broken into.[393] That wasn't all there was to it, however.

Miss Marshall and her staff were about to go on a cruise to Europe together. At the Cabbage Patch, Miss Marshall's frugality with the settlement's funds was legend; she would issue a new pencil only to someone who turned in a stub and provided postage stamps for only one letter at a time. When she took the staff off to see the world, however, she paid for the whole trip with her own money. She didn't want Cabbage Patch donors to find out for fear it would hurt her credibility when fund-raising.

Suddenly young men who had grown up amid the distinctly inelegant poverty of the Cabbage Patch found themselves on

---

393. Louise Marshall, report to the CPSH Board of Directors, July 20, 1964, CPSHR, FHS.

an elegant ocean liner taking the sort of trip that Miss Marshall loved—and that required them to wear coats and ties every day. It was an education on many levels, "the best of times and the worst of times," Jim Cooksey called it.[394]

The Cunard lines' "Queens"—*Mary* and *Elizabeth*— were known for transporting royalty, stars, millionaires, and others who craved glamour, comfort, and precision while traveling. The ships were known for their reliable five-day passages that left New York every Wednesday and arrived at Southampton or Cherbourg the following Monday. For the return trip, passengers boarded on Thursday and arrived back in New York harbor the following Tuesday, having enjoyed every comfort a traveler could want. Meals were a special point of pride.

The Cabbage Patch men found that the luxury liners provided "elaborate meals that go on forever" at tables with two assigned servers who would get to know a group—and individual wants—well. At breakfast the first day, Miss Marshall told the waiter, "Be sure to bring me my coffee hot. I like it to burn me."

The waiter brought the usual hot coffee.

"Ahhh, tepid!" she protested and sent it back. She sent the patient waiter back again and then again. "Can't you bring me some coffee that's hot?"

Finally, the waiter arrived with coffee that was nearly boiling. While the waiter watched, Miss Marshall took a sip

---

394. Terry Gibson, oral history interview by Victoria Groce, February 20, 2008, University of Louisville Department of History project, University of Louisville Archives and Special Collections; Dr. James J. Cooksey, PI, July 14, 2011.

that burned her lip. She swallowed the hurt and looked up at the waiter triumphantly. "Now *that's* the way I like it!"[395]

When the ship landed in Europe, the group followed plans that Miss Marshall had asked the AAA travel service to make for them, with stays in posh hotels and visits to tourist attractions that she knew well. In London, they stayed at the Grosvenor House, a Mayfair hotel that had hosted royalty ranging from Princess Elizabeth to the popular music sensation, the Beatles. The hotel was conveniently near the Natural History Museum and Buckingham Palace. In Florence, Italy, they checked into the very elegant Excelsior, beside the Arno River and Piazza Ognissanti, with a view of the Tuscan Hills. "She did it right," said Cooksey.[396]

Miss Marshall also wore out her companions, said Terry Gibson, a staff member who found himself on one of the trips. The group rented cars and got up at the crack of dawn for breakfast so they could set out to see all the sights that Miss Marshall dictated. Her list included everything.

"You need to see this," she'd say. "You need to see this." Miss Marshall was often too tired to go along, but when the exhausted men returned, she would quiz them. "What did you see? What did this mean?"[397]

The clandestine staff trips would be repeated over the years, taking the group across Europe to England, France, Switzerland, and Italy. On one crossing, the group traveled

395. Dr. James Cooksey, PI, July 14, 2011.

396. Dr. James Cooksey, PI, July 14, 2011.

397. Terry Gibson, oral history interview by Victoria Groce, February 20, 2008, University of Louisville Department of History project, University of Louisville Archives and Special Collections.

on the luxurious new *QE II* where everyone maintained a watch for glimpses of glamorous actress Elizabeth Taylor, who was also on board.[398]

The trips were all taken with great secrecy, much to the dismay of Mrs. Arthur Kappesser, the employee who was left in charge at the settlement with almost no notice and no instruction on how to handle the business that came up while the group was gone. In 1965, when the group returned from a six-week trip, Mrs. Kappesser complained that "it was not right to leave me alone with only two days' notice." Miss Marshall and the staff left again in 1966 for four weeks, despite Mrs. Kappesser's complaints that she felt vulnerable being left alone in the settlement. Finally, in 1967, when it appeared that Miss Marshall was about to leave again with the men in tow, Mrs. Kappesser gave two weeks' notice that she was resigning. Miss Marshall responded with a curt letter lacking the "Christian attitude" that Mrs. Kappesser thought due to someone who had worked at the Patch for 11 years. Miss Marshall enclosed a check for the wages Mrs. Kappesser was due and suggested that Mrs. Kappesser didn't need to work another two weeks.

"Please return the Settlement keys at the earliest possible date," the letter concluded. Because Louise remained as "Veechie" as any of the polite-even-when-contentious Veech side of her family, she ended the letter with a polite, "Cordially yours."[399]

---

398. Anne Majors Cooksey, PI, July 14, 2011.

399. Correspondence between Mrs. Arthur Kappesser, a CPSH employee, and Louise Marshall, May 4–11, 1967, CPSHR, FHS.

Even when they were back in Louisville, the men continued to travel with Miss Marshall between her two worlds. She seemed to want them to understand something about the line she had been walking between the nearly ascetic Cabbage Patch life she had chosen on one hand and her birthright on the other. She had a fur coat that she never wore to the Cabbage Patch neighborhood, she told Chin. She didn't want the people at the Patch to think she was flaunting her wealth.

"You know," she once said to Chin, "I could have bought a Cadillac if I wanted to." Instead, she bought a Chevrolet, something else her society friends simply didn't understand.[400]

Sometimes Mrs. Latta would invite Miss Marshall and the senior Cabbage Patch staff to her house for dinner. There the men would listen to conversations about finance and learn about a whole new world. At other times, Elizabeth Marshall Johnson, Miss Marshall's sister, invited them to dine at her home with monogrammed silver (the same pattern as Louise's) and fine china. The meals were an education on two fronts. The men continued to hone their social graces. And they discovered that they didn't know Louise Marshall quite as well as they thought. When they ate at the Johnsons, the Cabbage Patch men, who thought Miss Marshall's family didn't understand her as well as they did, discovered dimensions to Miss Marshall that they hadn't seen. At her sisters' homes, Louise could laugh and spar with her sisters just as other siblings might. Once her younger sister, Sallie Ewing Dosker, made Louise so mad that Louise called Sallie

400. Roosevelt Chin, interview by Sloane Graff, spring 2002, CPSHR, FHS.

a "stinker." Mrs. Dosker was furious—for the better part of a week. Then the sisters went out to dinner together again.[401]

Maybe the experiences in Miss Marshall's affluent world were an effort to repay the men for their work, just as they were sometimes inclined to believe. Maybe Miss Marshall, her friends, and sisters embraced the men as the sons she'd never had. And, maybe, she wanted Cooksey, Dietsch, and Chin, to have the experiences they would need to move in the same circles as Cabbage Patch board members and donors. Certainly, Miss Marshall took pride in the polish she'd helped them develop.

"Frankly, I think the biggest thing I've done is training and educating these men," Miss Marshall once told a newspaper reporter. "They have polish, finesse, and education, and they can go anywhere."[402]

"I'm devoted to them," she added. Cooksey, Dietsch, and Chin were devoted to her and found themselves more and more often performing the sorts of services that sons might provide—on whichever side of the social line Miss Marshall needed them.

At first, those duties included seeing Miss Marshall home at the end of a long day at the Cabbage Patch. They followed a ritual. Miss Marshall would fix herself chicken à la king for dinner in the Cabbage Patch kitchen. The men would close the gym at nine, and Miss Marshall would pack up her reading, an apple, and a banana before the short drive back to her room at the Puritan Hotel. Louise drove herself in a big 1964 Chevy Impala with "the biggest engine she could

401. James Cooksey, personal interview July 18, 2014.

402. Maureen McNerney, "The Cabbage Patch: A Treasured Home to Miss Marshall," *Louisville (KY) Courier-Journal & Times*, Louisville, May 16, 1971.

get." She would rev up that engine and take off from the settlement with a member of the staff following to be sure she arrived safely. One night, no protector was behind her when she drove home.[403] That night was a turning point.

403. Dr. James J. Cooksey, PI, July 18, 2014 and July 14, 2011; Roosevelt Chin, interview by Sloane Graff, spring 2002, CPSHR, FHS; Terry Gibson, interview with Victoria Groce, February 20, 2008, University of Louisville Department of History project, University of Louisville Archives and Special Collections.

CHAPTER 13

THE END OF
A LOVE AFFAIR

On May 16, 1971, Louise Marshall brought her two worlds together for one of the rare days when she permitted attention to focus on her and not on her Cabbage Patch Settlement. Those she loved gathered outdoors on folding chairs in the University of Louisville Quadrangle to see the university bestow the honorary college degree Louise had never earned with class work, Doctor of Humanities (Honoris Causa). No one but University President Dr. Woodrow Strickler was close enough to see for sure, but some people are certain she accepted with a twinkle in her eye and her usual funny little smile. Miss Marshall had read and studied all her life without benefit of even a high school diploma. She valued education and had pushed countless young people to get college educations that she often quietly financed herself. It was a big day for Louise and those who loved her.

"Many students and alumni of this university would never have reached their goals and realized their dreams without your encouragement and help," Dr. Strickler said in his remarks. The university was bestowing the degree on Louise, he said, "Because our society and all mankind have truly benefitted by your efforts."[404]

Louise had provided a long list of guests—family, friends, board members, and former Patchers—she wanted invited for the occasion. She could see some of them seated in front of the stage, and her niece Elizabeth Haynes's husband, Dr. Douglas Haynes, dean of the medical school, sat comfortingly close on stage behind her. What Louise didn't see was poignantly important. Despite half a century of conflict and painful silence between Louise and her brother Burwell, Burwell had brought his wife and son to see Louise honored. They were sitting, lost in the joyful crowd of graduates' families, where Louise didn't see them from the stage. She had wanted Burwell to be there—although Burwell may not have known that Louise had included him on the invitation list. For Burwell, the occasion was powerful. He sniffed and struggled with tears as his sister received her diploma and academic hood. However, he didn't seek her out after the ceremony. Louise and Burwell didn't speak that day, and time for making amends was running out. Two years later, Burwell died suddenly. It's unclear if the rift was ever healed.[405]

Louise didn't know about the opportunity she had lost until much later when, in her final years, she occasionally invited Burwell's son Keith to come to lunch on Sunday at the Puritan residential hotel where she lived. One Sunday, talk turned to the graduation ceremony.

---

404. Woodrow Strickler, remarks for University of Louisville graduation ceremony, May 16, 1971, CPSHR, FHS.

405. Burwell Keith Marshall III, PI, March 16, 2012; Elizabeth Johnson Haynes, PI, July 11, 2011.

"We were there," Keith Marshall said.

"You were?" Louise said, startled and deeply affected. She hadn't known. Even then, Keith Marshall did not learn for many more years that Louise had put his father on the list of people she wanted present. Keith, too, was startled and moved.[406]

The 1970s were like that for Louise Marshall; moments of pure happiness were interspersed with pain, sadness, and disappointment. For those who loved her, watching Louise, by then in her 80s, was like watching the air leak from a balloon. She was still dedicated to the Cabbage Patch and its people. She still drove her car—with odd springs attached to the sides as feelers so she would know when she came close to a curb or car. She still went to the settlement and barked orders. She presided over some board meetings. But the old stamina was gone. Miss Marshall just seemed tired.

Roosevelt Chin realized that Miss Marshall was getting old after an awful night in May 1973 when none of the men followed her home after the settlement closed at nine o'clock.[407] It was, after all, only a half mile to her room at the Puritan Hotel. Miss Marshall pulled up to the curb beside the Puritan and slid across the front seat to get out of the passenger's side as she usually did. But, on the sidewalk, someone was waiting. As Louise opened the door, the man shoved her back in and grabbed her purse. Louise wasn't about to let him have it, so he punched her in the face, again and again. Somehow, Louise started the car and took off with the man hanging out. After 100 yards or so, he finally let go.

---

406. Burwell Keith Marshall III, PI, March 16, 2012.

407. Roosevelt Chin, interview by Sloane Graff, spring 2002, CPSHR, FHS.

Louise drove herself to the city police substation in nearby Central Park. The police drove her to a hospital emergency room. No one remembered what happened to the purse.

At eight the next morning, Jim Cooksey received a call from the ER.

"We got a patient here who's been on a gurney all night," a voice on the phone said. "She wouldn't let us move her into a room until she could remember your phone number." It had taken a very shaken Louise all night to remember Cooksey's telephone number, but she finally did.

"Please come and get her," said the ER voice. Cooksey went and found Louise still on the gurney in the hall.

It took weeks for the bruises on Miss Marshall's face to finally fade, but, even then, something fundamental had changed.

"She was just shaken up by that," Roosevelt Chin said. "I think that was the first sign I had that this lady has had it."[408]

Cabbage Patch board meetings were cancelled in May and June because Miss Marshall didn't "feel equal" to attending. Charles Dietsch submitted the staff report to the board in July.[409] Miss Marshall's time-honored cure for doldrums was a cruise to beautiful places in Europe, something she'd done at least 16 times before. Louise's 17th trip to Europe was to be climatic. She asked a favorite Cabbage Patch volunteer, 19-year-old Kim McConnell, to go along as her travel companion.

Kim McConnell had been launched into volunteer work at the Patch as an 11-year-old when she went with her mother,

---

408. Roosevelt Chin, interview by Keith Cardwell, March 7, 1987, CPSOHP, CPSHR, FHS; Dr. James J. Cooksey, PI, July 14, 2011.

409. Charles Dietsch, reports to CPSH Board of Directors, May, June, July 1973, CPSHR, FHS.

Betsy, a Presbyterian volunteer and Miss Marshall's friend. As Kim helped with summer camps, Thanksgiving baskets, and Christmas programs in the years that followed, she and Miss Marshall grew close. She was one of the "few women Miss Marshall truly liked," Chin said. He said Kim reminded the staff of the young Miss Marshall. By 1973, Kim had started college. Miss Marshall asked her to delay the start of her fall semester at Purdue University by a few days so they could travel together. Kim said yes and started taking French lessons so she could summon help in case of an emergency.[410]

In August, just before they left on their trip, Kim found Miss Marshall standing by her desk at the Cabbage Patch looking at an old picture. Her brother Burwell had been on a trail ride and was found dead, Louise said simply. Kim remembered no lamenting or sorrowing.[411] Miss Marshall and Kim left for Europe on August 7, the day Burwell was laid to rest in his wife's hometown, Mt. Sterling, Kentucky. He had wanted to be buried with her.[412]

Chin may have thought that Miss Marshall had had it, but, at 85, her opinions and eccentricities were undimmed and the force with which she expressed them could still be daunting. Because Miss Marshall did not fly, Kim's mother, Betsy McConnell, drove Kim and Miss Marshall to the

---

410. Kimberly McConnell Schiewetz, email to Bill and Linda Raymond Ellison, September 24, 2014.

411. Kimberly McConnell Schiewetz, emails to Bill and Linda Raymond Ellison, September 25 and 28, 2014.

412 "Kentucky Deaths," obituary for Burrell Keith Marshall Jr., *Louisville (KY) Courier-Journal,* August 6, 1973; Burwell Keith Marshall III, PI, March 16, 2012.

Indianapolis railroad station to get a train to New York. They climbed aboard bearing a picnic basket that Kim and Betsy McConnell had lovingly prepared with Miss Marshall's favorite foods for lunch: fried chicken, pears, and Betsy McConnell's famous deviled eggs.[413]

In New York, the pair checked into the Hotel Barbizon Plaza, a 23-story hotel for women at Central Park South, renowned for its glamour and a long list of famous actresses, including Grace Kelly, who had stayed there. By the time Kim and Miss Marshall checked in that August in 1973, the hotel's glitter had tarnished, and many of the residents were conservative old women. It could still make Kim's eyes open wide, however, and, for the first time in her life, she had a hotel room all her own.

Miss Marshall announced that her first business in New York was to purchase a new purse, so she and Kim set off walking. They must have seemed an odd couple: the pretty, tall, willowy teenager and the tiny, upright, graying woman in a conservative black dress, sensible black shoes, and pearls. Each felt a strong responsibility for protecting the other. Their destination was a fashionable, upscale department store where they went straight to the handbag counter. Kim recalled that Miss Marshall plunked her old purse, "largish, very nicely made, and expensive" on the counter. She told the saleswoman she wanted its match. The woman disappeared and then reappeared, offering an identical bag. Miss Marshall "opened her bag really, really wide and just shook all the contents out of the old bag and into the new bag." She made

---

413. Kimberly McConnell Schiewetz, telephone interview, September 30, 2014.

sure everything was in the new one, presumably paid for it, and "wheeled out of there," leaving the old bag still sitting on the counter. Kim thought that was a "very strange and oddly wonderful" way to buy a purse.[414]

When they finally settled for the evening, Miss Marshall sat on her bed and yanked on her pearl necklace. To Kim's shocked surprise, the "pearls" popped apart. Wealthy women often took their less expensive jewelry on trips. Miss Marshall traveled wearing children's plastic "pop beads" that pulled apart and popped back together again.[415] That night Miss Marshall was strangely reluctant to let Kim leave for her own room, even in the fabled security of the Barbizon. The man who had stepped out of the Louisville night to hurt Louise had left an unseen scar. Miss Marshall, who had faced so much danger to protect her Cabbage Patch children, was frightened.

The next day brought sunshine, happy memories, and, for Kim, astonishment. Miss Marshall had booked first-class passage on SS *France*, the newest, longest, and very elegant transatlantic cruise ship. In 1969, *New York Times* restaurant critic Craig Claiborne had declared the *France*'s first-class restaurant the best in the world, "in a class by itself on what would seem a hundred dazzling counts."[416] To Kim, it all

---

414. Kimberly McConnell Schiewetz, telephone interview, September 30, 2014.

415. Kimberly McConnell Schiewetz, telephone interview, September 3, 2014.

416. "From SS *France* to SS *Norway* in the Port of New York," World Ship Society website, www.worldshipny.com/francenorwaypony.shtml (accessed September 25, 2014).

seemed like a fairyland. Kim and Miss Marshall boarded in time to have lunch in the restaurant, then went for a walk on the long, long deck.

As the ship slipped beneath New York's bridges and into the open sea, Louise recalled another trip to France 55 years before at the end of World War I and the men she had so enjoyed in Paris.

"There was someone in love with me," she told Kim. Then, from memory, Louise began reciting poetry, apparently the poetry that Bjorn Winger had written and that she had saved in her World War I scrapbook. The August sun bathed her in light and warmth as she clung to Kim's arm, and Miss Marshall was "very, very happy."[417]

The *France* offered travelers a variety of activities: walks on the long decks, deck chairs for sunbathing, and opportunities to meet people who ranged from interesting to famous. Miss Marshall had little interest in any of that. She seemed to value the voyage mainly for the opportunity to rest, read, and, perhaps, write notes. It's unclear exactly what she read or did during the hours when Kim took lonely walks on the deck. Miss Marshall's usual fare included a news magazine, *U.S. News & World Report*, and an assortment of books, many of them linked to faith, life, and mental health.[418] Louise's favorite authors— including evangelist Billy Graham, Presbyterian writer Glenn Clark, and Charles Jefferson—told stories of faith, prayers answered, and God's power in human affairs, reflecting her most closely held beliefs.

---

417. Kimberly McConnell Schiewetz, telephone interviews, September 3 and 30, 2014.

418. Dr. James J. Cooksey, PI, July 14, 2011.

Miss Marshall walked on the deck with Kim only once or twice after that first afternoon, and she emphatically did not want to be drawn into conversations with strangers. She imposed that discipline on Kim, too, starting with dinner that first night. The formally dressed waiter assigned to serve Miss Marshall's table for two at the early seating was young and attractive. As Kim studied the elaborate menu, she glanced up at him and made eye contact. In Miss Marshall's mind, that was a major violation of etiquette. She exploded, summoned the maître d' and demanded that the hapless waiter be reassigned for the rest of the trip. Kim, mortified, slipped back to the dining room later to apologize. "She is very old," the waiter replied.

Miss Marshall remained testy the whole voyage, ready to challenge everything. When Kim wore modest, white culottes on deck to get a little sun, Miss Marshall stared at her legs with eloquent, silent disapproval until Kim "couldn't take it any more" and changed. The *France*'s menu may have offered "a million choices" of the world's finest food, but Miss Marshall was not tempted by those either. Her lunch of choice was a ham sandwich on toasted white bread with ice tea. Breakfast was unerringly a boiled egg (in an eggcup), toast, and very hot coffee. Kim's ventures into interesting new cuisine prompted only disapproval—an issue that was to become important later in the trip.[419]

Despite her desire for solitude, Miss Marshall was lured into occasional conversations with strangers on shipboard, apparently because she had a weakness for very well dressed, attractive mature men, for whom she cocked her head to one

---

419. Kimberly McConnell Schiewetz, telephone interview, September 30, 2014; email to Bill and Linda Raymond Ellison, September 25, 2014.

side and smiled a funny little flirtatious smile. She permitted a conversation with a gentleman they encountered on deck who said he had sorted through the handwritten manuscript for *Gone with the Wind* that Margaret Mitchell sent in a suitcase to a New York publisher. Another couple, known to Kim only as Pat and Ray, passed Miss Marshall's test by revealing that they had once traveled from Michigan to buy antiques in Shelbyville, Kentucky. Pat and Ray relieved Kim's loneliness at meals and proposed that Kim and Louise meet them for dinner in Paris. To Kim's astonishment, Miss Marshall agreed.

Everything about the Paris restaurant Pat and Ray proposed suggested disaster to Kim, who feared Miss Marshall's displeasure. To begin with, the eatery featured a small, live, well-manicured pig in a pen outside. Kim need not have worried. Miss Marshall "thought that pig was the cutest thing you ever saw." She fell in love with it, scratched its ears, and petted its head. Then she launched up the steep stairs to the crowded, noisy restaurant itself. The eatery seemed to be everything Miss Marshall would hate. "She loved it."[420]

As with so many things on the trip, Paris was a patchwork of light and darkness—the happiest of memories and dark portents of what was to come. The Hotel Regina, where they stayed, was a "gorgeous, ancient" hotel with windows and balconies that provided spectacular views of Paris rooftops, the Eiffel Tower, and the Tuileries Gardens. For Louise, it also held memories of other trips to Paris. In 1918, the Regina was the American Red Cross's headquarters when Louise had mustered out of the Red Cross to go home. But the

---

420. Kimberly McConnell Schiewetz, telephone interview, September 30, 2014.

Regina, like the rest of Paris at night, also sheltered fears. Miss Marshall was convinced that someone had come into her room and stolen chocolates she had purchased for the staff at home. At night, even on crowded streets, she feared that "someone would knock us in the head," Kim said. In Paris, Miss Marshall also fell on some stairs and often seemed unsteady. She flared when Kim fussed, so Kim learned to keep her arm conveniently positioned where Miss Marshall could grab hold when she needed it. Sometimes Miss Marshall did.[421]

In the morning light and August heat of their first full day in Paris, Louise was ready to set out on an ambitious walk through the Jardin des Tuileries to a lunch spot she knew near the Arc de Triomphe. The heat was wilting, even for the young. Miss Marshall became so exhausted that she leaned on Kim's arm and allowed her to take charge. She didn't object when Kim ordered Cokes for an outrageously expensive 75 cents each. And she followed Kim down the steps to the Paris subway. Back at the hotel, Kim put her to bed. It didn't occur to either of them to take a more expensive taxi. The next day, Miss Marshall was still so tired that she sent Kim off to see the Palace of Versailles alone. Miss Marshall stayed in her room all day, regaining her strength. Before they left Paris, she wrote a note to Kim's mother, who had sent Miss Marshall red roses that were "just a little less beautiful than your lovely daughter." Miss Marshall pronounced Kim "a darling" but complained that Kim seemed to think that she (Miss Marshall) was unable to handle her own affairs. "I have been here only 10 times," Louise noted.[422]

421. Ibid.

422. Louise Marshall to Mrs. William McConnell, August 17, 1973, in possession of Kimberly McConnell Schiewetz.

After three nights in Paris, a travel agency's representative scooped Miss Marshall and Kim up and deposited them on a first-class sleeper train to Florence, a city she enjoyed every time she visited. Florence also promised another comfort: Charles Dietsch, one of the young men Miss Marshall had taken on earlier trips, flew in to join them and drive their rented car. Dietsch brought his hearty laugh and an ability to take things in hand. He knew Miss Marshall and her travel habits very well.[423] He and Kim coordinated their selections for the cheese course so they could sample more cheeses. (Miss Marshall didn't like cheese.) They exchanged tastes of desserts. And, each night they agreed who would be responsible for checking the next morning to see that Miss Marshall was up and moving, "not exactly pleasant duty." Once up, Miss Marshall seemed to take forever to get going.[424] In AutoTrains and a rented Fiat 132, the trio spent a week working their way north, through breathtaking Alpine scenery and along lakes fed by glaciers. The travel agency helpfully suggested "attractive excursions," but Miss Marshall had favorite stops of her own.[425] Sometimes she and Kim would venture out without Dietsch to have lunch and explore the shops. Many years later, Kimberly McConnell Schiewetz still treasured memories of golden moments they shared when Miss Marshall, bathed in sunshine, looked onto a beautiful landscape and radiated her own happiness.

---

423. Tilford Travel Service document, "Final Itinerary for Miss Louise Marshall, Miss Kim McConnell, Mr. Charles Dietsch," August 1, 1973, in possession of Kimberly McConnell Schiewetz.

424. Kimberly McConnell Schiewetz, email to Bill and Linda Raymond Ellison, January 12, 2015.

425 Tilford Travel Service itinerary.

The route took the travelers near the village of Hohfluh, home to Eleanor "Bambi" Leuenberger, a former Cabbage Patch volunteer and staff member who had married the Swiss pastor of a little Swiss Reformed Church. Miss Marshall invited Sam and Bambi Leuenberger to lunch in the village, then went to their apartment in "Heidi country," on the side of a mountain overlooking a glacier. Miss Marshall was excited about seeing their home. She was lively, animated, and talkative that day, enjoying the encounter with a young woman she loved. Samuel Leuenberger remembered that Miss Marshall expressed admiration for Switzerland, for its cleanliness and the people's honesty. (Miss Marshall had once left a watch in Interlaken, she said. When she went back years later, the people still had the watch and returned it to her.) Interlaken remained one of her favorite places to visit.[426]

Other moments that caught Miss Marshall's fancy were less easy to explain. One occurred in the elevator of a very elegant lakeside hotel in Italy, where Miss Marshall, Kim, and Dietsch stayed on an upper floor. One day, as Kim and Miss Marshall took the elevator down, it stopped. A man blocked the door from closing while he carefully looked them over. He nodded to another man and suddenly Kim knew: "These were bodyguards." One of them flipped open his jacket to reveal his black revolver. Satisfied that the women posed no threat, the guards motioned for a third man, short, middle-aged, and dressed to fit the stereotype for a mafia chieftain.

"He had on the best looking suit you ever saw," Kim Schiewetz remembered. "I mean he was buffed and puffed."

---

426. Eleanor Gorin Leuenberger, PI, January 9, 2015, and Samuel Leuenberger, conversation with the authors, January 9, 2015.

Miss Marshall was oblivious to everything but the man's elegance. Reflexively, she started flirting, batting her eyes, smiling, and speaking to him. The man nodded and smiled at her, then the descent ended. One of the guards held the women back until the security team ensured that the path was safe, then fell into step as the man got off.

Miss Marshall was left breathless. "Oh, Miss McConnell," she said, "have you ever seen a finer gentleman in your life? Did you see the way he was dressed? Im*peck*ably dressed." Miss Marshall went on and on. Kim made a snap decision not to tell Miss Marshall the men had guns. "I just thought it was one of those things I couldn't explain, and she wouldn't get it."[427]

By the time Miss Marshall, Kim, and Dietsch got back to Paris, Miss Marshall was showing worrisome signs that trouble was coming; she had fallen twice and sometimes dropped the silverware at meals. None of them quite understood the significance of those omens. Miss Marshall still wanted to enjoy the trip.

In Paris, they went to the Paris Ritz for a subdued, formal dinner.

Miss Marshall had a special fondness for raspberries, and for Peach Melba, made with ice cream, peaches, and raspberries. As they ate, one of Miss Marshall's raspberries escaped and bounced across the table, leaving a thin, red trail on the crisp, brilliantly white cloth. A young man with a crumb brush arrived to brush it onto a tray, but off the raspberry went, across the table, trailed by a line of red dots.

"Oh no," thought Kim. "She's going to be mad at this guy."

---

427. Kimberly McConnell Schiewetz, telephone interview with authors, September 30, 2014.

Miss Marshall looked at the raspberry and started to laugh. Then Dietsch and Kim started to laugh as the waiter chased the raspberry across the table. Miss Marshall laughed until tears came to her eyes. "That's the only time I remember seeing her just go off in gales of laughter," Kimberly Schiewetz said years later.[428]

The giddiness was gone by the time Dietsch flew home to Louisville, and the travel agency deposited Miss Marshall and Kim in first-class train seats bound for Le Havre, the SS *France*, and New York. At breakfast on shipboard, Miss Marshall ordered her usual boiled egg and made no effort to hide her disgust at the fish Kim decided to try. She announced that she and Kim would no longer have breakfast together; they could meet for lunch.

Sure enough, the next morning Kim ate alone. But Miss Marshall didn't appear for lunch either. A nagging worry began to build in Kim. She called Miss Marshall's room, but Miss Marshall didn't answer. By mid-afternoon, Kim was worried enough to knock on Miss Marshall's door and to listen carefully for a response. There was none. Kim paced back and forth in front of the door, debating whether to ask for help from a steward.

"If that door swings open and she's lying in that bed reading her Bible, she is going to take me apart" for bringing a man into her room, Kim thought. Then Kim took her nerve in hand and found the steward to open the door.

Miss Marshall wasn't in the bed or at the desk. The steward rushed into the bathroom where Miss Marshall, in her long-

---

428. Ibid.

sleeve pink nightgown, lay on the floor between the tub and the toilet, her hip broken. "Get him out of here," she barked at Kim. The steward was already on his way to get help.[429]

Miss Marshall was taken to the ship's hospital in the bowels of the *France*. The ship doctor phoned Cooksey in Louisville and told him that he could keep Miss Marshall comfortable but could do little more. Miss Marshall wanted Cooksey to come to New York to meet the ship.[430]

"They did not take good care of her" on shipboard, said Kimberly McConnell Schiewetz. "They weren't giving her fluids or anything." So Kim, 19, took on Miss Marshall's care. Kim took Miss Marshall her own nightgown printed with small coral flowers. The short sleeves left Miss Marshall's thin arms bare as Kim began spoon feeding Miss Marshall ice and broth. One morning, Miss Marshall reached up and touched Kim's face. "Mother," she said.[431]

"I knew she was dehydrated, and she was out of her mind," Kimberly Schiewetz said years later. Kim was distraught. The sequence is a little unclear, but Kim arranged to call home on a ship-to-shore radio to alert Cooksey and for a tearful talk with her mother.

"Whatever it is, you can handle it," Betsy McConnell told her daughter.[432]

It seemed a long trip, but when the *France* finally docked

---

429. Ibid.

430. Dr. James J. Cooksey, PI, July 14, 2011.

431. Kimberly McConnell Schiewetz, telephone interview with authors, September 30, 2014.

432. Ibid.

in New York City, Cooksey had bought a plane ticket to get Kim home and back to school. He took Miss Marshall to a New York hospital where a well-respected surgeon operated to pin Miss Marshall's hip—but botched the job, leaving Miss Marshall in pain and unable to walk normally.[433]

No one remembered how Cooksey got Miss Marshall back to Louisville and to the Mt. Holly Nursing Home. Her recovery proved to be long, painful, and taxing for everyone: Miss Marshall, the young men on her staff, the Cabbage Patch board, and her family. Miss Marshall wasn't about to retire from the Cabbage Patch. As her sleeping place moved from the nursing home to her sister's home, and then back to the Puritan, Miss Marshall was determined to return to her work at the Cabbage Patch and to find a surgeon who would risk operating on a frail 85-year-old woman's painful hip. She wanted freedom from the terrific pain, the walker, and the wheelchair that limited her.[434]

"We thought, well, that's it. She'll be in a nursing home the rest of her life," Chin said. Everyone who thought that was wrong, but the period prompted well-grounded anxiety and uncertainty among the staff, volunteers, and board members, who were beginning to understand how critically important Miss Marshall was to the Cabbage Patch.[435] The worried question on everyone's mind was the same: Could the Cabbage Patch be the Cabbage Patch without Miss Marshall?

---

433. Dr. James O. Cooksey, PI, July 14, 2011.

434. Ibid.

435. Roosevelt Chin, interview by Keith Cardwell, March 7, 1987, CPOHP, CPSHR, FHS.

It was a good question. Miss Marshall brought her unique mix of vision, love, and determination to the settlement, but she left a problem. Good management practice had never been Miss Marshall's strong point. In many ways, her understanding of how to manage employees and a complex organization had not improved since the very early days of the Cabbage Patch, despite her painful experience with employees like Joe Burks and Lloyd Redman. What had matured was Miss Marshall's ability to use her vision, charm, and the force of her will to control the settlement's operations and to power it forward. By the time she reached her mid-80s, however, her control was fading and the haphazard management she had fostered was threatening her settlement's future.

The Cabbage Patch board was well schooled in the ethic that they should do only what Miss Marshall directed. But by the 1970s, the board was also well laced with attorneys and businesspeople who recognized that the Cabbage Patch wasn't being run like a business. Miss Marshall's settlement had no budget, no staff reporting structure or job descriptions, and minimal financial records. Staff salaries were spartan, and basic employee benefits were missing altogether. Financially, the settlement was a hand-to-mouth operation. As Miss Marshall's health faltered, board members grappled with the growing knowledge that they were going to have to take a stronger hand in Cabbage Patch affairs—whether Miss Marshall knew and approved or not. Suddenly, the always-unanimous board began having real discussions and substantive disagreements on issues that had always been heavily colored by Miss Marshall's fears and prejudices.

One of the most important debates concerned the settlement's continuing relationship with the Presbyterian Church. For 40 years, Miss Marshall had considered the local presbytery's leadership and financial support both inadequate and unwelcome, even if it was necessary. As the Northern and Southern branches of the national Presbyterian Church moved closer to closing the rift that had divided them since the Civil War, Miss Marshall's fears grew to alarm. If the denomination united, the larger, northern church's values, which she regarded as misguided and, still worse, progressive, would be imposed on the Cabbage Patch. She feared losing control of the board and settlement to the northern church's power structure, which she called "vile" and which reminded her of the evils the Apostle Paul had warned against in the Bible.

Board member Dr. Henry Mobley, a Presbyterian pastor, favored continuing the settlement's Presbyterian ties, which he argued provided a stabilizing influence. Jim Cooksey, Roosevelt Chin, and Charles Dietsch, who spoke for Miss Marshall, favored a break, lest the Presbyterians change the ways that Miss Marshall had always done things. As with most important Cabbage Patch decisions, the debate went on for years before the settlement and the Presbyterian establishment formally parted ways.[436]

As the differences between the board and the staff suggested, leadership was also an issue. Miss Marshall had always intended for the young men she groomed to carry on her work, but cracks were beginning to show in that plan,

---

436. Louise Marshall, report to the CPSH Board of Directors, August 6, 1970; Minutes, CPSH Board, February 28, 1972, CPSHR, FHS.

too. Cooksey was feeling a growing call to become a clinical psychologist and, in 1969, he left the Patch for a yearlong residency. Dietsch, too, was a reluctant leader, who once refused to step in to chair a board meeting, even when Miss Marshall was sick.[437] Cooksey would return and Dietsch would later lead, but even Miss Marshall's iron will could not control others' lives forever. In the short run, Miss Marshall needed the men's help for almost everything. They were her sons, and she used them unsparingly.

Miss Marshall was determined to return to the Cabbage Patch, a formidable daily undertaking for those who had to load and unload Miss Marshall and her wheelchair from the Cabbage Patch van and install her on a red sofa in the old Mother's Club Room (her "throne room," one board member called it).[438] There she could keep tabs on comings and goings and talk, almost constantly, it seemed, on the old, black rotary phone that served as her fund-raising tool and link to the world. Sequences are unclear, but by February 1974, Miss Marshall was able to attend the Cabbage Patch board meeting, even as the settlement's management deteriorated, threatening her life's work.

Miss Marshall's skill at raising what the settlement needed had become both a strength and a weakness because she never told staff members which donors she called to ask for help or how she did it. Staff members only knew that when they took her a problem, she would make a phone call to solve it. Telling her secrets hardly seemed necessary to Miss

---

437. Minutes, CPSH Board, May 19, 1969; staff report, CPSH Board, February 13, 1970, CPSHR, FHS.

438. Lynn Gant March, PI, June 14, 2011.

Marshall because she wasn't about to give up command of the settlement.[439]

In February 1975, just before her 87th birthday, Miss Marshall found a surgeon willing to replace her hip. The result was remarkable. After weeks of physical therapy, she could walk again with minimal help from a walker. She attended a board meeting in May, returned to her apartment at the Puritan, and continued to dream ever-expanding—and very expensive—dreams for the Cabbage Patch.

Miss Marshall wanted the settlement to have its own campground, 100 acres of land and a spring-fed lake.[440] That was not easily found, and when the settlement finally did buy property outside the city limits, it proved to be a swamp. It was a bad decision the settlement couldn't afford. Miss Marshall's absence showed everywhere, but especially in the settlement's finances. As programs were trimmed, she warned the board not to approve any expenditures the Patch's checking account couldn't cover. She was used to making do.

However, nothing in Miss Marshall's past prepared her for the challenges facing the settlement in the mid-1970s as segregated housing patterns led to resegregated schools. Louisville had successfully opened schools to black students in the 1950s, but county school officials resisted calls for renewed integration in the 1970s. Officials decided to merge the predominately white Jefferson County system with the poorer schools in Louisville where many black families lived, creating one huge school district with many starkly segregated schools.

---

439. Roosevelt Chin, interview by Sloane Graff, spring 2002, CPSHR, FHS.

440. Thomas R. Chambers, PI, July 13, 2011.

Finally, a federal district court ordered the county school system to bus black and white children across the county to fully integrate schools. Some children, especially those who were black, spent hours on buses and no longer had time for Cabbage Patch activities, Dietsch's report to the board said in November 1975. The school busing plan was a heavy blow to the Cabbage Patch's afternoon programs such as the sewing school and athletic practices. Recruiting children became more difficult. Some longtime programs closed. Life had changed for Louisville's children at a time when the Cabbage Patch's flexibility was limited, when the children badly needed the settlement's stability, and when Miss Marshall demanded the staff's help with the most basic of activities.

While the city changed outside the settlement, Miss Marshall continued to hold court on the red sofa, helped in the afternoons by a visiting nurse.[441] If Miss Marshall dozed through board discussions, Dietsch later filled her in on what she needed to know. At night, a team of staff members lifted Miss Marshall from the couch and took her to her efficiency apartment at the Puritan for a nightly trial that lasted for hours. The team put an ill-tempered Miss Marshall to bed, fed her tomato soup, and left "wondering how she was going to get along." A parade of sitters was brought in to help, but none lasted. "She must have used every sitter in the City of Louisville," Chin said. "She'd get somebody she could get along with and then something would happen and they'd quit on her."[442]

441. Lynn Gant March, PI, June 14, 2011.

442. Roosevelt Chin, interview by Keith Cardwell, March 7, 1987, CPSOHP, CPSHR, FHS.

Miss Marshall's vision, charisma, and will had kept the Cabbage Patch strong over the years when settlement houses in other cities had folded or become community centers. Now, the Cabbage Patch needed leadership that Miss Marshall could no longer provide. At first, the staff ran the settlement "like a family running a store," Chin said. "You're the store clerk, and I'll do the mopping and everyone just did it." Then, when board members stepped in, they were amazed. "How does anyone know what they were doing?" the board's sophisticated businesspeople asked. No one knew.[443] All the weaknesses in Miss Marshall's management style were revealed. The board formed a fund-raising committee in 1977 and finally came to a dismaying realization: No one understood the "financial set-up of the Cabbage Patch." The board formed another committee to figure it out. Finally, they asked Miss Marshall to send out an old-fashioned money-raising letter right away.[444]

As problems mounted, there was one issue that everyone had a hard time discussing with Miss Marshall. She had become quite wealthy, and no one could convince her that not a penny of her fortune would go to the Cabbage Patch unless she made a will. Both her family and the staff knew why.

"She thought she would never die," said Charles Dietsch. "She felt that the type of work she was doing was so important that she would probably just never die."[445] Finally, in November 1977, a trusted board member and friend, Morey Booth,

443. Roosevelt Chin, interview by Keith Cardwell, March 7, 1987, CPSOHP, CPSHR, FHS.

444. Minutes, CPSH Board, September 19, 1977, CPSHR, FHS.

445. Charles Dietsch, telephone interview with Linda Raymond, December 31, 2014.

convinced Miss Marshall to sign a simple three-paragraph will leaving almost everything to the Cabbage Patch Settlement.[446]

That same month, the fund-raising committee presented a report with six ideas that were businesslike and varied. But the report emphasized again and again, Miss Marshall's ultimate resource would be necessary to pull the settlement through all the trouble; the committee needed prayer—everyone's prayers.[447] Louise Marshall needed prayers, too. The New Year would bring her 90th birthday and a crushing disappointment.

The first hint of that sadness arrived during lunch at one of Miss Marshall's favorite downtown eateries, the Colonnade Cafeteria, where she had gone with Chin and other friends. Jim Cooksey arrived with an attractive young woman, Anne Majors. He decided that the unplanned opportunity was the right moment to introduce Miss Marshall to his fiancée. In fact, there was no good time. Miss Marshall wouldn't talk to them, not then, not later.

"Things changed after that," Anne Majors Cooksey said. Miss Marshall had groomed Jim Cooksey to assume a consuming, lifelong leadership role at the Cabbage Patch, something he couldn't do if he had a wife. Miss Marshall's close relationship with Cooksey changed profoundly.[448] She had lost Lloyd Redman and Joe Burks to their families and to jobs that would support them. Cooksey's decision was a wrenching third blow.

---

446. Louise Marshall, last will and testament.

447. D. B. Kurfees, CPSH "Report of Fund-Raising Committee," November 29, 1977, CPSHR, FHS.

448. Anne Majors Cooksey, PI, July 14, 2011.

As the other staff members Louise Marshall had trained left for other jobs, Charles Dietsch took on more and more responsibility for the settlement and its aging founder. He was her choice as her power of attorney, executor, and settlement director. *Courtesy of Cabbage Patch Settlement House Archives*

"She was just really hurt," Jim Cooksey said. Cooksey had passed up opportunities to leave the Patch for jobs in the mental health field because he didn't want to leave the settlement in a bind. Still, he felt a growing call from God to move into a new career that used his training as a clinical psychologist. In January 1978, he gave six months' notice that he planned to leave the Patch. Miss Marshall didn't tell Cooksey to leave at once as she had Joe Burks and other Cabbage Patch employees who resigned, but "she made herself scarce" where Cooksey was concerned. For Cooksey, there were no more casual chats, no more meals together, no more inclusion in the meetings Cooksey had always attended.

"I was just given the cold shoulder," he said. Once again, the hurt ran deep on both sides. Chin and Dietsch wanted to attend Cooksey's wedding and continue their friendship, but Miss Marshall made it clear that was not permitted.

On Cooksey's final day on the job, the settlement got quiet earlier than usual. When he looked around, Cooksey found that everyone had left. He was the last person in the building. He left his keys on the hall table, went out, and locked the door. No one said good-bye.[449]

The year did have happier moments. For Miss Marshall's 90th birthday, the board invited everyone to an open house to celebrate—and raise money. Throughout the year, people came by to pay their respects. One was Mike Caswell, the lovable, mischievous kid who had stayed in trouble with Miss Marshall from the time he was a tot trying to sneak into the settlement until he left as a teenager to care for his family. By the time he came to say hello to Miss Marshall, he was 26 and had filled out considerably. Dietsch and Chin met him to warn—needlessly, it turned out—that Miss Marshall's sight wasn't good and that she might not recognize him. "Mike Caswell," Miss Marshall called out from her sofa, "you old fat thing, come here to me."[450] Another point of happiness was Kim McConnell's marriage to Ken Schiewetz. Miss Marshall went with her walker, a smile and, uncharacteristically, a print dress, black with bright red flowers.

Miss Marshall attended most of the board meetings in 1978 and ended the year by taking an action that finally

---

449. Dr. James J. Cooksey, PI, July 14, 2011.

450. Mike Caswell, interview by Keith Cardwell, January 31, 1987, CPSOHP, CPSHR, FHS.

reflected reality: She established an annuity trust fund that would leave the Cabbage Patch more than $150,000 when she died and could provide it with an extra $7,000 a year while she lived. The gift was announced January 22, 1979, at the last board meeting Louise Marshall ever attended. A health problem sent her briefly to the hospital and then to Twinbrook Nursing Home, where she could look out on land her grandfather Veech once owned near the Bowman Field Airport. In February, the board report said Miss Marshall was recovering "very nicely." In March, she was said to be doing as well as expected and that she was quite content at the home. In truth, her fabled energy had simply run out.[451]

In the months that followed, Miss Marshall gave Dietsch her power of attorney and the board endorsed him as executive director of the settlement, a title that sat uncomfortably on his shoulders. Charles Dietsch had been an inspirational coach and a competent administrator, but leading people who were used to Miss Marshall's ways was harder. Employees would yield to Miss Marshall's odd habits like issuing stamps for one letter at a time or requiring a pencil stub before issuing a new pencil. Dietsch couldn't pull that off. Staff members who'd worked well with him as an equal weren't ready to accept him as a boss. He couldn't flirt with donors as Miss Marshall did, either. And he'd never been trained to manage any way but Miss Marshall's way. The board took charge and made business-like decisions on staff benefits, job descriptions, and salary.

For Miss Marshall, days at Twinbrook Nursing Home were marked by visitors. Morey Booth, the trusted board member,

---

451. Reports to the Cabbage Patch Settlement Board of Directors, 1978–1979, CPSHR, FHS.

went often. So did Dietsch and Chin. Miss Marshall seemed grateful that they'd come even if she was too weak to talk much. Kim McConnell Schiewetz and her brother Mike McConnell, a former Patch volunteer who became a federal judge, sent letters of encouragement. The people Miss Marshall had loved so much were what kept her going, Dietsch told them.[452] Jim Cooksey went often, too, sitting beside her and talking even when Miss Marshall didn't respond. It was hard to tell if the silence reflected emotional hurt or great weariness. Miss Marshall had communicated to Cooksey that she was miffed, but she'd run out of steam. When her great energy finally gave out, Miss Marshall seemed to go downhill quickly, Cooksey said. At Twinbrook, she looked "like a nursing home patient."[453]

The people who sat beside her during those months don't remember Louise Marshall ever needing to discuss death. She wasn't fearful or even overly concerned about dying, Dietsch said. "She knew that there was a time when she would no longer be here with friends and people she was working with."[454] She was prepared. "She was a real Christian," said Cooksey, "and I think she felt she had a relationship with the Lord that was going to cover that."[455]

By February 1980, Dietsch reported that Miss Marshall was just holding her own. She would hold on for another year. On February 5, 1981, Louise's much-loved niece Elizabeth

---

452. Charles W. Dietsch to Mrs. William McConnell, February 25, 1980, in possession of Kimberly McConnell Schiewetz.

453. Dr. James J. Cooksey, PI, July 18, 2014.

454. Charles Dietsch, telephone interview with Linda Raymond, December 31, 2014.

455. Dr. James J. Cooksey, PI, July 18, 2014.

Johnson Haynes had just turned the lights out for the night when she got a call from Twinbrook Nursing Home. Louise Marshall, 92 years old, had died.[456]

Peg Harvin, the longtime board member whose friendship spanned both of Louise's worlds, handled the funeral arrangements. Louise would be buried with her parents in the historic—and fashionable—Cave Hill Cemetery. Dr. Henry Mobley, the Cabbage Patch board member who gave Miss Marshall such trouble, led the service. Niece Elizabeth Chambers suggested two hymns, "The Church's One Foundation" and "The Strife is O'er," but Dr. Haynes went to choir practice to deliver a message that only "goopy hymns from the Victorian era" should be sung.[457] Naturally, the service was held at Second Presbyterian Church where Louise had worshipped so long—but not in the new, main sanctuary constructed after a fire had destroyed the downtown church. Louise thought the construction had cost entirely too much. Her funeral was in the smaller chapel. When Mobley finished writing his meditation for the funeral, his secretary Ruth Chaffins, typed his notes. She did it with a full heart; Ruth Tolmerlin Chaffins had been a Cabbage Patch kid, a dedicated volunteer, and a lifelong admirer of Miss Marshall. Mobley's sermon mixed humor and sadness, she said. "He did a good job."[458]

---

456. Elizabeth Johnson Haynes, PI, March 1, 2013.

457. Elizabeth Chambers to Margaret (Peg) Harvin, September 4, 1979, CPSHR, FHS; Dr. Douglas Haynes, personal journal, February 5–7, 1981, in possession of his widow, Elizabeth Johnson Haynes.

458. Ruth Tomerlin Chaffins, telephone interview with Linda Raymond, July 6, 2014.

People from the Cabbage Patch turned out in large numbers for the visitation to tell stories about how Louise Marshall had helped them. Some sent flowers, but not many. The family had asked for expressions of sympathy to go to the settlement. For the funeral, a cross of Louise's favorite pink carnations and vine leaves covered the coffin.

"A great multitude of family" members sat in the chapel's front two rows.[459] Jim Cooksey, who had probably spent more time than anyone with Miss Marshall during her final days, slipped into the back of the church. Niece Elizabeth Chambers walked all the way down the aisle to ask him to join the family in front. Miss Marshall's "boys" were her family, she said. They should sit where they belonged at her funeral.

As people who knew and loved—or simply knew of—Miss Marshall turned to eulogy, her two lives merged. For many, Miss Marshall was the Cabbage Patch Settlement, which the *Louisville Times* pronounced "among the most successful examples of the settlement house movement," the result of the love with which it was founded. "She was one who really cared," the headline said.[460] The Cabbage Patch board struggled to write its own tribute, too, and focused on the people Miss Marshall had touched, the thousands of alumni who, the resolution said, "read as a Who's Who of the city."[461]

As the years passed, Miss Marshall's legend grew, and stories often focused on her eccentricities rather than the pain

---

459. Dr. Haynes, personal journal, February 7, 1981.

460. "She Was One Who Really Cared," editorial, *Louisville Times*, February 6, 1981.

461. Resolution, Cabbage Patch Settlement Board of Directors, March 16, 1981, CPSHR, FHS.

she caused or the faith that underlay her work. Those who loved her most understood and remembered, however, and, like Miss Marshall herself, were unapologetic about who she was.

"She made creative use of her neuroses to do what she actually did," said her favorite nephew, Lewis Marshall Johnson.[462]

Charles Dietsch, whose dedication to Miss Marshall and her principles never wavered, summed her up simply: "Miss Marshall was a devoted and dedicated Christian who knew what her mission in life was and pursued that mission 100 percent."[463]

Louise Marshall would have doubtless dismissed all the attempts to assess her life. She had summarized it herself in a 1974 newspaper interview. "I love people big and little," she had said, "and, oh my dear, I knew at 16 what I wanted to do, and it's never changed.

"It's been one long love affair."[464]

---

462. Lewis Marshall Johnson, telephone interview with authors, January 1, 2013.

463. Charles W. Dietsch, letter to Ruth Tomerlin Chaffins, August 1, 2011, shared with the authors.

464. Lucinda Inskeep, "Miss Louise Marshall of the Cabbage Patch," *Louisville Times*, May 17, 1974.

THE LEGACY

With all the concern about the Cabbage Patch Settlement's future in the months after Miss Marshall died, no one paid much attention to skinny little Kim Hazelwood when she slipped into the settlement with other children from the neighborhood. She was easy to miss, a shy, quiet 13-year-old with a tendency to hang back. But Kim, who grew up to be Kimberly Hazelwood Glass, would come as close as anyone could to reflecting Miss Marshall's legacy.

People who know the Cabbage Patch tend to describe that legacy in two different ways. For some, Miss Marshall's legacy is the still-vibrant settlement house itself and the still-successful methods Miss Marshall used there to lift people—especially children—from poverty to proud self-sufficient citizenship. For others, Miss Marshall's gift is the people themselves, the ones she touched and changed and who in turn continue to touch and change others, creating ripples of good. Kim Hazelwood's story supports both assessments.

By all accounts, Kim came to the settlement when its finances seemed inadequate, its buildings were wearing out, its management was in disarray, and its leaders stressed. Everything at the settlement had worked because Miss

287

Marshall made it work. Her succession planning had focused on the young men she had pulled from the neighborhood and groomed to follow her. But, with Jim Cooksey's departure, only Charles Dietsch and Roosevelt Chin remained. Both had coached, mentored, and inspired hundreds of children. Both had enormous gifts. Neither was up to the challenge of leading the Cabbage Patch without Miss Marshall.

As Miss Marshall's health failed, the Cabbage Patch Board had designated Charles Dietsch, who had Miss Marshall's power of attorney, as the settlement's director. He believed passionately in Miss Marshall and her methods, but his gifts didn't include managing staff and raising money without her. The board, now eight men and nine women, proclaimed a "Transition Year" and set goals that would not have occurred to Miss Marshall: establishing a bookkeeping system, financial reports, and formal policies for employees. Transition did not mean changing everything, however. The board's staff policy remembered that the Patch was founded by "dedicated Christian leaders." New hires needed to demonstrate similar dedication, Christian character, and love.[465]

Everyone wanted to keep Miss Marshall's magic; no one was sure if they could.

In December 1982, the board made a critical hiring decision that would have an impact on both Kim Hazelwood and the settlement's ability to honor Miss Marshall's philosophy and her methods for another half century. They hired Rod Napier, one of Miss Marshall's boys whom she had nurtured,

---

465. "General Philosophy and Qualities for Selection of Cabbage Patch Settlement Staff," Minutes, CPSJ Board of Directors, October 14, 1982, CPSHR, FHS.

trained, and tormented from the time he was an 11-year-old. Napier's parents were country people who had moved to Louisville to find factory work in the 1950s. Young Rod was left to occupy himself and noticed that all the neighborhood kids disappeared around one o'clock on summer afternoons. He followed them and discovered the Cabbage Patch.

In the years that followed, Napier took part in almost everything the settlement offered: sports, crafts, games, camps. He was not "totally noticeable," he said, but Miss Marshall noticed him and hired him to work in the office for 50 cents an hour. Napier fell under the influence of the legendary Cabbage Patch coaches, like Joe Burks and Lloyd Redman, and chaffed under Miss Marshall's demands. "*Napier!*" she'd yell, and Rod Napier would cringe. He doesn't know why he stayed, but he did. By the time he left for college, "I hated her," he said. "She suspended me more times than you could guess for things like chewing gum."[466]

Although Miss Marshall offered to finance his education, Napier went to the University of Louisville on a track scholarship and majored in physical education and recreation. (Miss Marshall didn't approve of track because it isn't a team sport.) He got a master's in education at Temple University and started work on a doctorate in recreation and leisure studies at Indiana University. His studies gave him an appreciation for the theoretical foundation of the Cabbage Patch program and for Miss Marshall's philosophy that demanded quality, character, and accountability. When Napier started teaching at the University of Louisville, Charles Dietsch asked Napier

---

466. Rod Napier, PI, June 22, 2012.

to work summers at the Patch. Napier accepted and had a chance to have long, mutually respectful conversations with Miss Marshall while she lay on the red couch in the Mother's Club Room. Napier rediscovered why he had loved Miss Marshall even as he'd hated her. When Charles Dietsch asked him to stay on full time at the Patch, he agreed, intending to stay only two years. Instead, Napier found a personal ministry at the Cabbage Patch that lasted more than 35 years.

"I do it a lot like Miss Marshall," he says. He also makes sure that newcomers to the Cabbage Patch staff know how Miss Marshall did it.[467] Napier wrote a three-page document, "The Patch Way," to teach new staff and remind old staff of the settlement's culture. The guidelines sound like pure Miss Marshall: "Stretch the dollar as far as you humanly can, then do more," "Do not make changes for change sake," "No double standards between staff and youth . . . lead by example," and "Patch Pride—we will strive to always be the best."[468]

When Napier met Kim Hazelwood, he saw a child much like he had been, and he focused on her much as Miss Marshall had focused on him. He encouraged Kim to become involved in activities, even activities she resisted. She wasn't a natural athlete, but he insisted that she go out for teams.

"Mr. Napier, look at me" she'd moaned, looking at her skinny legs sticking out of over-big gym shorts, but she played baseball and basketball. And she made friends.[469]

---

467. Rod Napier, PI, June 22, 2012, and February 2, 2015.

468. Rod Napier, "The Patch Way," guidelines he wrote to explain CPSH culture to new staff, 2011.

469. Rod Napier, PI, February 2, 2015.

Thirty-three-year-old Tracy Holladay was the Cabbage Patch board's choice to succeed Louise Marshall. His hat touts one of the settlement's fund-raising activities. *Courtesy of Cabbage Patch Settlement House Archives*

When they weren't occupied running the Patch's programs, Napier and his longtime colleague Roosevelt Chin speculated on how the board was going to solve the settlement's leadership problem. For all his dedication and skills as a programmer, Dietsch simply wasn't working out as director. The board launched a search for an executive director who could both run the settlement and raise money. Chin thought they should hire a "minister type." Napier saw the settlement as a business with huge financial and management needs that needed an "MBA type."[470]

In March 1984, the board settled on an engaging 33-year-old man with a red beard and a not-yet-awarded master's

---

470. Rod Napier, PI, June 22, 2012.

degree from the Southern Baptist Theological Seminary. Tracy Holladay's background included managing a rental cars business, advertising, and real estate; managing a band called Fresh Heirs; and directing Louisville Young Life, a non-sectarian, interdenominational Christian outreach to high school students. He knew almost nothing about the Cabbage Patch. He proved to be an inspired choice.[471]

Tracy Holladay was personable, pastoral, practical, and skilled. He graduated from the seminary in May 1984. Then, even before his official July date to start work, Holladay bucked the board on its strong inclination to fire Charles Dietsch.

"The man's worked 30 years of his life here," Holladay told them. "Why don't you let me see if I can find a spot for him where he can live out his work life here."

The proposal prompted some of the most vigorous board debate in Cabbage Patch history, but Holladay won the day. Dietsch stayed as a staff assistant to Holladay, working until he retired at age 65 after more than 50 years of serving Miss Marshall and the Cabbage Patch.[472]

When he visited the settlement as a job applicant, Holladay had been impressed by the programs and activity behind the nondescript facades of the houses the settlement occupied on Sixth Street. As director, he found that Miss Marshall had

---

471. "Tracy Holladay . . . One of the People to Watch in 1985," *Patch-Work*, a publication of the Cabbage Patch Settlement House, January–March 1985, CPSHR, FHS; Joan Kay, "Cabbage Patch's Spirit Attracted a Man of Faith," *Louisville (KY) Courier-Journal*, February 17, 1985.

472. Minutes, CPSH Board of directors, March 15, 1984, and June 21, 1984, CPSHR, FHS; Tracy Holladay, interview with authors, October 16, 2014; Charles Dietsch, telephone interview with Linda Raymond, December 31, 2014.

left formidable problems. The buildings were in disrepair and depressing. The roof leaked. The gym needed work. All the settlement's walls were a practical battleship blue, the linoleum floor uniformly black. The board had only hinted at seething "staff tension." That turned out to mean some members of the staff simply couldn't tolerate each other. Some programs had been closed down because of a poor understanding of how much money was available. The Cabbage Patch Park that Miss Marshall had so wanted was sucking money voraciously as the board tried to make the park's playing fields playable and as the staff worked on ways to use fields that were a bus ride away from the settlement.[473] If Holladay was dismayed, that wasn't recorded. He bought into Miss Marshall's philosophy and embraced many of her methods.

"You try to go where the people are, instead of expecting them to come to you," he said. "You try to meet needs in the community."[474]

He launched into solving the problems as the settlement prepared to celebrate its 75th anniversary in 1985 with a budget that had already grown 17 percent from 1984. Holladay announced a "painting party" to give the Patch a friendlier face.[475] Like Napier, he also focused on Kim Hazelwood.

Under Holladay and Napier, the Cabbage Patch began formalizing some of Miss Marshall's informal programs.

---

473. Tracy Holladay, PI, October 16, 2014.

474. Joan Kay, "Cabbage Patch's Spirit Attracted a Man of Faith," *Louisville (KY) Courier-Journal*, February 17, 1985.

475. Minutes, CPSH Board of Directors, January 17, 1985, CPSHR, FHS.

Young teens who seemed to have promise were channeled into a leadership development program that offered the youths formal classes in public speaking, leadership, grooming, and building relationships. Leadership trainees were also challenged with High Adventure camps that took them out of their comfort zones and built their confidence. With considerable encouragement, Kim did everything the Cabbage Patch offered: the day camps and classes, the athletic teams where she never excelled, the camps on tour, and memorable canoe adventures—to Missouri's Current River in cold weather and to Ontario, Canada, for fishing during mosquito season. Kim was perfectly ready to paddle and portage and camp under difficult conditions, but she drew the line at fishing. Napier worked by Miss Marshall's rules. Everyone on a fishing trip was required to catch and fillet a fish. No exceptions. But Kim wouldn't do it; she didn't want to hurt the fish. When the group paddled into a Canadian lake, her pole hung defiantly over the bow with the lure dangling above—not in—the water. However, even Nature seemed determined that Kim would not fail the test. A 26-inch Northern Pike jumped out of the water, took her lure in mid-air, and started to run with it. "Grab the rod," Napier shouted. Kim did. Napier continued to shout instructions until a hysterical Kim finally landed the fish. From then on, she paddled happily with her partner and without a fishing pole. She could go home saying that she had succeeded.[476]

By the time she finished high school, Kim was a young woman "with skill, integrity, and intelligence," said

---

476. Rod Napier, PI, February 2, 2015.

Holladay. She not only had a group of close friends, she had "meaningful relationships with people who were different from her."[477] Kim Hazelwood, the former wallflower, was liked and respected by everyone. She had also developed a mental toughness that she would need.

That's the kind of transformation Miss Marshall believed in. That's what she accomplished thousands of times. That's what the Cabbage Patch still does with the principles Miss Marshall dictated.

"Meeting needs, doing it with . . . a sense of compassion and service, providing diverse opportunities to kids and families . . . significantly improving their lives, not just keeping them off the streets," Holladay said.[478]

The people Miss Marshall touched with her own hand are getting old now. Some still meet their friends from the settlement and talk about their days at the Cabbage Patch. Shirley Rose Alvey is among them. There is no question that the Cabbage Patch changed her life; she met her husband there at a wiener roast. Every month, she and her Cabbage Patch friends meet to enjoy each other and to remember.

"Miss Marshall taught me a lot," Mrs. Alvey says. "She taught what's good to do and what's not good."[479]

While Cabbage Patch alumni—and the young volunteers who helped Miss Marshall—went into many different jobs and professions, many became teachers and coaches. They,

---

477. Tracy Holladay, "Words of Remembrance" at memorial service for Kimberly Hazelwood Glass, December 30, 2014.

478. Tracy Holladay, PI, October 16, 2014.

479. Shirley Rose Alvey, telephone interview with authors, 2015.

too, used what Miss Marshall had taught them to shape successive generations. The Burks family is a good example.

Legendary coach Joe Burks had left the Cabbage Patch as an employee so he could earn enough to support his family. He taught and coached in the public schools for years, but Miss Marshall eventually asked him back to the settlement to help lead summer camps. He brought with him his own son, Joe Jr., a teenaged camper who also went on to proudly graduate from college and become a teacher and then principal of Louisville Male High School.

Eleanor "Bambi" Leuenberger, who had left her Cabbage Patch job to marry and move to Switzerland, sent her own son back to Louisville for high school. She was amazed to find an American public school that emphasized discipline, high standards, and pride. It wasn't until her son's graduation that she discovered why Male High School incorporated those virtues. She met the principal, Joe Burks Jr.

"I grew up in the Cabbage Patch," he told her.

"All of a sudden, everything fell into place," Eleanor Leuenberger said. "My son got to go to school under a principal who was influenced by Miss Marshall. It went through me like electricity—that my son was actually in that line of influence . . . It was a blessing for our son."[480]

Such blessings were repeated again and again by other Cabbage Patch alumni whose students never knew that the teachers and coaches who shaped them had been shaped by Miss Marshall. That legacy continues.

When Kim Hazelwood was a high school senior, her

---

480. Eleanor Gorin Leuenberger, PI, January 9, 2015.

mother called Napier. "She wants to go to college, and I don't know what to do," Janet Hazelwood said. "Let me think about it," said Napier.

It was time for the Cabbage Patch to institutionalize Miss Marshall's ad hoc program for sending young people to college—often with her own money and help from her own contacts. Tracy Holladay began by establishing an educational opportunities fund, and awarded Kim Hazelwood the first Cabbage Patch Scholars scholarship. She decided she wanted to become an architect, a choice that made her a pioneer in a field that was overwhelmingly male and resistant to women. When it was time for her to leave for the University of Cincinnati, Napier loaded Kim and her things into his own van, drove her to Cincinnati and helped her set up her first college dorm room.[481]

Over the next four years, Mrs. Hazelwood called Napier when Kim needed something—a slide rule, for example—that she couldn't provide. Somehow, Kim got what she needed. When Kim needed to interview for internships, Napier took one look at her and decided that her appearance needed attention. He called board chairman Don Kurfees, who called his own daughter. Kim emerged from their shopping trip with a wardrobe, followed by a new hairstyle and makeup. Suddenly, she was a very attractive young woman. When she graduated, Holladay made some calls, as Miss Marshall had once done, to scout architectural jobs for Kim. She got one. In the years that followed, Kim became a pioneer in her field for women and for the environment. She was probably the

---

481. Rod Napier, PI, February 2, 2015; Holladay, "Words of Remembrance."

first Louisville architect certified for her expertise in designing environmentally friendly buildings. She married Doyle Glass, embraced a stepson, and had a daughter. Someplace along the way, Kimberly Hazelwood Glass's relationship with the Cabbage Patch flip-flopped. She joined the Cabbage Patch board of directors and began giving back.[482]

Kim Glass joined a board very different from the ones Miss Marshall had tapped, and she joined at a critical point in the settlement's history. Under Holladay, the board had grown to about 30 people, reflecting a range of denominations and experience. (When the board had its first Catholic board president, Holladay found himself wondering: "Is Miss Marshall turning over in her grave?") Holladay insisted that new board members understand clearly that the settlement has a working board whose members work on committees and raise money, no matter how much they hate fund-raising. Board meetings are a crisp 90 minutes. Holladay doesn't prepare lunch; it's brought in. But the board does still start with prayer. Board members have vigorous discussions but find the meetings somehow different from most other organizations they serve.

"It's the only organization that I'm involved with that I always come away feeling that the board meeting is uplifting," said former board president Bill Grubbs.[483]

Kim Glass found her place on the board quickly. In 1988, the Cabbage Patch launched a wonderfully successful fund-

---

482. Rod Napier, PI, February 2, 2015; obituary, Kimberly "Kim" Hazelwood Glass, *Louisville (KY) Courier-Journal*, December 30, 2014.

483. Tracy Holladay, PI, October 16, 2014; William Grubbs, PI, January 27, 2015.

raiser originally called Street Ball Showdown, a three-on-three basketball event that eventually attracted 50,000 spectators and 3,000 amateur basketball players before it ended 19 years later. The games were played on a summer weekend on parking lots or city streets that required 70 basketball courts to be marked on the pavement. Kim Glass volunteered to handle the job. Laying out the courts was hot and laborious; board member Katherine M. Davis remembered 95-degree temperatures as a small team of volunteers began laying down tape to mark court boundaries.[484] Kim Glass was still there when everyone else left. That was not the most ambitious job Kim Glass took on for the Cabbage Patch, however.

Kimberly Hazelwood Glass was a Patcher who grew up to become a settlement board member and benefactor.

Courtesy of Cabbage Patch Settlement House Archives

---

484. Holladay, "Words of Remembrance"; Katherine M. Davis, telephone interview with Linda Raymond, September 27, 2014.

While Miss Marshall's principles didn't change, the Cabbage Patch's programs were evolving as its leaders refocused to meet the needs of a new day when more than 80 percent of the children were black, and some reflected a shifting demographic mix that included white, Asian, Hispanic, and Muslim youth. Many children traveled farther to get to the safety of the Patch. And they lived with all of society's evolving problems with drugs, gangs, and family dissolution. The settlement had ended some programs, like those for preschoolers and the elderly, and focused on serving at-risk youth and their families.

New programs needed new spaces, and the old Sixth Street houses simply didn't offer much flexibility. Kim Glass helped the settlement design an ambitious renovation and expansion that would redo the gym and double the space for programs. Because the settlement is in a historic preservation area, getting city approval for the plans required a gantlet of meetings and hearings with people "not particularly thrilled" with parts of the plan. Kim Glass went to the meetings with Holladay, stood her ground, and respected everyone involved. When construction started, she put on a hard hat and steel-toed shoes, and, at five feet, two inches tall, she commanded respect from the construction workers.[485]

For those who remember the drab, cramped old Cabbage Patch quarters, the new facilities are stunning, full of open spaces and bright, child-friendly colors. Children now have a computer lab, spaces for homework help and classroom instruction, cooking lessons, weight room workouts, art, and, of course, sports.

---

485. Holladay, "Words of Remembrance"; Rod Napier, PI, February 2, 2015.

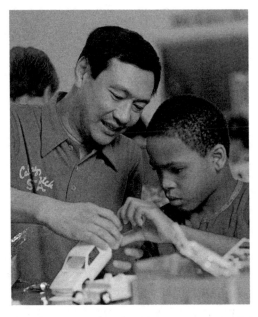

Roosevelt Chin devoted his entire adult life to serving the Cabbage Patch Settlement, especially its children. The renovated gym was named in his honor. *Courtesy of Cabbage Patch Settlement House Archives*

The beautiful new gym was named for Roosevelt Chin, the "gentle soul" who died in 2007 after giving his entire life to the Cabbage Patch. Holladay estimated—conservatively—that Chin had helped shape 25,000 lives over half a century. He quietly buried Chin's ashes at center court before the new gym floor was laid. Later, when an adult Cabbage Patch alumnus learned he was in Chin's presence during a tour of the new facilities, he broke away from the group, knelt in the center of the gym, and kissed the floor.[486]

---

486. Paula Burba, "Cabbage Patch Worker Roosevelt Chin Dies at 73," *Louisville (KY) Courier-Journal*, January 19, 2007; Lea Fischbach, PI, February 3, 2015.

The expansion required a major fund-raising campaign just as the country was entering a deep recession. That made for considerable anxiety and some hard decisions, but the board held its course. Today, raising money is always a matter of concern but not cause for handwringing, former board members say. The budget for March 2016–April 2017 was nearly $2.1 million, 37 percent of that from contributions and 23 percent from special fund-raising events. As Miss Marshall wished, the Cabbage Patch still does not accept money from government or Metro United Way. Holladay has worked to build an endowment that now produces 40 percent of the settlement's annual income.[487] His plans for endowment funds allowed Kimberly Hazelwood Glass to make her last major contribution to the Cabbage Patch. She and her husband established the Cabbage Patch Kim and Doyle Glass Educational Opportunities Fund. After a long, hard fight with cancer, Kimberly Glass, 46, died December 27, 2014, but her gift is supporting one of the Patch's most important programs: making college graduates of Cabbage Patch youth.

The Cabbage Patch dedicated a wall in the settlement to recognize alumni who graduated from college (Kim is one of the bright stars). Under Tracy Holladay, the Cabbage Patch Settlement has formed a "strong partnership" with the University of Kentucky, which will accept and provide $10,000 annually to Cabbage Patchers who meet basic entrance requirements and stay on track through their college careers. In the 2015–16 school year, Holladay said the Cabbage Patch had nine scholars at the University of

---

487. William Grubbs, PI, January 27, 2015; "Facts about the Cabbage Patch," CPSH Fact Sheet.

Kentucky getting aid from both UK and the Patch. His five-year goal is to increase the UK cohort to 35.[488]

That, however, is just a part of a remarkable support program that is at once sophisticated, personal, and reminiscent of Louise Marshall.

"You've got to be willing to do that stuff that pretty few programs are willing to do," things like filling out forms, coordinating with admissions, and renting apartments," said Holladay. "It is a very extra-mile kind of approach—which works."[489]

Jamayle West's story illustrates both how the new program works and how little has changed about the Cabbage Patch's approach to changing lives. Like thousands of other children, Jamayle came to the Patch as a lonely, wary 11-year-old. His reception that first day stunned him. "They just welcome you with a hug." Suddenly he felt at home. "I don't have to be scared," he told himself. "I can be myself." From then on, Jamayle was at the Cabbage Patch's door when it opened at three p.m.[490]

He was still focused on basketball and fun when the staff started pulling him into activities he never imagined that he would do: canoeing, camping, whitewater rafting. His confidence grew. Jamayle started thinking about college and let the staff pull him into an ACT prep class. He failed the first practice test he took, but the staff was excited.

---

488. Tracy Holladay, email to Bill and Linda Raymond Ellison, January 25, 2016, and PI, October 16, 2014.

489. Tracy Holladay, PI, October 16, 2014.

490. Jamayle West, PI, January 29, 2016.

"Now we know what you need to work on, and you'll do great on it," they told him.

They were right. When he took the ACT, his scores earned him scholarship offers from the University of Louisville, University of Kentucky, and Western Kentucky University. Suddenly he had options. After a series of campus visits with the Cabbage Patch staff, he settled on a business major at the University of Louisville.

"That was the time I needed the Patch the most ever," he says. The big freshmen classes seemed cold and unwelcoming, the teachers uncaring. His first grades were low. He felt as if he had hit a stone wall, but the staff at the Patch offered encouragement, mentoring, help finding tutors, and a summer job working with younger children. Eventually, he earned a bachelor's degree in PanAfrican studies, then a master's degree in exercise science.

Now, as part of the Cabbage Patch staff, Jamayle West teaches new generations of frightened children to be confident canoers and gives his phone number to new groups of young people headed for college. When those fledgling college students call in the middle of the night he tells them, "You have people who want you to succeed. You can push through."[491] He's not the only staff member who helps with whatever the students need. When freshmen head to the University of Kentucky with scholarships from UK and the Cabbage Patch, they carry the phone numbers of every member of the settlement's education department on their cell phones.

---

491. Jamayle West, PI, January 29, 2016.

"They help you from when you first go to the Cabbage Patch all the way up until you graduate college," says one of those students, Abdi Omar. "It's crazy. We're grown men and grown women . . . but there they are, every step of the way, they help . . . If you have a dream, they are going to do everything to help you achieve that."[492]

That continuous contact and support separates the Cabbage Patch from other youth organizations that help young people finish high school and then send them off to college to make their own way. And the Cabbage Patch approach is not new. Stories of Patchers like Jamayle have been told again and again since Miss Marshall founded the settlement in 1910. It's the story of Ben Hynes, Joe Burks, Jimmy Sedbrook, Dorene and Ruth Tomerlin, Jim Cooksey, Sherman Lewis, Charles Dietsch, Rod Napier, Roosevelt Chin, Ron Butler, Mike Caswell, Kim Hazelwood, and many others. They all wandered into a neighborhood place to have fun and found something more: People driven by faith who treated them with love and accepted nothing but their best. At the Cabbage Patch, children whom society labeled as "at risk" or worse, were treated as individuals. They learned to respect themselves and others in a place where nothing is free and actions have consequences, where everything must be earned with work, effort, or good behavior. They learned that the world is bigger and their futures more expansive than they had imagined. As one generation of Cabbage Patch teens increases their confidence and sense of accomplishment, the youngsters around them grow, too, establishing a chain reaction of success.

---

492. Abdi Omar, telephone interview with Linda Raymond, February 16, 2015; Rod Napier, PI, February 2, 2015.

"I found as I did better, my peers stepped up with me," said Vernon Wolfork, a Cabbage Patch alumni who went on to graduate from college and become a decorated officer in the US Army.[493]

Like all those stories of other young people, Jamayle West's and Kim Hazelwood Glass's stories are a part of Miss Marshall's legacy as much as the nondescript wooden houses on Sixth Street. As Tracy Holladay approaches retirement, the revitalized buildings are well maintained, bright, attractive, very functional, and very busy, serving the staff, children, and programs well. The settlement's management is sound by all accounts, and the programs are well run by staff members with advanced degrees and expertise. Some leaders have begun thinking about succession planning for Holladay's retirement. The board includes people who are hardworking, talented, and who grasp Miss Marshall's vision. Finances are in hand, and Holladay is working to build the endowment so that it can provide half the settlement's income. The management mess Miss Marshall left is long gone.

What remains are the principles she practiced and passed on through people like Rod Napier, who is also approaching retirement. He has done his best to cement those principles into the Cabbage Patch culture, so that the staff members who never knew Miss Marshall use them when they embrace children like Kim Hazelwood and Jamayle West. Kim and Jamayle are, in turn, passing the legacy on. Kim Hazelwood Glass died determined that the endowment fund she and her husband Doyle established would help maintain Miss

---

493. "Vernon Wolfork, Captain in the U.S. Army," interview in *Patchworks* (a publication of Cabbage Patch Settlement House), December 2011.

Marshall's life-changing legacy, forever. Jamayle West used his Patch scholarship to graduate so that he now teaches and shapes the lives of children as the Cabbage Patch shaped him.

From the outside, the settlement still looks pretty much as it always has except that the much-painted chain-link fence and Miss Marshall's flower garden are gone. Instead, the Kentucky Historical Society planted a marker in front of the settlement in 2010, the Cabbage Patch's 100th anniversary year. It credits Louise Marshall, the great-great-granddaughter of US Supreme Court Chief Justice John Marshall, with founding the settlement and serving as its director from 1910 until her death in 1981. For 100 years, the sign says, the settlement has been profoundly changing the lives of local children and families.

Sometimes people wonder what Miss Marshall would think of the settlement now. No one doubts that she would find things she would want to shape up. Mostly, though, her followers think that she would like what she would see: love, faith, pride, respect, hard work, discipline, and care being lavished on individuals. She'd like the happy children, too, just as she always did. Some people suspect that she is still watching. Stories are told about a staff member who worked late one night in the old nursery schoolroom where Miss Marshall enjoyed visiting the very little children. That night, the staff member was startled to hear footsteps outside the room. But no one was there. She couldn't find any reason for the sound.

Those who tell the story know what it means: Louise Marshall never left her Cabbage Patch Settlement.

ACKNOWLEDGMENTS

The very best part of researching this book was talking to people who knew Louise Marshall. They brought color and life to the details we dug from archives and made Louise Marshall live for us—and, we hope, for readers of this book. Kim McConnell Schiewetz, whose notes and memories, gave vivid insights from far-off Washington state, earned our special gratitude. You'll find all those who told their stories listed in the bibliography and quoted in the book. Here, we'll just say "thank you" again. You were terrific.

We owe special thanks to Tracy Holladay and the Cabbage Patch staff and board—past and present—who had no role in shaping the content of this book but who worked with patient faith to provide access to all the material we needed. We are deeply grateful for their help and enthusiasm for our project.

The extended Marshall family has been graciously supportive and helpful with memories, family lore, and photos. Elizabeth Johnson Haynes has been especially generous, answering our endless questions and digging out photographs at unpredictable moments over the six years of our work.

The Filson Historical Society and its staff have been a rich and wonderful resource, helping pull what we needed from boxes of documents even before some had been fully curated. We are especially grateful to Jennie Cole, now manager of collections access. The University of Louisville Archives staff was knowledgeable and helpful. And Mary Margaret Bell, coordinator of the Jefferson County Public Schools Archives and Records Center, helped dig important details from her archives.

We never got to meet some of the people whose work was most useful—the people who powered the Cabbage Patch Settlement's oral history project in 1987. They asked the right questions, coaxed answers, and listened when the people they interviewed said unexpected things. Thirty years later, their results are pure gold. Keith Cardwell, Andrew Chancey, Margaret Harvin, Carolyn Kline, and Lynn Gant March gave us all a great gift.

All writers need critics, and we had terrific readers who suffered through our early drafts, asked questions, and made suggestions that improved this work. We are especially thankful for Ruth Tomerlin Chaffins, a Cabbage Patch kid, who was a source and cheerleader for the project and a demon proofreader for successive drafts. Pat Wheaton provided an outsider's perspective. Bill Grubbs and Virginia Carter read portions of the book and made it better with their reactions. Our daughter, Susan Ellison, served as reader, counselor, advisor, and meltdown inhibitor.

Finally, we appreciate the support, advice, and professionalism of Carol Butler and her staff at Butler Books. We are especially grateful to Susan Lindsey, our editor, for her care and attention to detail.

BIBLIOGRAPHY

ABBREVIATIONS
Frequently cited sources have been identified in notes by the following abbreviations.

CPSH: Cabbage Patch Settlement House

CPSHR: Cabbage Patch Settlement House Records

CPSOHP: Cabbage Patch Settlement Oral History Project

FHS: Filson Historical Society, Louisville, Kentucky

PI: Personal interview with Bill and Linda Ellison, tape and transcript in authors' possession

Primary Sources

CABBAGE PATCH SETTLEMENT HOUSE RECORDS
In 2010, the 100th year for the Cabbage Patch Settlement House, CPSH began transferring its archives to the Filson Historical Society in Louisville, Kentucky. Since then, the collection housed at the Filson has grown to several thousand documents that occupy more than 40 cubic feet. Most of those documents pertain to the period from 1910 until 1981, when founder Louise Marshall died, and the period immediately afterward. Although the bulk of the records deal with institutional information, the collection includes some of Miss Marshall's personal correspondence, a short handwritten diary she

kept during her late teen years, and her scrapbook covering the time she spent as a Red Cross volunteer in Paris just after World War I ended. Miss Marshall was a very private individual, so her personal information in the collection is scant, but illuminating.

The institutional records say a lot about Miss Marshall's faith, her values, and her beliefs on how best to provide support for the needy families the settlement served. The collection includes CPSH administrative and financial records and correspondence, as well as information about publications, recreation and education, social ministries, and Cabbage Patch Circle records. An important part of the collection includes an oral history project described below.

CPSH ORAL HISTORY INTERVIEWS

After the Cabbage Patch Settlement House celebrated its 75th anniversary in 1985, a decision was made to document the settlement's history by conducting oral history interviews with the Patch's past participants, staff members, volunteers, and board members. A lengthy interview with the settlement's founder, Louise Marshall, had been recorded by board member Lynn Gant in March 1974, and was included in the collection. In 1993, CPSH published a booklet, *The Story of the Cabbage Patch Settlement House Founded in 1910 by Miss Louise Marshall as Told by Those Who Lived It*, based on those interviews and edited by Martin E. Biemer. The Filson collection includes the tapes and transcripts of the following oral history interviews. The authors have quoted from many of these interviews; other interviews informed their work in a general way.

Blanford, Margie McGill, past CPSH participant, interview by Andrew Chancey, September 24, 1987.

Burks Sr., Joseph, past participant/staff, interview by Keith Cardwell, January 31, 1987.

Carter, Mike, past participant, interview by Keith Cardwell, February 18, 1987.

Bibliography

Caswell, Mike, past participant, interview by Keith Cardwell, January 31, 1987.

Chaffins, Ruth Tomerlin, past participant/volunteer, interview by Carolyn Kline, April 4, 1987.

Chambers, Elizabeth, Louise Marshall's niece/supporter, interview by Margaret Harvin, March 19, 1987.

Chin, Roosevelt, past participant/staff, interview by Keith Cardwell, February 28 and March 7, 1987, and interview by Sloane Graff, spring 2002.

Cooksey, Dr. James J., past participant/staff, interview by Andrew Chancey, October 15, 1987.

Dosker, Sallie Ewing Marshall, Miss Marshall's sister/supporter, interview by Margaret Harvin, February 23, 1987.

Dover, Frances A., past staff, interview by Keith Cardwell, March 7, 1987.

Glur, Ray, past participant/staff, interview by Keith Cardwell, February 4, 1987.

Green, Anita C., past staff, interview by Andrew Chancey, September 24, 1987.

Harvin, Margaret (Peg) Pleune, past board member, interview by Keith Cardwell, February 20, 1987.

Marshall, Louise, CPSH founder, interview by Lynn Gant March, June 25, 1974, and an undated tape fragment, interviewer possibly James J. Cooksey.

Masters, Alice, past participant, September 14, 1987, by Andrew Chancey.

Masters, Georgia Beeler, past participant, February 6, 1987, by Keith Cardwell.

Mobley, Laura Wheeler, past participant, February 14, 1987, by Keith Cardwell.

Palmer-Ball, Thames Castner, past board member, interview by Andrew Chancey, September 18, 1987.

Parle, Dorothy Johnston, past and current participant, interview by Andrew Chancey, September 23, 1987.

Pasley, Pat Osbourne, past participant, February 21, 1987, by Keith Cardwell.

Purcell, Mary, neighborhood resident, and her daughter, Jeanne Purcell, past participant, September 18, 1987, by Andrew Chancey.

Raley, Ann Anderson, past board member, interview by Margaret Harvin, February 24, 1987.

Redman, Lloyd, past staff, interview by Keith Cardwell, February 12, 1987.

Scott, Alice Probst, past participant, interview by Keith Cardwell, February 5, 1987.

Smith, Gussie, CPSH neighborhood resident, September 18, 1987, by Andrew Chancey.

Stewart, Gene, past participant, October 15, 1987, by Andrew Chancey.

Thome, Dorothy Simon, past participant, January 30, 1987, by Keith Cardwell.

Tomerlin, Escue and Geneva, past participants, interview by Carolyn Kline, April 2, 1987.

Weikel, Bertha Mann, past staff, interview by Andrew Chancey, October 1, 1987.

ORAL HISTORY COLLECTION
EKSTROM LIBRARY, UNIVERSITY OF LOUISVILLE
The University of Louisville also has recorded interviews from a separate oral history project.
Burks Sr., Joseph, interview by Chris Petzold, March 2, 2008.
Defazio, Michael, interview by Sasha Caufield, March 17, 2008.
Gibson, Russell, interview by Victoria Groce, March 16, 2008.
Gibson, Terry, interview by Victoria Groce, February 20, 2008.

Bibliography

INTERVIEWS BY THE AUTHORS
The authors conducted personal interviews and telephone interviews
and, in some cases, they exchanged emails with the following
individuals. In many cases, they also had follow-up telephone
conversations, meetings, and email exchanges. The authors have
possession of the recordings, transcripts, and notes from those
interviews. Details can be found in footnotes.

Alvey, Shirley Rose
Burks Sr., Joseph
Burks, Kathleen
Butler, Ron
Chaffins, Ruth Tomerlin
Chambers, Thomas R.
Cooksey, Anne Majors
Cooksey, Dr. James J.
Davis, Katherine M.
Dietsch, Charles
Fischbach, Lea
Grubbs, William
Harvin, Margaret (Peg) Pleune
Haynes, Elizabeth Johnson
Holladay, Tracy
Johnson, Lewis Marshall
King, Frances Laughton
King, Rob
Leuenberger, Eleanor Gorin
Leuenberger, Samuel
Lewis, Sherman
March, Lynn Gant
Marshall III, Burwell Keith
Napier, Rod
Omar, Abdi
Peak, Patsie
Runyon, Meme Sweets

Schiewetz, Kimberly McConnell

Stopher, Dorene Tomerlin

Webb, Mary

West, Jamayle

Young, Margaret Ann

NEWSPAPERS

The Louisville Free Public Library has an extensive collection of Louisville newspapers on microfilm. Specific articles are cited in the footnotes.

Christian Observer, Louisville, Kentucky

Louisville Courier-Journal

Louisville Evening Post

Louisville Herald

Louisville Post

Louisville Times

New York Times

Louisville Cardinal (University of Louisville)

Other Sources

Addams, Jane. *Twenty Years at Hull House*. New York: MacMillan, 1920.

Ancestry.com. *Virginia, Prominent Families*, Vol. 1–4 (database online), Provo, UT: Ancestry.com Operations Inc., 2001.

Aubespin, Mervin, Kenneth Clay, and J. Blaine Hudson. *Two Centuries of Black Louisville: A Photographic History*. Louisville, KY: Butler Books, 2011.

"Authority to Form a Chapter" and minutes of meetings, October and November 1917, Louisville Chapter of the American Red Cross Archives, Louisville, Kentucky.

Boewe, Mary. *Beyond the Cabbage Patch: The Literary World of Alice Hegan Rice*. Louisville, KY: Butler Books, 2010.

————"Back to the Cabbage Patch: The Character of Mrs. Wiggs," *Filson Club History Quarterly 59*, no. 2 (April 1985): 179–204.

Bibliography

Browning, James R. "Anti-Miscegenation Laws in the United States," *Duke Bar Journal 1*, no. 1 (1951): 27–41.

Bullitt, William Marshall, Papers. Pocket diary and correspondence. Filson Historical Society, Louisville, Kentucky.

Caron's Louisville City Directory. Louisville, KY: Caron's Directory, 1903–1910 editions.

Coalter, Milton J, John M. Mulder, and Louis B. Weeks, eds. *The Confessional Mosaic: Presbyterians and Twentieth-Century Theology*. Louisville, KY: Westminster/John Knox Press, 1990.

Cott, Nancy F. *No Small Courage: A History of Women in the United States*. New York: Oxford University Press, 2000.

Crocker, Ruth Hutchinson. *Social Work and Social Order: The Settlement Movement in Two Industrial Cities, 1889–1930*. Urbana: University of Illinois Press, 1992.

Davis, Allen F. *American Heroine: The Life and Legend of Jane Addams*. New York: Oxford University Press, 1973.

———. *Spearheads for Reform: The Social Settlements and the Progressive Movement 1890–1914*. New York: Oxford University Press, 1967.

Davis, Mark. *Solicitor General Bullitt: The Life of William Marshall Bullitt*. Louisville, Kentucky: Crescent Hill Books, 2011.

Elshtain, Jean Bethke. *Jane Addams and the Dream of American Democracy: A Life*. New York: Basic Books, 2002.

Fabricant, Michael B. and Robert Fisher. *Settlement Houses under Siege: The Struggle to Sustain Community Organizations in New York City*. New York: Columbia University Press, 2002.

Farrell, Irene. Letter to Dearest Mother, June 2, 1919. World War I Research Institute website. http://ww1institute.org/bios/ifarrell.php.

"Fiftieth Annual Report of the Girls High School, Louisville, Ky. 1905–06." Jefferson County Public Schools archives, Louisville, Kentucky.

Football game program, University of Louisville vs. Georgetown,

October 25, 1946. University of Louisville Archives.

"From SS *France* to SS *Norway* in the Port of New York." World Ship Society website. www.worldshipny.com/francenorwaypony.shtml.

Haldeman II, Walter N. Haldeman Family Papers. Filson Historical Society, Louisville, Kentucky.

Hardy, E. J. *Manners Makyth Man*. New York: Charles Scribner's Sons, 1887.

Haynes, Dr. Douglas. Personal journal in possession of his widow, Elizabeth Johnson Haynes.

Holladay, Tracy. "Words of Remembrance." Delivered at the memorial service for Kimberly Hazelwood Glass. December 30, 2014.

Jennings, Kathleen. *Louisville's First Families: A Series of Genealogical Sketches*. Louisville, KY: Standard Printing, 1920.

Kleber, John G., editor in chief. *Encyclopedia of Louisville*. Lexington: University Press of Kentucky, 2001.

K'Meyer, Tracy E. *Civil Rights in the Gateway to the South: Louisville, Kentucky, 1945–1980*. Lexington, KY: University Press of Kentucky, 2009.

Knight, Louise W. Citizen: *Jane Addams and the Struggle for Democracy*. Chicago: University of Chicago Press, 2005.

"Louisville Fifty Years Ago." Louisville Board of Trade, March 9, 1923. At Louisville Free Public Library, Louisville, Kentucky.

"Louisville Girls High School Record 1853–1908." Jefferson County Public Schools archives, Louisville, Kentucky.

Lucas, Marion B. *A History of Blacks in Kentucky: From Slavery to Segregation, 1760–1891*, Vol. 1. Frankfort, KY: Kentucky Historical Society, 1992.

Marshall Sr., Burwell K. Last will and testament, filed with Jefferson County, Kentucky, Circuit Court Clerk, July 7, 1932.

Marshall, Louise. Last will and testament, filed with Jefferson County, Kentucky, District Court, February 19, 1981, with supporting documents from probate and final settlement of the estate.

————. Letter to the editor of the *Courier-Journal*, republished in memorial booklet for The Reverend John Marinus Vander Meulen, June 7, 1936. E. M. White Library, Louisville Presbyterian Theological Seminary, Louisville, Kentucky.

Minutes of Louisville Presbytery, a governing body of the Presbyterian Church in the United States, renamed Mid-Kentucky Presbytery of the Presbyterian Church (USA), offices at Louisville Presbyterian Theological Seminary, Louisville, Kentucky.

Mustered Out, yearbook published by the Louisville Boys High School Class of 1917, at Louisville Free Public Library, Louisville, Kentucky.

Napier, Rod. "The Patch Way" (guidelines to explain the Cabbage Patch Settlement House culture to new staff members).

Newmyer, R. Kent. *John Marshall and the Heroic Age of the Supreme Court*. Baton Rouge: Louisiana State University Press, 2001.

Otter, Melville. Memory book for 1914. Melville Otter Briney Papers, 1855–1986. Filson Historical Society, Louisville, Kentucky.

Ousley, Stanley. *Limerick, An Irish Neighborhood,* booklet published to commemorate Kentucky's bicentennial, 1974.

"Paris Reviews the Victorious Troops." Vogue, September 15, 1919.

Rice, Alice Hegan. *The Inky Way*. New York: D. Appleton-Century, 1940.

————. *Mrs. Wiggs of the Cabbage Patch*. New York: Century Company, 1901.

"The South Atlantic Route," 1926, YodelOut! Travel website, http://travel.yodelout.com/the-southern-atlantic-route/ (accessed April 12, 2017).

Stuart, Paul H. "The Kingsley House Extension Program: Racial Segregation in a 1940s Settlement Program." *Social Service Review* 66, no. 1 (March 1992): 112–20.

Sullivan, Mark. *Our Times: The United States 1900–1925*, Vol. 1, The

Twenties. New York: Charles Scribner's Sons, 1935.

Thompson, Ernest Trice. *Presbyterians in the South*, Vol. 3. Richmond, VA: John Knox Press, 1973.

Tilford Travel Service. "Final Itinerary for Miss Louise Marshall, Miss Kim McConnell, Mr. Charles Dietsch," August 1, 1973. In possession of Kimberly McConnell Schiewetz.

"Tracy Holladay . . . One of the People to Watch in 1985." *Patch-Work*, newsletter of the Cabbage Patch Settlement House, January–March 1985.

Trolande, Judith Ann. "From Settlement Houses to Neighborhood Centers: A History of the Settlement House Movement in the United States." *In Hundred Years of Settlements and Neighbourhood Centres in North America and Europe*, ed. Herman Nijenhuis, 41–56. Utrecht: Gamma, 1986.

Trustee for Richard and Helen Marshall. Periodical Settlement of Accounts, October 23, 1934. Lincoln Bank and Trust Company. Jefferson County Circuit Court Clerk.

"Vernon Wolfork, Captain in the U.S. Army." Interview in *Patchworks*, a publication of Cabbage Patch Settlement House, December 2011.

Wade, Louise Carroll. "Settlement Houses." In *Encyclopedia of Chicago*. http://www.encyclopedia.chicagohistory.org/pages/1135.html.

Wright, George C. *Life behind a Veil: Blacks in Louisville, Kentucky 1865–1930*. Baton Rouge: Louisiana State University Press, 1985.

INDEX

Index

ABOUT THE AUTHORS

Linda Raymond and Bill Ellison are retired journalists with a strong interest in history. After retiring from long careers at the *Courier-Journal* and and *Louisville Times*, they pursued their interest in history, and Raymond taught writing for 15 years at Bellarmine University and other Louisville-area colleges. Together they wrote *Like Jacob's Well: The Very Human History of Highland Presbyterian Church*, which won the 2008 Angell Award for best first book by Presbyterian writers.